Somewhere
in the
Music,
I'll Find Me:
A Memoir

Eric in
Real Life!
Thanks for your
support & I hope
you enjoy the
book!

Somewhere in the Music, I'll Find Me: A Memoir

LAURIE MARKVART

For Mable

CONTENTS

ACT ONE, ON THE VERGE 1

1 - PRIDE 3

ACT TWO, LEARN, ESCAPE, BREAK, REPEAT 9

2 - FILLING THE GAPS WITH MUSIC 11

3 - PRIVILEGE 20

4 - SMALL TOWN SECRETS EVERYONE KNOWS 25

5 - THE STUMBLE INN 28

6 - BUT YOU'RE A GIRL 33

7 - ROCK YOU LIKE A HURRIcANE 39

8 - NOTHING BUT A DREAMER 43

9 - CRUSHED BIG APPLE 49

10 - SMOKING HOT MINNEAPOLIS MUSIC SCENE 55

11 - BREAKING ALL THE RULES 59

12 - COVER BAND 65

13 - THE ROAD 68

14 - HAIRCLIPS 81

15 - SMELL LIKE MICK JAGGER 86

16 - BLEW MY CHANCE 96

17 - THE MILES BETWEEN 102

18 - CULTURE SHOCK   111

19 - ALL THE WORLD'S A STAGE   114

20 - FIND A GOOD MAN   122

21 - BAND WANTED   129

22 - DREAM BAND   141

23 - CLOUD NINE WITHOUT A SILVER LINING   144

24 - PLEASE WAKE UP   152

25 - LIBERTY LUNCH   159

26 - DESTRUCTION   165

27 - THREE STRIKES   171

28 - ECSTASY   177

29 - STRIP CLUB   183

30 - CRAZY   189

31 - TRAILER PARK CONFESSIONS   196

32 - IMPOSTER   207

33 - PLAYBILLS AND WORN HEELS   214

34 - HELL'S KITCHEN MARGARITA   225

35 - DOMESTICATION   236

36 - THE CITY OF ANGELS   246

37 - TO HONOR   253

38 - PURPLE VELVET   256

39 - PROCREATE TO VALIDATE   259

40 - UNPREDICTABILITY   270

41 - DETERMINATION   274

42 - CIRCLE OF LIFE   281

43 - UNDER PRESSURE   285

44 - BEAT THE ODDS   292

45 - TRADE YOU   297

46 - THE BEAUTY OF A MOMENT   306

47 - NUMB BUT NIMBLE   315

ACT THREE, THIS LIFE PRESENT DAY 2011   322

48 - HERE WE GO   323

49 - IN THE DRIVER'S SEAT   330

50 - ROADKILL   338

51 - WRISTBAND   343

52 - WHY ISN'T THIS LIFE ENOUGH?   347

53 - BUDDHA IN A SHOE   350

54 - A GOLDEN TICKET   357

55 - REPRESENTATION   367

56 - TOO OLD FOR THIS SHIT   370

57 - TICKET EXCHANGE   376

58 - NOW OR NEVER   384

59 - GAME ON   386

60 - STAND ON THE X   388

61 - CONCRETE AND SOLITUDE   395

62 - BREATHE   400

Author's Note   405

Acknowledgements   407

About the Author   409

Resources   410

ACT ONE

ON THE VERGE

1

PRIDE

Los Angeles Sports Arena, March 2011

"Tickets and wristbands, please," the daunting security guard in black jeans and t-shirt repeats like a drill sergeant straight out of Central Casting. As I get closer to him, my heartbeats speed up.

With a trembling hand, I show him my seat ticket and the purple wristband attached to my wrist for the last 36 hours. He glances and waves me on. Grasping the railing to steady my wobbly legs, I descend the stairs to the arena floor, realizing that— I beat the system.

My group from Section 12—30 strangers—gather around a show staffer, a twenty-something gal. Half my age, she's petite but assertive, waving her arms above her head, drawing everyone to her like she's presumably done with hundreds of previous singers on this audition assembly line. We cluster in closer. An intense aroma of makeup, hairspray, and body order permeates the group. A contestant behind me forcefully sighs, and her breath smells like stomach acid. My gut lurches in response. Well, this *is* Round One for "X-Factor." *Keep it together, Laurie. This is just an audition. You've been through far worse than this.*

On the arena floor, it's apparent how loud the upper arena is: packed full of contestants, families, and friends, cheering, talking, and clapping. The clamor radiates off the concrete floor, like at a sporting event.

I fumble in my purse for my iPhone. I need to listen to my music to gain perspective, even as my eyes remain deadlocked on the staffer. She's still wrangling people, so I have time to get it together. I roll back my shoulders and stretch my neck from side to side to calm my nerves.

A fellow contestant taps me on the arm. I pull out one earbud. "You, okay?" he says. He appears in his late fifties and looks like a street magician from Venice Beach. He's scruffy, has a drastically receding hairline, and his thin ponytail is a *too dark for your age* shade of black. He wears a faded black tux tail over a ragged floral print Hawaiian shirt. The only thing on him that looks current is the purple wristband, just like mine.

I'm surprised by his curiosity and attempt to interact. If anything, I'm annoyed. What does he care?

"Hey, I'm in my zone, and you just messed it up."

He gapes at me, lifting an eyebrow. His face softens. "You just look really nervous. Relax. You're about to be discovered," he says with sparkling eyes. "Be proud you've made it this far."

"Proud?" I shake my head, then smile remorsefully. With my head hung low, I stick my earbud back in. I'm such an asshole. As well, I'm lying. I'm not in my zone. The only zone I'm in is one warped with anxiety and confusion.

However, proud? My husband Neil said the same thing this morning as I left our house to go on this wild goose chase. As I paused at our front door, Neil followed closely behind. I sensed the warmth and calmness of his tall body behind me. I assumed he had something to say. In a somewhat uncomfortable but sweet send-off, he muttered, "Good luck today or break a leg or damn, which is it?"

"It's break a leg." I chuckled and turned to him. I reached up for a hug and melted into his strength. He kissed my forehead. I wish things were better for us. If only we hadn't suffered so much. I whispered, "Thank you. I'll be in touch throughout the day."

As I walked to the driveway, he added, "I'm proud of you." That comment stopped me in my tracks.

"Why are you proud of me?" I asked, turning to him, a quiver of curiosity in my stomach.

Leaning against the door frame, Neil removed his hands from his PJ bottom pockets and folded his arms across his muscular chest. "Well, I mean, the last few years have been tough for you. I hope this is what you're looking for. What you need."

I hesitantly nodded in return, got in the car, took a deep breath, and let out a loud, satisfying sigh. I reminded myself, again, that I'm someone who is getting the chance to audition for a reality TV show. Finally, there is no age restriction. I can no longer complain or hide behind ageism. However, I also can't hide behind my anxiety, all that has happened, or my mom's long held expectations of me becoming a famous singer or mine, for that matter. Proving it might be enough to fix things. To fix me.

Backing out of the driveway, I realize that no matter how stressed, frustrated, or ill-minded I've felt leading up to this, I desperately miss this part of my life—making music, auditioning—the apprehension, energy, and the full-on engagement of the moment. It's an instant of being fully alive, too mentally and emotionally high to be touched by heartache or loneliness.

Now, standing with aching high-heeled feet on the cement arena floor next to the Venice guy, I'm no longer worrying about my song selection or how I look. It's too late for that. I'm next in line for the audition booth. While I try to ignore my sweaty armpits, I steady myself with deep breathing. *I got this.* Of course, I do. I've been singing since I was a kid. My first performance was at church. A duet of "Jesus Loves Me" with my only sibling and older brother David. We were barely six and seven years of age.

I revert to thinking of my song choice. Which one will I do? I hum each one in my head. Does one feel better than the other? Ignoring all around me in our tight group, I hum the songs out loud to check how my voice feels. My humming turns into words, louder and louder, with no concern about who can hear me. I can barely hear myself, muffled by the intrusive sounds of the arena and those next to me doing similar vocal warmups.

My voice is cold and unsteady, restricted and tight, like any muscle until it's warmed up. I want my voice to feel as nice as a warm glove. Instead, it's as frozen and unforgiving as the winter pond I skated on as a child growing up in Wisconsin.

ACT TWO
LEARN, ESCAPE, BREAK, REPEAT

2

FILLING THE GAPS WITH MUSIC

Waterloo, Wisconsin, the 1970s

By Midwest farm country standards, our two-story red brick house on one of the main drags, Madison Street, was in the hustle and bustle of little Waterloo.

Waterloo had two thousand people. There was one stoplight in the whole town, and it marked the four corners of the town center, where the two main thoroughfares of Madison and Monroe Street met. I could see the light blink from my front yard.

Our town center consisted of a pharmacy, bowling alley, shoe and clothing store, bank, movie theater, fire station, diner, and six taverns. Yes, six. And all within walking distance of our house. Our town also had four churches, all within walking distance from our house and town center. Occasionally, the clergy from those churches patronized those six taverns. Mom would say,

"The best sermons are on a Saturday night to a bunch of drunks, then on Sunday to the hungover."

Waterloo was not much different from other small towns in Wisconsin. Still, I thought Waterloo was beautiful, with soft hills making up Fireman's Park filled with tall Oak, Ash, and Pine trees forming canopies over summer's deep green lush grass. The tree branches turned to icicles twinkling like diamonds in the sun when we used the hills for sledding in the winter.

The chocolate brown slow-flowing Maunesha River ebbed through the park, lined with Pussy Willows and marsh shrubs. A dam at the Mill House forced some of the Maunesha up into a large-sized pond, which in summer was home to ducks, geese, and the occasional fisherman frustratingly hoping for a catch. When December would come, the pond became a frozen sheet for childhood shenanigans of snowball fights, hockey, and ice skating.

If it wasn't for the strong smell of manure that would waft through the town from the many nearby dairy farms, as a little child, I thought Waterloo was damn perfect until it wasn't.

Everyone in Waterloo knew each other, and they didn't just say hello in passing on the street or at the local diner. Long conversations would ensue about family, friends, and the latest happenings about town or, God forbid, national politics or worldly events. In the 70s, those conversations were curated from the Sunday newspaper, evening news, and the radio and spiced up with small-town opinions.

My mom would always direct the conversations to local gossip, which she found more attractive, even though she sometimes was part of the story. And my dad, having grown up in Chicago, served 20 years in the military through World War II and a year in Korea during the Korean War, would never engage in the gossip that he called "small town nonsense." Still, he'd willingly debate politics with the right person.

A typical grocery store run was the excitement of the day for Mom, and she conversed with everyone from the entrance to the exit. From the vegetable aisle to the meat counter, she never missed a chance to "bullshit." When I was a pre-teen, I'd usually bide my time waiting for her by looking at *People* and other entertainment magazines hanging near the checkout, fantasizing about a more exciting life. But by the time I was in high school, Waterloo was isolating and boring to me. Although I was not the popular type, I had good friends and enjoyed school. But with only 70 kids in my class, popularity was not my priority. Variety was.

Every day around Waterloo, I saw the same people repeatedly, and while my mom found this comforting and enjoyable, I was restless. The folks of Waterloo were genuine and caring, and the sense of community was strong, but I yearned for diversity and excitement.

The closest city where I believed the real action and activity happened was Madison, twenty-six miles to the west. Madison had nearly two hundred thousand people, and I could feel the energy every time we visited for shopping or birthday celebrations. If we approached the city at night, the thousands of streetlights lit up the dark sky, and it was a beacon to something more thrilling.

The city had various ethnic restaurants, the state capital, indoor malls, an airport, people of different colors and religions, a university, and giant lakes, Mendota and Monona, that looked like oceans to my adolescent eyes when I first saw them. But Waterloo did have a quaintness that my mother loved. And at times, I embraced it too. Primarily for her sake and especially when I was young and yearning for her attention.

***

As a young child, every Sunday morning, I pleasantly woke in my upstairs bedroom of our house to the sound of needle scraping vinyl on the downstairs record player. Classical music boomed from Pioneer floor speakers in our living room. My dad—that ex-military early-bird, predictably rose at 6 a.m. (when the bugle sounds!) and played his favorites after he poured his first cup of coffee. I assumed that this was part of my father's routine to wake up my brother and me: a friendly pronouncement, the Head of the house was up. Or so I thought at the time.

As the years progressed and my parents' relationship grew more strained, I wondered if he might have done it to piss off his typically hungover, depressed wife.

But I loved the music. As I rested on my white eyelet canopy bed, surrounded by stuffed animals, I listened to every note with anticipation and memorized every lyric, even in French or German. I'd fade in and out of sleep, content, amused by the swells of the music, the sudden lulls, the dramatic operatic vocals.

My father had said, "In every opera, someone always falls in love, and someone always dies, but in between, there is a lot of beautiful music."

My dad had a small-framed body and carried his shoulders back with poise and confidence, especially when discussing opera. Even though his weekend sweatshirt and white Converse high-tops wouldn't suggest that he was an opera enthusiast. Nor would his machine shop green coveralls from his day job. No matter the attire, grease lingered under his fingernails and his hands smelled of machine oil, as did what was left of his hair. But I liked the smell. It smelled like him.

My brother David would shut his door on Sunday mornings in response to Dad's orchestral onslaught. However, the door to my parents' room—with my mom presumably sleeping—was always closed, although a closed door wasn't enough to silence the music. My door was left open. The cacophony told me I was not alone. Dad was there. I was safe. My father was the stable force in our unpredictable home.

I could assume my dad's mood, and my mom's likely condition, by his musical choices. He was in a carefree spirit if he listened to piano concertos like Tchaikovsky's or operas like *Tosca* or *Carmen*. He'd be enjoying the Sunday paper. Sometimes he'd hum as he made his way around the house, and the sound would bring me great pleasure. It also meant my mother was sober, happy, and making breakfast. On these days, I would not linger in bed; I'd rush downstairs to join them.

Beethoven, especially *Moonlight Sonata*, meant he was stressed. I would find him amiable but unhappy. He was busy doing my mother's chores: making breakfast, cleaning the kitchen, and disposing of liquor bottles from the night before. He was an old-school man who'd say, "These are the wife's duties, not mine."

Mozart's *Requiem in D Minor* meant a dark mood. I would find him unapproachable, further evidenced by deep furrows on his brow and puffy eyelids. I could only assume he and my mother had fought the night before. He had every reason to use Mozart to insulate himself from her. Thankfully, I was confident that he loved me. Even if he was not incredibly welcoming, as he sat with legs crossed tightly against the base of the living room armchair, his hand wrapped tightly around a cup of coffee, offering a reduced smile for me. I would head to the kitchen, hoping my mom was preparing breakfast before church. However, when *Requiem* was playing, she was never there. She was still in bed.

I was angry at my mom for putting my dad in such a state. Also, I was lonely, the only one to sit at the breakfast table with no one to make food for me, provide comfort, and ask if I slept okay.

As a ten-year-old, I could put Lucky Charms in a bowl and pour milk on it. Then again, compared to my mother's *good* Sundays, when she would prepare pancakes, waffles, bacon, toast, and fresh juice, cold cereal was disheartening. Until my brother would join me, these quiet moments of eating alone were sad and crushing, especially with *Requiem* in the background.

On Mom's good Sundays, when she was not depressed or hungover, she was engaging, loving, caring, and had an outrageous sense of humor. She dished out hugs, back rubs, and kisses to our foreheads and cheeks and never missed a second to say, "You mean the world to me." She had pet names for us: sweetheart, darling, honeybunch, pumpkin, kiddo. Her attention was devotional. But also confusing. How could she be so unavailable on some days and emotionally stifling on others?

My mother was a pretty woman with pleasant straight light brown hair that would curl into her neck as it reached her shoulders. Her clear blue eyes and high arched eyebrows were probably her most delicate features. She was of average height and weight but slightly taller than my dad. She'd put on weight when depressed and then lose some when she was in a good state. She would dress in contemporary clothes and shoes if she felt mentally well, but nothing fancy or flashy. She loved clip-on earrings and long-chain necklaces, and she incorporated purple, her favorite color, into her wardrobe every chance she could. But the most constant part of her attire was a cigarette. A Salem was her fashion statement. And her comfort.

When Mom was in a good state, she ran the stereo on Saturday mornings; it was rousing fun. She'd play upbeat music, popular on the radio: *Candy Man* by Sammy Davis Jr. or *Raindrops Keep Falling on my Head*. Those Saturdays would not be complete without Johnny Mathis.

Mom spun Johnny Mathis vinyl like his voice was an oxygen tank for her lungs. She owned every album he recorded. She documented her collection on ruled school paper, with columns drawn with a ruler in pencil to section out release dates, album and song titles, and duets, and she placed it all in a 3-ring binder. The spine simply labeled Johnny.

Much to my dad's displeasure at the cost of Mom's obsession, every time a new Johnny album arrived in the mail, Dad would say, "Johnny put out *another* album?" Mom also belonged to Johnny's international fan club and swooned like a teenager when she received an annual birthday card with his photo and replica autograph. She'd tack it to the bulletin board in the kitchen for all of us to see. Johnny's tender chocolate eyes and apparent genuine cheerfulness made me adore him too. Along with his smooth, charismatic velvet voice, I understood Mom's attraction and wished I could sing like him. Mom told me she heard he gave up a successful shot as an Olympic high-jumper to be a singer. I often wondered why he had to choose between the two.

Ella Fitzgerald, Nat King Cole, Stevie Wonder, Glenn Campbell, Joan Baez, and Carole King were also Mom's favorites. She'd tout, "Laurie, did you know Carole King writes her music? That's a big deal, kiddo." Those words stuck with me. Even as a very young child, I would stare at the cover of Carole King's album *Tapestry* and wonder if *I* could write a song.

When Mom played musicals, like *South Pacific* or *Oklahoma!*, I was inspired to sing along, happy because I wasn't alone. Sometimes Mom and I'd dance around the living room; afternoon sun rays shining on us through the window like a spotlight. We'd twirl and spin like novice ballroom dancers; rug burns on our feet. Holding hands, we'd lip-sync until the song's end, and on cue, Mom and I'd fall dramatically onto the couch in an embrace of sweat and laughter.

"Laurie, someday I'll take you to New York City, and we'll see Broadway!" she would exclaim, throwing her hands in the air for a loud clap, her eyes dancing. She would quickly fall into the fantasy world show tunes offered. I had no problem joining her. Nevertheless, the song always ended.

3

PRIVILEGE

One day on the weekly drive to the grocery store with Mom, she paused the car a bit longer after pulling out of our gravel driveway.

"Laurie, your dad and I have noticed you love music; you're always singing. So, you're going to take piano lessons."

"Sure, Mom. If it makes you happy." I never thought twice about making her happy, and she was right. I loved music, and when I'd listen to it, I was intrigued by how to play any of it. How does music happen? How did these opera vocalists get so high with their voices or hold a note so long? How did the horns peak at the right time with the strings? How did any of it happen? I guess it must start with piano if that's where they want me to start? "Learning a musical instrument is a privilege." She glanced my way, winked, and then gunned the gas pedal, my head forced back against the headrest. I knew with the wink she was happy for me.

"I never had the chance. Understand how lucky you are that we can afford to buy a piano for you to take lessons."

James Archie Sr., my mother's father, was a classically trained vocalist. He descended from a long line of family musicians. He was a well-known regional singer in the 1940s when my mom was young.

My mother idolized her father and his success. She would say, "Your grandfather was very popular. Hundreds would come from far away to hear him sing. I couldn't believe I was the daughter of someone famous!" Then her expression would sadden. "But he was also a drunk, and my parents had awful fights."

I was never sure if my mom exaggerated the stories of their fights or her father's musical success. Although, one of his live shows was recorded, and she would play the LP vinyl for us. His tenor voice sounded beautiful and pleasant, and he sang with tremendous emotion. When Mom was melancholy, especially when she was drunk, she'd play that record and drift off somewhere else, eyes closed, swaying back and forth. My brother and I would never disturb her then.

My grandfather had supported his family the best he could on a singer's salary, but he spent most of his money on alcohol. Eventually, he was forced to quit performing and work a stable job to keep the lights on. Attempting to keep my grandfather off the sauce, his father opened a dry-cleaning business. My family had a saying that my granddad learned how to clean up other people's clothes, but not himself. He was in his early sixties when he died of a heart attack. I was only three but well remember my mother's pain; she cried for weeks. Her sadness scared me. That had been the beginning of her unavailability, the start of my profound loneliness and desire for her attention and approval.

From the time I was five, my mother went to a psychiatrist twice a week. My brother and I went too-to the waiting room. It was an appealing office in Madison with soft cushioned couches, magazines on tables, and tall leafy indoor plants. The best part, the Coca-Cola machine in the waiting room would dispense endless amounts of glass bottles for our drinking pleasure. The receptionist never stopped my brother or me from sliding the top of the machine open for more drinks. I was happy if the bubbles kept coming but eventually, I'd get a stomachache. Also, there was never enough pop to satisfy my curiosity why my Mom was talking to the man "behind the door."

Mom had been diagnosed bipolar with a severe anxiety disorder. She had massive mood swings: being happy and energized, then wholly depressed and shut away in her bedroom. When my dad would come home from work, he would discreetly open the back door and whisper to my brother or me, "How is she today?" During this period, she was admitted to a psychiatric hospital twice. It was the first time I heard the words "suicide attempt." She was gone for two weeks to a month. Each time Mom left, a deep sense of abandonment took over.

In her absence, my father was loving, sometimes reading to us before bed. Although he was also despondent, he took on her housekeeping chores. But between his job and visits to her, we were stuck with our grandmother for much of our caretaking. My mother's mom came with all sorts of demands and expectations regarding bedtime, dinner, and politeness. Her coldness was far different than our mother's warmth and love, and sometimes we could be downright rude to her. She was an easy target for frustration over our mother's absence.

Our grandmother was highly emotional and would swing between anger and weepiness with predictability that amused my brother and me. When grandma would look for us, we'd giggle, hiding in closets or under beds. We played a game of hide-and-seek that she didn't know she was playing. She always wore a white apron that looked ready to burst; it was tied so tight around her plump waist. "Children, I've asked you to come downstairs now!" This stock high-pitched shriek from her perpetual white Mylanta-lined lips came after other failed attempts to rouse us for dinner. We'd ignore her until she'd crawl up the carpeted flight of stairs on all fours, like a monkey, due to her bad back. She'd whine in tears, her blue eyes squinting in frustration as she approached us. They were the same blue as my mother's eyes, filled with sadness. And mine, filled with curiosity.

"Wait until I tell your father!" That was her final warning, shaking her finger close to our faces when she found us. And it worked. I never wanted to make things worse for my dad.

My mom did not like her mother, as she told me numerous times. I assume this knowledge added to my disregard of my grandmother's feelings and my annoyance of her in my mother's absence. Grandma would say, "Your mother makes excuses. She's just like her father, bless his soul, a drunk and ill-minded. She has everything in the world--a lovely home, you two beautiful children--and yet she chooses to be ill!"

I knew my grandmother was wrong. My mom didn't choose this. Something was wrong with her, and I had a growing need to protect her. To make her healthy and bring her back to me.

4

SMALL TOWN SECRETS EVERYONE KNOWS

As the years went by and Mom's illness intensified, I was taught that mental illness was a private affair, never admitted to—not in our small town, where everyone seems to know everything. "No one will speak of your mother's condition. This stays within the family," my grandmother would fiercely state. Personally, it was another matter when she'd yell at my mother. "Mary Ann, you can't take your kids to school in your pajamas! You're a slob, and your drinking is embarrassing." Mom would return to her bedroom in tears but not before bellowing, "Oh, go take another Valium, Mom!" Both were dealing with a similar illness, but no one spoke of it.

Sometimes Mom would experience Agoraphobia and not leave the house for weeks, sitting in front of the TV like a zombie, smoking one cigarette after another watching *The Price is Right* or *Wheel of Fortune*. Sometimes she'd spout out the answer with clarity. Or for days she'd stay in bed, in the same clothes. At her worst, she would remain in her bedclothes for weeks, not showering, her hair not brushed. Their bedroom darkened, drapes pulled, sheets wrinkled a thousand times over from her continuous use and an ashtray full of the butts that never satisfied her despair. My dad would sleep on the couch during those times.

Every couple of weeks, she would alternate between depression and mania. When manic, Mom would get her hair done, and she looked beautiful to me, like in her flawless senior high school portrait that hung above our fireplace.

She had endless energy to make sure all the household chores were completed, attending school events and cooking, yet she also wanted to socialize at local bars where she had many friends. Her mania encouraged her drinking and her propensity for telling vulgar jokes, to the amusement of many, and she argued with those who were annoyed by her lack of verbal filter. I recall overhearing someone at our town grocery store say, "That Mary Ann, she's a loose cannon."

At the time, I didn't know what that meant. Years later I figured it out in a McDonald's parking lot in Madison. A stranger had us blocked in our parking spot, and he wouldn't move his car even though my dad beeped and flashed car lights at him. Unexpectedly, Mom lunged out of the passenger side of our Plymouth station wagon. She swiftly marched to the stranger behind the wheel like a bull approaching a Matador. Through his driver side window, she angrily screamed, "Go fuck yourself!" while tapping her middle fingernail on his window. He didn't look at her. But he did move his car. I slunk down in the backseat, embarrassed.

During times of delusions, she thought everything, and anything was possible. She would tell me, "Dream as big as you want. You have a great voice, just like your grandfather. Keep practicing your piano. Someday you'll be discovered and be famous like Elton John!" To me, those words were magical, and I believed everything she said.

But it was different when she was in her dark, depressive state. Those times left me confused, insecure, and desperate for her attention. Thankfully, my father's dependable presence provided a degree of normalcy. I assumed he made excuses to neighbors and schoolteachers to explain her long absences.

However, by the time our car broke down during the dead of winter on the way to elementary school, and my mom got out, lifted the hood for a look, I assumed everyone knew her condition. As she hailed a neighbor for jumper cables, her shabby house slippers sunk into the snow and her see-through tattered pink night dress swirled in the icy winter air, exposing pale arms and unshaven bare legs. No bra, no coat, no gloves. At least she wore my dad's winter hat--the knock-off Russian kind that covers your ears. She hadn't lost all sensibility.

5

THE STUMBLE INN

Folger's coffee percolated the air on Monday mornings. When I was twelve, I'd sit at the kitchen table, watching Mom sort her weekly meds into her plastic pill organizer with the precision of a pharmacist. She'd count out loud as she dispensed the pills and diligently wrote each drug name, dosage, and side effects on a pocket-sized notebook, she'd carry in her purse. I was impressed by the rainbow array of different colored tablets and capsules.

She openly spoke to me about Lithium, Sertraline and eventually Prozac, as well as her many benzodiazepines. I assumed she told me to prove she was trying to heal or prepare me for the sporadic side effects she would exhibit like drowsiness, slurred speech, agitation. The mere mention of the meds evoked an uneasiness within me.

"Mom, I don't need all the details. I just want you to be happy," I'd say.

"You know, Laur. I keep trying all these damn pills, and I hope one of them is the magic one. One of these days, sweetheart. One of these days." Her face would sink, and I was sad for her.

I had two years of piano under my belt and an impeding recital. The piano became an outlet for the melodies occupying my head, and maybe a way to reach my mom.

The piano sat against the wall in our living room, the liveliest area in the house. Sitting on the cushioned piano bench, I could ignore the chaos around me, focusing for hours on sheet music, transforming notes on pages into music radiating from the instrument. I liked how repetition improved my ability, and the beauty of the music would seep into my body and provide instant gratification. If I got frustrated with a new piece, I'd look up at the bronzed Beethoven bust on top of the upright Kimball, convinced he was staring back. My dad told me that Beethoven had lost his hearing and yet still created music. If Beethoven could do that, I could keep practicing. Sometimes, exhausted, I'd fall asleep, my head on folded forearms draped over the keys.

For the recital, I chose Beethoven's *Ode to Joy*. Most likely due to the Beethoven bust. When I completed the piece, the applause from the teacher, Mom and Dad, and other kid's parents, tickled my tummy. I felt immense joy and pleasure at their reaction. I wanted to stay at the piano and relish in my feelings, but the teacher shooed me back to my seat. The praise stirred my desire to practice more and even to compose my own music. An ache to become a musician awakened.

As an early teen, my mother's episodes decreased as her psychiatric meds evened her out. On some levels, her pills worked. She was more available, dependable and calm during the week. She was emotionally supportive to my questions on boys and first crushes. However, her weekend binge-drinking worsened. Like clockwork, shortly after dinner, most Friday and Saturday nights Mom and Dad would leave for one of the six bars in our small town. Some Friday nights my brother and I would join for the family fish fry. When the bar kitchen closed at 8 pm, and patron conversations turned louder and raunchier, Mom and Dad would pull us from our game of pool and pitcher of Pepsi and send us home.

Typically, around 10 pm, Dad would come home after he'd had a couple of beers, enough for him. He'd say, "She's still at the bar. She'll come home when she's ready." I learned this meant she'd close the bar down.

Some weekends, I'd overhear Dad call the bar at midnight and ask the bartender to send her home. Occasionally Mom would oblige and return with a round of choice cuss words directed at Dad. Most times she'd stay at the bar. Dad would go to bed, but I remained up for her.

Looking up the sparse tree-lined town street from my second-floor bedroom window, I could see some of the bars. Their neon beer signs flashed in a rhythmic cadence against the black night. In my dark and quiet room, I'd kneel on the red shag carpet, chin on my arms on the windowsill, watching. Pins and needles marching into my legs as they'd fall asleep. I'd adjust to crisscross, eyes focused on the door of The Stumble Inn. Eventually, she'd stagger out alone or sometimes with a group of swaggering friends. They'd part ways with boisterous laughter, and she'd sway and weave as she walked down the sidewalk. When she shut the front door behind her, I'd return to bed and let my heavy eyelids close for sleep. It was 2 am.

My parents' marriage declined as her drinking increased. Their fighting escalated. Screaming and name calling at the heart of their fights. My father would sometimes have enough of it, grab a suitcase - never filling it, and abruptly leave the house - with a slammed door behind him.

I would dash to my bedroom, lock my door and put earphones on, and crank up the music to avoid Mom's crying. The music or my heavy panting was not enough to quiet the sound of her smashing beer bottles in the kitchen sink. Sometimes she'd scream: *You're so stupid, Mary. You're just a drunk!* One summer after one of their battles, she threw all her clay potted plants of various sizes and flowers off the back deck, screaming obscenities as she tossed them at the grass. She had no specific target but to release her frustration, and I assumed she hated her actions that caused my dad to leave. If it were winter, and they argued, I escaped to the frozen millpond behind our house and skate. My tears warmed my cold face as they'd fall in sequence to my metal blades that screeched the hard, fractured ice like the sound my parents made when they fought.

Eventually, no matter the season, my dad would return after a few hours, easing the same door open with caution, with beer on his breath, not drunk. I never saw him drunk. After he returned, he would usually go straight to the couch to sleep or retreat to his basement workbench where he had a cot. He never said a word to my brother or me, and the next morning, he and Mom acted as if nothing happened. Their silence was worse than the argument.

6

BUT YOU'RE A GIRL

It was 1980. I was thirteen. When I wasn't in school, the headphones were plastered on my head, with bands like Queen, Heart, The Police, Journey, and Blondie pounding against my eardrums. I didn't want to leave the turntable, as I sprawled out on the living room shag, attached by a coiled cord to the stereo system. Listening to the band Rush tormented me in an alluring way. I wanted to learn every musical note, vocal inflection, but it was almost impossible. I couldn't figure it out just by listening to them again and again.

With tenacity, I begged my parents to allow me to attend the upcoming Rush concert at Dane County Coliseum in Madison. My dad was going to drive my brother and two neighbor friends to the show. They were fourteen, the age my parents deemed okay to go to a concert. I thought I was close enough to convince them. At first, my parents resisted.

"You're too young, Laurie," Mom stated. "You're a girl," Dad injected.

"Dad, that's not fair! Because I'm a girl?"

They finally submitted to my foot-stomping, crying, and teen antics, and allowed me to go with a few conditions: no drinking or smoking pot. Who knew that was even an option?

As my dad dropped the four of us outside the concert, he told my brother, index finger firmly pointed out the driver window, to look after me. Also, he advised me to stay close to David.

"I'll be back in three hours at this exact spot. Meet me here and don't get in trouble," he said. His white-knuckled hands on the steering wheel and his squinted blue eyes gave away how reluctant he was to leave. I leaned in through the window, kissed his cheek, and reassured him I'd be fine. He departed, and we started our walk to the arena doors.

While Dad's taillights faded away, we took an unexpected detour. We're hailed by older teens tailgating to partake in their beer if we had anything in exchange. I was confident we had nothing to offer. On the contrary, joints fell out of one of our friend's jean pockets like stolen candy. I was astonished. My brother appeared unmoved, sipping their beer. He wasn't smoking, but our friends dove in quickly. They pounded beers and blew out plumes of pot smoke that I tried to dodge by waving the smoke away from me. I didn't want my parents to smell it on me.

I waited, impatient with hands on my hips, occasionally leaning against the stranger's black Camaro with a gold eagle painted on the hood. AC/DC blared out of its windows. Almost every other car had a similar party going on. It was kind of fun to watch, but I was more concerned with the steady stream of people entering the Coliseum. I was there for one thing only: Rush.

I yanked on my brother's arm and begged him to leave the tailgaters. He pushed my hand away but eventually obliged. "Guys, we gotta go. Meet you inside," he told our friends. As we walked away, he whispered, "Don't tell Mom and Dad."

Inside, it was a sea of long-haired rock fans in black rock concert t-shirts, and a significant pot haze that hovered over the crowd like a mushroom cloud. There was no way I could escape the strong smell of marijuana. The stage drew my attention, taking up the other end of Coliseum, painted black, surrounded on both sides with a towering wall of speakers that appeared 20 feet tall and 30 feet wide. Now I didn't care about the weed. I made a beeline to the arena floor to get as close as possible.

"Laurie, hold on! We have to stay together," Dave yelled over loud recorded Black Sabbath music that played through the stage speakers.

"I'm going to the front," I yelled.

He shrugged and joined me. "It's gonna be loud and crowded!"

"I hope so," I said eagerly.

We found a small opening, 30 feet from center stage. We're jammed in tightly together, and I had to stand on tippy toes in my all-white Nike high-tops to see the scene on the stage: workers dressed in all black scurrying around, moving cables, tuning guitars, getting ready for showtime. How exciting! One of them was testing the drums. Every time he kicked the bass drum, it felt like a shock wave beat on my chest. Oh, man, that's Neil Peart's drum kit. I got goosebumps.

I was sweating; a cool breeze passed over my face. A fog machine pumped out white spirals from the stage, temporarily eliminating the weed and cigarette smoke. So, this is a rock show? Hell, yes. I couldn't imagine being anywhere else except on that stage. *Imagine all these people looking at me?*

Finally, the Coliseum lights went down. The audience screamed, and it was the loudest thing I'd ever heard, like an airplane taking off. It hurt my ears, as a reflex I covered them, but then I gave up. I loved how loud it was. The whole place was pitch black, except for cigarette lighters held above the heads of some fans. Standing directly behind me, with barely an inch to spare, packed like sardines, my brother patted my shoulder numerous times--his show of excitement. Unexpectedly, a surge of bodies from behind moved towards the stage. Like a wave engulfing us, I was caught off guard and tumbled on top of the person in front of me. My brother grabbed my t-shirt and yanked me back up. A significant amount of water poured down my back, and it cooled me off, except I soon realized from the smell it was beer. Oh, well. A guy to my left, twice my age, with a beer and cigarette in one hand, turned to me and screamed something I couldn't make out. His thick Fu Manchu mustache surrounded his broad smile, and he put his free hand up for me to slap. I did without pause.

The excitement in the air was magical, and I was ecstatic. I turned my head around to smile at my brother. He responded with a squeeze of his hands, now firmly placed on my shoulders to keep me close. The audience swayed and moved like a boat on a turbulent sea. With each surge forward, I laughed riotously as my brother's grip tightened. The screaming was finally squelched by the thunderous music booming from the stage: Rush! I recognized the song, 2112: Part 1: Overture. *Holy Crap.*

During the show, I jumped, screamed, clapped, sang out loud, even cried. The experience was spiritual. How can I be a musician like this? I must get on stage, too.

After the concert, we found our friends outside. One of them didn't make it into the show. He got too wasted on weed and beer and passed out in a bush. Oh, no, this won't go over well with my dad. And, like the sergeant he was, he lectured the beer-stinking, sweaty, stoner neighbor for 30 minutes straight, all the way from Madison to Waterloo.

As for me, I thought my new Rush concert t-shirt would cover up the beer smell, but it didn't. I stunk like one of the town bars Mom and Dad would take us. And my previously pristine white high-tops, now covered in dirty footprints and beer stains were a dead giveaway. My parents agreed that I didn't consume anything, but they still grounded me from live concerts for a year. A year! Their only explanation: *You're a girl. You shouldn't be around such corruption.* As for my brother, no ban for him. I was pissed, sad and angry, but at least I saw Rush. And contrary to my parent's intentions, their ban ignited my curiosity and passion for rock music even more.

***

In late 1981, I was almost fourteen. The live concert ban was still in effect. It didn't matter. I glued my face to the new cable TV network MTV. I was taken aback by the vibrant artists I watched, especially Queen. The video for *Bohemian Rhapsody* made a regular rotation, and it was heart-stopping. I'd heard the song before, but this was the first time I *saw* Freddie Mercury. He pounded a white piano and strutted like a god in a white satin jumpsuit. I was swooning. He was everything I wanted to be.

The Wilson sisters of Heart and The Runaways were my first exposure to women playing rock guitar, and they became my first artist girl-crush. But Chrissie Hynde fronting The Pretenders showed me how a woman commanded a stage, fronting a band of guys, without depending on her sexuality to sell it. Her presence was so strong and demanding attention that she just *was* sexy. All these women incited a lustful desire to become like them. They looked in control and powerful. Their lives, full of fame and money, must be way better than my lonely life in Waterloo. Rock 'n Roll was the only way to go.

7

ROCK YOU LIKE A HURRICANE

A few weeks after the Rush concert and the stains on my Nike high-tops faded, I asked my parents for a guitar one night over dinner. It was clear, at least to myself: I wanted to be a rock star. "Mom, Dad, I like to play piano, and it's cool. I already sing a lot at school, but I really want to play guitar. I want to play rock music."

There was a quiet lull over the Tuna Helper.

"Well, I don't like rock music," Dad said finally. "However, you've proved with the piano that you can stay focused and respectful to the instrument. So, if we get you a guitar, you need to take lessons. And no electric guitar or any of that loud stuff until you prove you've learned the instrument."

"Yes!" I screamed, jumping up so quickly to hug him, I banged my knee into the bottom of the table. However, the excitement I felt, and his chuckle quelled the pain.

"And keep playing piano!" Mom added. She moaned, "We didn't pay for all those lessons for nothing."

"I will, Mom. I still love singing and musicals. It's just that rock music is so, so, cool." I moved to hug her gently from behind and kissed her cheek. My brother sneered at my enthusiastic display. He had shown little interest in learning to sing or play an instrument and was not bewitched with music like me.

In the small music store in Madison, I touched every guitar before I picked out my first acoustic, a budget Yamaha. The polished, light tawny-colored lacquered wood on the face of the guitar and the rough steel strings under my fingers was mesmerizing. Even the new aroma of the black hard-shell case was intoxicating. I buried my nose deep in the case, like smelling a flower for the first time. When we drove home, I held the guitar case like a mom grasps a baby to her chest. I was excited, if not delirious and already in love with an instrument I couldn't yet play.

I immediately began weekly lessons. After learning the basic open chords, then bar chords, it was strumming and picking technique. After two months, *Landslide* by Fleetwood Mac was the first full song I learned. Next, *Stairway to Heaven*. I listened to The Beatles and Prince, trying to figure out their songs by ear.

I *had* to be on stage, singing lead and playing guitar. I needed to perfect my rocker stance. My makeshift mic was the blade of a hockey stick, balanced between piles of books under my bed. Singing at the top of my lungs to the stick handle, playing guitar, I fantasized in front of the mirror. I'm famous, playing at an arena, as far away as possible from this room, this house, this life in Waterloo.

I practiced guitar and singing every day after school for two to three hours at a time. I succeeded in mastering enough chords and progressions to prove to my parents I was ready for an electric. They honored their word; six months after they bought me my first, they bought my second: A Fender Jazzmaster. It had a creamy-white body, cherry-red pickguard, three single-coil pickups, and a tiny practice amp to go with it that was not much bigger than a shoebox for a pair of winter boots. The small amp had limited volume, so I turned it up as loud as I could until Dad banged on my bedroom door.

A schoolmate Paul took guitar lessons at the same place I did, and we had an instant musical bond. We loved the same bands, and both wanted to be rockers. We formed a group with two high school friends interested in the same goal. Our high school was small, 300 kids in total. It was easy to know who the other rockers were. With Jeff on drums, Guy on bass, four amateur but talented fifteen-year-old kids wanting to be rock stars became Trooper. We practiced nightly in Jeff's family's basement. I'm sure the noise drove Jeff's parents nuts, but I was so excited to play, I never asked. We had been offered a gig at our high school dance after we begged our high school band teacher to let us play. We mustered up cover songs of KISS, Journey, Van Halen, Scorpions, Jefferson Starship and REO Speedwagon.

At the dance, we played on the elevated gymnasium stage, curtains, lighting, and all. Outside of tangling guitar cables and some missed cues, we all got our bearings quickly. Naturals.

I wore a tight black blouse and jeans and one single red bandana wrapped around my head. I felt like I was in the rock band Loverboy. I happily played rhythm guitar and sang lead. I loved singing into that mic, commanding the gymnasium stage, and strutting. I especially enjoyed singing the word "bitch" when we played *Rock You Like a Hurricane.* Under the stage lights, I felt like a real rocker, a grownup, famous. Not the unsophisticated fifteen-year-old with dental braces. Also, our friends and other teens applauded like we were Def Leppard. Moreover, I was also doing something for me—instead of for my ill mother.

Still, Mom was supportive. She came to our show that first night and stood in the back of the high school auditorium, alone. Dad chose not to go. She congratulated me and never mentioned my use of foul language.

8

NOTHING BUT A DREAMER

When I was a little girl, my mom made a mania-induced promise to take me to New York City—a promise she kept in 1984 when we visited my Aunt Nan, an actress. By that time, I'd already expressed my desire to move to New York after high school graduation next year and pursue a career in rock music or theater. Mom acknowledged my dream but would caution me back to reality. Her mental health was more stable these days. She said, "Honey, I've told you many times that you'll be famous, but you know I was sick? Just because I said you'd be famous doesn't mean it will happen." I ignored her comment and her taping hand on my seated leg. I gazed out the airplane window descending into New York City. The high noon sun sparkled off the high-rise metal buildings of Manhattan in the far distance like fine jewelry on display. All I saw was glitz, glamour, and opportunity. *Sorry, Mom, you've already planted that fame seed.*

The first second we walked up out of a subway by 5th Ave and The Plaza Hotel, I was knocked into by a passing stranger. I nearly fell over. No apology. He never looked back. I didn't care. I liked the oblivious manner of strangers. Mom, not so much. "Hey asshole, you almost knocked my daughter over!" she yelled, thrusting her middle finger at him. "That would never happen in Waterloo!"

"Mom, neither would this." Spellbound, I pointed to the endless array of buildings, Central Park and white decorative horse carriages waiting for passengers. It was like a fairy tale. I looked left, then right. City blocks extended for miles with endless opportunities on the streets: break-dancers performing to hip-hop blaring from a giant boom box; musicians, guitar cases open, busking. It was extraordinary: people yelling over loud taxicab horns; the strong smells of street food, car exhaust, garbage; the enthralling energy of New York City. This was where *everything* was happening: music, life, people, people and more people. My eyes dried up from not blinking.

"It is extraordinary, isn't it?" Mom said. With her arm in mine, she appeared caught up in the energy, too. Her eyes were big and full as she looked around at the city.

"Mom, you know I can make it here, right?"

"Honey, you're sixteen. Just hold your horses and calm down. Let's move slow, okay? Also, I've heard we shouldn't be near Central Park after dark so let's get to Aunt Nan." She squeezed my arm tighter.

***

I always idolized Aunt Nan. I had vivid memories of her and Uncle Wally, my dad's younger brother and their visits. They'd sweep in from the Big Apple to our sleepy farm town. Aunt Nan and Uncle Wally always looked dashing: he in a tailored suit and her in trim black bell-bottom pantsuits. Their attire was far different from farm town clothes: denim jeans, plaid shirts, baseball caps and muddy boots. She spoke with a smooth, long-winded, theatrical tone, and her evening cocktail was a martini, not the typical Wisconsin Schlitz can. She used a long cigarette holder, delicately balanced at the end of slender fingers.

Nan was petite, and her straight dark brown hair pulled back tightly into a neat bun. She embraced life, always smiling, laughing, hugging. Also, she carried herself the way I assumed a real stage actress should, with class and dignity. She always looked stage ready, with shoulders back, head held high as if performing a monologue. As a young girl, I had no idea what it was like to be an actor, but I was intrigued.

***

During my birthday trip to New York, I witnessed the stark reality of living the artist's life in that city. And the demise of my elegant aunt. My uncle Wally had passed away five years earlier of a massive stroke. It left Dad heartbroken and my aunt a widow, trying to survive on a limited income in an expensive city.

After Uncle Wally died, Aunt Nan moved from Manhattan to Forest Hills in Queens. Her tiny studio, all that she could afford, had one window, and it faced the elevated subway tracks. Every time a train passed, the floor would shake, and pictures rattled on the wall, and we'd raise our voices to speak. Her entire cluttered apartment was no bigger than our living room in Waterloo.

Nonetheless, with pride, she showed us around her oasis. She made it her own, with lovely trinkets lining the lone bookshelf that separated her living area from her bedroom. The walls were adorned with framed performance photos, celebrating years of acting. Her home was far less luxurious than what I'd fantasized. Cockroaches crawled the sinks and the only living room furniture a loveseat and armchair--were both covered with new throw blankets. (The store packaged creases gave away their freshness.) When we'd sit on either piece, the blanket collapsed and exposed the shabby furniture underneath. However, all I saw was the love in my aunt's eyes for her home, her city, for us.

Aunt Nan was in her early sixties and her acting opportunities had diminished to character roles. To make ends meet, she found side work at a department store selling cookware. Her cigarette smoking and alcohol consumption had reached a new level well beyond what I remember from childhood visits. On this visit, a lit cigarette never left her unsteady hand, and she'd start the late afternoon with a highball. Evenings would end with slurred speech and an overflowing ashtray, which included my mom's contributions.

Thankfully, my mom drank minimally, shooting me a look when Nan poured another round. Mom said, "Oh, Nan. Please enjoy your cocktail. No more for me."

"Oh, Mary. You're on vacation. Enjoy!"

My mom would smile and let her pour the vodka, but Mom would only take sips to appease Nan. The drunker Nan became, the less my mother pretended, and all together stopped sipping. I could tell it was difficult for Mom. Her hands trembled, and I imagined the unfamiliar environment and small apartment made her uneasy as well, being claustrophobic. Yet, at night, there was laughter and many good stories between the two over those cigarettes and cocktails. Moreover, there was love--lots of hugs and words of endearment. Late into the evening, their rousing conversations about family, politics, and love would finally drive me exhausted to Aunt Nan's bed, just on the other side of that bookshelf. On her thinning blanket, I comfortably dozed in and out, fantasizing my adult life in New York City. Mostly, I listened to their sweet voices, which occasionally shrieked in laughter or gained in volume as a train passed.

When morning came, and my aunt leaned against her dresser gasping, straining to put on her work clothes, I realized her life in the big city was difficult. My aunt and uncle never made it beyond *off, off* Broadway. Maybe I would? I'm a musician and a singer! They were only actors. Would I have more options?

While visiting, Mom and I took in Dustin Hoffman in *Death of a Salesman,* and *La Traviata* at The Metropolitan Opera. I was impressed with both performances and felt even more inspired to pursue the arts. Now, if only we could go to a rock bar. It was a long shot, but I asked Mom if we could visit CBGBs, the rock club I'd read about in *Hit Parader* and *Creem*. Her reply was, "CB what? Hell, no."

Even after seeing my aunt's hard life, I still wanted to move to New York City after high school. Maybe if I went to acting school, I imagined, I could appease my parents. Of course, I'd also hit up the rock bars.

But as the days in New York City continued, so did Mom's anxiety. She'd pick at her thumb with her index finger until it bled. She'd cover both fingers with a Band-Aid to stop the compulsion. Also, she added an extra anxiety pill to her morning and evening meds. When we were out in the city, she would hold me close while we walked, frequently commenting, "Oh, there are so many people here, and things move too fast."

After returning to Wisconsin, and in the months preceding my graduation, I secretly wrote to Aunt Nan, expressing my interest in moving to the city. She was supportive, even offering to introduce me to her agent. "I'll tell Lewis about your talents. He may have more luck with you darling, and finally someone in this family will be famous." She also was a tad discouraging of my ambitions. "It costs a lot to live here. You'll have to work many side jobs before you even set foot on a stage. But this city is for dreamers, sweetheart. And you certainly are one."

9

CRUSHED BIG APPLE

Dad knocked on my bedroom door a few times, interrupting my guitar practice. He politely asked me to meet him and Mom at the kitchen table for a talk. The kitchen table had always been the family meeting place, the location of all household discussions. At times, their outcomes had been delightful, like learning we'd vacation at Disney World. Also, there were times of despair, like when Dad told us his brother Wally died, Aunt Nan's husband.

I slowly walked down the stairs, not in a rush to get to the kitchen on this late February afternoon. I assumed our talk was about my plans after I graduate high school in four months, and we'd most likely disagree. I paused at the window at the bottom of the stairs and looked out at the end of the winter snow. The once fluffy stuff had now melted down to hard patches blackened by car exhaust, and the lower half of cars look like they were spray-painted white from the salt that splattered up from the roads. The exact salt that was spread to melt the ice also rusted vehicles, stained boots and if you got a good whiff, it smelled like an over-chlorinated public swimming pool. If you had a collectible car, you never took it out in the winter. But we had a family station wagon, and it was parked in the driveway with salt and rust climbing up its sides like unwanted vines.

Sitting at the table, I provided an audibly loud swallow that held my anxiety down to my stomach. Mom was holding her coffee mug close to her chest, with both hands wrapped around it like she was protecting a baby bird that lived inside it. Dad was sitting sideways in his chair at the head of the oval kitchen table, his legs crossed, and his hands casually placed over each other. The only digit moving was his index finger on the lower hand, in a slow pulse, tapping the fake wood laminate table.

"I know what you want to do, Laurie. You've made it clear on many occasions. However, leaving folded notes with NYC circled in a heart on my work desk does not convince me. Neither does your leaving a pamphlet from Stella Atler's acting school on my bed pillow."

"Dad, it's Stella *Adler*. Not *Atler*."

"New York City is too big, Laurie, and too far away from Wisconsin." His voice softened like he was talking to a toddler. "Sweetheart, you live in a town of two-thousand people. You're only seventeen, soon graduating high school. Now is not the time to go."

He changed strategies. "Look, you've shown interest in the travel industry, and there is a reputable trade school in

Minneapolis, and we think it's a suitable alternative to New York. You need to get some education and still be close to home."

"Dad, I've shown interest in travel because I want to get out of Waterloo."

I was frustrated. I knew he was right. In the past, I talked about how it would be cool flying around the world as a flight attendant or working for an airline. I thought their jobs looked exciting and their uniforms elegant. Something was intriguing and sexy about going to new places with new people. But I thought I'd accomplish that by being a musician.

"Dad, I know to work for an airline or travel agency is cool but it's not New York or music."

"Laurie, it's either stay here in Waterloo and find a menial job or go off to the school in Minneapolis. I'm giving you an option, a damn good one, and you should be grateful. Oh, and there will be no more discussing it." He appeared comfortable and unfazed; in this house, he held the gavel.

I sat to the left of my dad. I slowly rolled side-to-side on the armless swivel chair. My hands were out of sight, under my legs. My fingers were scraping along the trim of the dark-brown vinyl seat. *Tom Sawyer*, a song by Rush, was playing in my mind. Anytime I wanted to escape reality; music was the remedy.

Mom sat across from my dad, still holding her mug closely. Her face was flat. I couldn't read her. Then again, I'm not sure she'd debate him in front of me. He was the alpha; and he was fifteen years her senior. He automatically led her-as he should, she was the unstable one. But I had ways of convincing him: Daddy's little girl tried once again.

"Okay, Dad. I get it. But I've been talking about going to New York forever. After last year's visit to Aunt Nan, I really feel I can do something magical there."

My father crossed his arms over his chest, leaned back in his chair, and raised an eyebrow. Most likely my word choice—"magical"—had not helped. I paused, sensing the tension. His stiff posture revealed he's unsympathetic. On this topic, there was nothing I could say or do to sway him.

"Well, I guess if Minneapolis is all there is, it's better than staying here in Waterloo," I said, resigned.

I glanced towards my mom. She ignored me and looked to my father. His bald head, reflecting the hanging red and yellow iridescent lamp above the table, was a shiny hue of orange.

He looked up and warmly smiled. "I think it's a good option, Laurie."

"But, Dad, you know I want to pursue music and acting too" He frowned. He's taping his finger again. This time, faster. "Okay, I'll go to the travel school. It's a good back-up. But I want to see what's happening with music in Minneapolis, too." "Laurie, drop it!" He slammed down his fist on the table hard enough to be heard but not hard enough to shake his coffee mug. "Go to school and get the certificate before you consider music or theater. Concentrate on school first. And grow up a bit."

He pushed himself back from the table and stood up, tucking his golf shirt into his pants. He sighed, meaning he was done with a conversation. Before leaving the room, he turned to me, jiggling the keys and coins in his pockets.

"Laurie, it's a big world. You have a lot of time to see it. And you will. This time, do it for me, okay? Just stay focused on school," he said.

He glanced at my mom. She set her coffee mug down on the table. She was now looking directly at me, her eyes welled up with tears. I saw the truth in her face. She was the one behind the decision to make me go to Minneapolis--not him. She was leading this cause.

Even though I was unsatisfied, I reached for her hand resting on the table. She took it tightly and let out the deep breath she'd apparently been holding. I had no idea how she must had felt, but she looked frightened. She was so damn vulnerable. I didn't want to hurt her.

My dad remained in the kitchen, one hand leaning on the counter for balance as he somberly watched us.

"Okay, I'll go and focus on school," I said, conceding. "I'm lucky you're giving me a chance." I smiled at my dad. He bowed his head in return and left the room. I looked at Mom, still holding my hand. Her face was red and eyes wet; on the contrary, her smile was broad. It took my breath away when she jumped up and hugged me, giving me no chance to stand. I guess she knew I'd push hard for New York. She had told me on many occasions: You can be as stubborn as your dad.

"Honey, I know how much you love New York, but I'm not comfortable with you being that far away."

"Mom, then why did you take me there? I thought you want me to be famous." I pulled away from her hug, continuing to hold her hand as she sat back down.

She didn't reply. She gripped my hand tighter. "Mom, I would be okay in New York."

She didn't shift.

"Okay, I understand. I'll go to Minneapolis if it makes *you* feel better," I said. Pushing her hand away, I stood to leave. "Honey, you, hold your horses. No one wants you to succeed more than me but at the right time. I need you to take it slow. For me." She stood and hugged me again, even tighter.

Dammit, it's always for her! But again, even with her mental illness, she's a smart, wise mother. Possibly she knows something I don't.

"Okay, Mom. Okay."

My mother's hug remained strong, with no inkling it would dissipate soon. Pressed against her large breasts-which only the women on her side of the family were gifted-I smelled her Fendi perfume. It brought me comfort. I will miss her. She drives me mad, yet she is my mom. Maybe New York is too far away. For now.

10

SMOKING HOT MINNEAPOLIS MUSIC SCENE

What my parents didn't realize was the Minneapolis music scene was on fire. It's the city of Prince, Husker Dü, The Replacements, and many others. Paul, my bandmate from our high school band, Trooper, had just moved there. My mind swirled with excitement for the music that would be at my fingertips.

In August of 1985, a few months shy of turning eighteen, I arrived in downtown Minneapolis with my parents as nervous chauffeurs in the family station wagon filled with dorm essentials. My music dreams were forefront but kept hidden from my parents. I stood on the street outside the all-girl dormitory and read the plaque on the building. *The Pillsbury Club--supported by the Woman's Christian Association.* I stared at the tan brick eight-story building in dismay. *Christian Association?* Was this Mom's doing? I scanned the streets for public transportation options for future escapes.

As my parents unloaded the car, I gaped at the city in front of me. This was not at all like the feeling I had when I visited New York City, but it would do. There were blaring car horns, tall buildings, sidewalks filled with people of all races, classes, and attitude, moving at a pace that left Waterloo far behind. This was an exciting reality for me; I already liked the vibe-except for the girls' dormitory. Although the dorm did put me smack dab in the middle of downtown Minneapolis. Also, I wouldn't be alone in the nunnery; some other high school girlfriends were moving from Waterloo to attend the travel school and live in the dorm, too.

Before my parents left, Mom and I explored downtown, walking to Nicollet Avenue a few blocks away. We walked arm and arm, holding each other close. I was thankful that my mom, now medicated for years, kept her makeup, hair and appearance attractive and conventional. There was a part of me that didn't want her to leave, yet I couldn't wait for her to go. We looked at department store windows, luring us in to ogle and laugh at things we couldn't afford. We left the stores empty-handed, strolling back to the Pillsbury Club dorm.

"Well, my darling daughter, Dad and I need to start the drive back. It's five hours," she stated, her voice serious.

"Yes, I know, Mom. We just drove five hours up here," I said, laughing. Usually, I would expect, "Oh, you're a smartass," at my comment, but this time she was quiet.

"Laurie, I love you. More than you'll ever know. We'll see you in October when you come home for your birthday." She looked away when she started to crumble and cry.

"Mom, you'll be fine. I'll be fine! I love you so much," I said, pulling her to me. I tried to hold her as tightly as she had held me at the kitchen table.

My dad interrupted the hug--the hug all parents eventually give their kids when they leave home. As a kid, you might wish you could wiggle out of a hug like that. Then years later, you may want to wiggle back in when things fall to pieces.

"Come on, Mary. We need to go," he said, gently pulling her from me. She obliged and let my dad come forward for his hug. I watched her, in tears, walk away to the car. He pulled my attention back to him, grabbing both my hands and looked directly into my eyes.

"You know where home is. We're a call away. Stay close to the dorm, study hard, and be safe. Be smart. Always walk on the sidewalk, don't cut through parking lots. And remember, bad choices will catch up to you. So, don't do stupid stuff."

"Jeez, Dad, now I feel stupid when you say it like that. Like I have stupid potential. I'll be good, don't worry," I said as I tried to release his hands. He increased his strong hold on mine.

He looked at me sternly, his eyes not blinking, "All kids have stupid potential, Laurie. It's expected. Just stay off Hennepin

Avenue, here in downtown. I've heard bad things." He grabbed me for a firm, brief hug, and patted my shoulder.

"What've you heard, Dad?" He let go of me. His face hardened. He zipped up his jacket to his chin, warding off the crisp autumn breeze.

"Just watch yourself. This isn't Waterloo." "Okay, Dad." I decided not to push it.

"Goodbye, Laur." He patted my shoulder again. He appeared uncomfortable to leave, forcing his hands deep into his jacket pockets. He studied my face before he turned to walk away.

I didn't wait to watch them drive away. I didn't need to see them leave. I already felt their absence, and I was already thinking about when to go to Hennepin Avenue.

11

BREAKING ALL THE RULES

Just as Dad suggested, I spent the first month getting accustomed to the sights, sounds, and intensity of big city Minneapolis. The cockiness I had being on my own when my parents drove away turned to waves of homesickness in the first few weeks. I called my mom every other day just to hear her voice and stayed close to the comforts of The Pillsbury Club. Dormitory life was safe, if not bland and boring. Also, quiet. So fucking quiet. By the end of the first month, my desire and curiosity to explore the city had grown. It eventually gripped me and distracted from the *Pillsbury Club Dorm Rules*; the rules by which all wholesome, young Christian women should live by:

1. No men allowed
2. No alcohol or drugs
3. No smoking
4. No loud music
5. No parties

6. No animals
7. 10 pm curfew on weekdays. 11 pm curfew on weekends. Doors lock at curfew and do not open until 6 am
8. If you do not plan to return by curfew, you must call to report your absence

By the end of the third month, I broke rules 2, 4, 5 and 7. I almost broke number 1, but I knew they'd notify my parents because *it puts all the women at risk if a man is in the dormitory!* Rule 7 I broke a lot, because of number 1. So, I broke 8, too. Now the age of eighteen, *my* Pillsbury Club rules: dorm life by day, city life by night.

I hung out more with Paul from Waterloo, who was like a second brother. He made me comfortable in the city. He had the biggest laugh. Everyone was drawn to his great sense of humor and genuineness. His one-bedroom apartment near Uptown, its walls lined with rock posters and beer signs, became a party magnet, especially for us dorm dwellers. He'd also developed into a badass lead-guitarist, with '80s-rocker hair: flawless, shoulder-length, frizzy, spiked on top. He was the quintessential party headmaster.

Paul held ritual weekend bashes, with three expectations of those entering: Drink, laugh, and listen to loud-as-fuck music. He entertained the McConnell Travel School girls, and his fellow Brown Institute buds, with cheap-ass Cold Springs beer or whatever else we could modestly buy from Chicago-Lake Liquors to get us hammered. Zeppelin, Van Halen, Kiss or Cheap Trick screamed off the vinyl. There was always a knock at the door from the Super to "Turn it down," or "You kids need to go somewhere else to party!"

A few months after my arrival, Paul and I saved enough cash from our parent's weekly allowances to hit a budget music studio, where we recorded an original song we co-wrote called *Boy-oh-Boy*. It was my first time in a studio, but I wasn't nervous, just excited. I felt at ease and at home in a sound booth or at the mixing board. Funny thing is, we had no idea what to do with the song after we finished except play it over and over for our friends. For the time being, that satisfied my rock star desires.

We both attended tech schools by day, but by night we hit every bar we could get in to catch live music. We headed to Uptown, and other areas around the city, for small venues with sticky floors, horrible pours, cheap door prices, and bouncers who didn't always check your ID. Like Mr. Nibs on 26th. Mr. Nibs became our go-to. We continued this routine for months, mastering an ability to keep awake during school, hungover, and finding live music shows at night. Paul seemed to like the rock star fantasy, but it was not his big dream anymore. "Rock 'n roll is cool. I mean, I like playing guitar. A lot! Fuck, I wish I was Eddie Van Halen, but that's not happening," he confessed one night over some Rolling Rocks. "But Laurie, this is what you came here to do. You gotta find a band."

I complained that not being nineteen yet, the legal drinking age, there were bars I couldn't get in. My options were limited, though we did make it to Hennepin Avenue and downtown's First Avenue and 7th Street Entry. First Avenue was everything I imagined it would be, just like I saw in *Purple Rain*–this was Prince's home base: an altar to Minneapolis music. However, since I could only get into all-age shows, we explored further on Hennepin to an area called Block E. It was full of street creeps, homeless, and drug addicts, all floating around outside skanky bars like Moby Dick's, which had rumors of naked women walking around inside. The endless run of police cars up and down Hennepin recalled my dad's admonishment to stay away. I could hear his voice: *Bad choices will bite you in the ass later.* Or something like that. The street life entertained me, but I wanted to find bars with live music.

After eight months of studies at the McConnell Travel School, as I promised my parents, I proudly got my travel agent certificate. To have been a more realistic representation of my studies, my diploma should have had beer stains and White Castle grease marks on it.

The backup plan was in place. I moved into an apartment with Paul and another Waterloo alumnus, Amy. The apartment afforded me freedom with men, liquor, and loud music--all of which my former dorm overseers would have found deplorable.

My parents supported the move when I convinced them I'd find travel agent work. I also found a part-time job at Dayton's Department Store. I had come clean that I was looking to find a band; however, I was not honest about the amount of time I was spending on that goal.

In May of 1986, the drinking age in Minnesota was nineteen. Later in September that year, the state would change it to twenty-one. If you were already nineteen as of September 1, they'd grandfather you in, and you could still get in bars. That was great for Paul and my other friends who were a year older, but I didn't meet the criteria. I would turn nineteen in October, missing the grandfather clause by six weeks. It meant I'd have to wait two years until I was twenty-one to get into bars. I couldn't let a six-week cutoff stand in my way. I wanted to find a band!

Instead of applying my efforts to travel agency applications, proving I knew the three-letter code for worldwide airports, I focused on becoming a fraudulent nineteen-year-old. I took my birth certificate and, ever so gently and precisely, erased the seven in 1967 and added a six to change it to 1966. I made a copy to disguise the forgery. I took it to the Minnesota Department of Transportation and applied for an identification card. For some reason, I imagined it would be illegal to obtain a driver's license with an invalid birthdate, but less so for just a state-issued identification card. Though my logic was skewed, it worked. Besides, I didn't have a car. With the arrival of my identification card in the mail, I became nineteen.

A newspaper ad caught my eye: a local hard-rock cover band was looking for a female singer. The ad took me to a dive bar in St. Paul, where I watched a live show of four long-haired, hard-rocker dudes. They were in their late twenties, wearing ultra-tight t-shirts with strategically placed rips, and red or yellow bandanas tied randomly around their heads, arms, and legs. Their jeans were so tight, the blood flow to their nuts must have been cut off. Their show was decent, not great. It might be a good place for me to start. After the show, Mike, the band leader invited me to come back the next week to their practice. He told me to prepare *Barracuda* by Heart and *Whole Lotta Love* by Led Zeppelin. Up close, I noticed his long hair was clip-in hair extensions. His façade slightly bothered me, but I was still stoked for the audition.

Nervous but excited, the next week I showed up to their basement rehearsal room below Mike's music store in St. Paul. On limited funds, I worked on the best Wendy Melvoin look I could come up with. I sang *Barracuda* and played rhythm guitar on *Whole Lotta Love*. I knocked both out on their loaned electric guitar and equipment, as I only had my acoustic guitar with me. They offered me to sing lead on girl cover songs, and to play rhythm guitar on the guy covers songs sung by Mike. It was his band, named for his last name: Runner.

It was official! I was in a band! A real band in the Twin Cities. I felt so damn cool. I told all my friends with excitement as if I had just joined Prince's band.

I didn't call my parents and announce the news. It hurt I couldn't tell my mom. I usually told her everything. She'd be excited by this but maybe not just yet.

12

COVER BAND

The band Runner was soon playing local gigs around the twin-cities, at least two shows a week: dive bars to start, within weeks, larger clubs as we got better. My fake ID was paying off. I was singing!

One of our gigs was at a St. Paul bar that shared a passageway, a door between venues, with a strip club. Same owner, different stages. After headlining a weekend gig ending at 2 am, we put off breaking down our gear until the next morning. That next day after loading equipment, the guys in the band wanted breakfast at the strip club: band perk is free food.

It was the first time I saw a female other than myself completely naked. I'd looked at porn magazines when I stumbled on my parent's collection but seeing another woman in the flesh was shocking. She was petite, bleached short hair, big breasts, masturbating with a dildo on an enclosed stage framed by a six-foot-wide by a nine-foot-high cage of Plexiglas. Patrons could feed her money through a bank teller style window. Three burly, unshaven men sat in front of her, eating their breakfast burritos, watching her go about her business. I sat ten feet away at the bar with the guys, going about our business, eating free food. My bandmates ogled the stripper, although never tipped her. I acted nonchalant although I couldn't help curiously looking up from my eggs at the display. I'm not sure what struck me more: men eating Sunday breakfast watching a woman masturbate like it's a sporting event, or my knowing the difference between her stage performance and mine. While I dressed scantily on stage, I'd never take my clothes off. I used my voice, not my tits.

During the day, when not singing, I offered pleasantries and politeness to customers at my part-time Dayton's job. I wore a below-the-knee skirt and a turtleneck, one-inch-heeled dress-shoes, pantyhose, and minimal makeup. At night, I was a small-time rock-star, in a one-piece lace nightie over torn fishnets, four-inch spike-heeled boots, and black eyeliner streaked an inch wide across my eyes from temple to temple, screaming "Fuck yeah!" into a microphone to an audience that roared in response. My hair was ratted sky high, and I was having a blast, playing guitar, getting my finger-tip calluses built up. I loved to sing lead, hearing the crowd shout with excitement at each song I introduced. I enjoyed seeing people happy. They accepted me. I wished we were playing original music, but I had to start somewhere.

The emotional high I got from playing was unimaginable. I shivered with pleasure with each kick of the bass drum and the roar of the guitars. The sound on stage was ear-deafening, and I couldn't get enough of it, mainly when I knew I was one of the people creating the onslaught of noise.

I was having so much fun at night, I started to hate my day job in equal measure. Every time I showed up at Dayton's, I thought, *I can't fucking do this.* I wanted to rock out all the time. I considered leaving my job, but this band wasn't making money. I had to continue offering daytime pleasantries to obtain nighttime debauchery. I reminded myself that within a year of arriving here, I was playing live on stage in Minneapolis, doing what I wanted.

As for my parents, I told them I found a band, as a singer. It was casual, I added, part-time and they shouldn't be concerned. They were unmoved, distracted, and that made more sense when Mom told me during one of her phone calls that they were divorcing after twenty years of marriage. It was not surprising. I wondered why it hadn't happened sooner. But she said her illness, while it was better, was too hard for the two of them to continue a relationship. She needed to focus on herself. She tried to reassure me that we'd all be okay. But her words didn't ease my discomfort, however, knowing our family would never be the same. What would happen to our house in Waterloo? To our family dog? I was sad, tearful and I had many questions. Yet I didn't have much time to think about it. I was head deep in music.

13

THE ROAD

Notes from the tour bus:
Mike Runner – Band leader, guitarist and singer
Nikki – Lead guitarist
Narly – Bass player
Keith – Drummer
Doug - Roadie

Mike found us gigs outside of Minneapolis on a multi-state touring circuit across Minnesota and North and South Dakota. "These gigs on the road should bring us more money," he explained. "There are way more venues to play outside of Minneapolis. We can head out of town in a couple of weeks when I get it all lined up. We'll *kill* it out there on the road. Who's in?" he asked the band one night at practice. His hair clip-ins still bothered me, but not his enthusiasm. He was a showman with his gold watch and pinkie ring. He reminded me of a used car salesman.

I was interested in more money and more experience, but with a cover band? At nineteen? Oops, I meant eighteen? Did I even know what the road demanded? Dayton's hadn't been the happiest with me. I'd been showing up late when I'd had a gig the night before. Once, I was caught asleep on a large bag of unopened new clothes in the storage room. I needed to keep the job unless we made enough on the road to sustain me. I was torn. I imagined everyone I would seek counsel with-my parents, roommates Paul and Amy– would tell me not to go. However, no one understood the emotional high, the giddiness, I got on stage when performing. On stage, I'd forget everything wrong in life: my lack of money and my parent's divorce. I was present in that moment, the performance. Decision made: I was going.

A week before we departed for our first of out-of-state gigs, Mike pulled us from rehearsal to the street. With his hand extended like Vanna White, he showed us a haphazardly repainted dark-blue 1970s school bus he'd converted for touring. The windows were blacked out with spray paint, except for the first three on each side. It was ugly, but the right kind of ugly for a low- budget rock band. Nothing glamorous about it.

"Dudes, you gotta see the inside. I've got this thing converted into a touring party pad. It's awesome!" Mike leaped up the bus stairs, "Come on!"

Entering the bus, the aroma of fresh raw-cut wood, used for making six unpainted bunk beds and an eating table, overtook me. The intense smell of motor oil diminished it.

"Mike, does this thing actually run? Will it even get us out of the state?" I inquired, hand partially covering my nose.

"I'm more concerned if it will get us back," said Narly, the bass player. He was 6'4" but not a towering guy. He was always bent over, giggling from smoking too much pot. But, his welcoming smile, even while framed with a porn styled mustache, made me feel initially the closest to him, like a brother.

"Guys, it runs fine." Mike's hands were on his hips, seeming to indicate disappointment in our lack of appreciation. "Look, I got a good deal on it. But bring your sleeping bag. This isn't the fucking Four Seasons."

"No shit, man. Where'd you get it?" asked Keith, the drummer, as he tried to open a jammed window, sweat dripping from his brow. Keith was a different story from Narly. Keith was a bit gruff, crabby about practice schedules and which songs we'd play. He'd say many times that I was the "new kid." Mike had mentioned to me that they had previous singers, and I was the first chick. I sensed Keith felt stuck with me, just as he did that jammed window.

"Doesn't matter, man, how I got the bus, it's all good," Mike said.

"Ya, I guess. But it's summer, man. It's hot. Does this thing have AC?" whined Keith.

"No, it doesn't have AC. It's a fucking school bus! Open a window if you get hot."

"Ah yeah, man, trying?" Keith replied while still fidgeting with the jammed window.

"What about a toilet?" probed Nikki the guitarist, observing with his arms crossed. Nikki always wore leather pants, jet black, same color as his eyes and his spiked hair that looked like a Troll doll's mane, except - sexy.

"Really, Nikki? Just hang it out the window! Shit. I thought you'd all dig this," Mike stated.

"Nah, it's cool, man. It's cool. We dig it," Narly responded. He patted Mike on the back. Mike brushed him off and walked out of the bus, shaking his head, mumbling something along the line of *ungrateful assholes*.

"Well, it's better than a van," Keith said, giving up on the window.

"I kinda like it," I said. "It's ugly as hell and smells like a gas station. I call top bunk," I asserted as I dashed to the bunks.

"Rock 'n roll, baby, rock 'n roll!" Narly yelled. He raced behind me to claim the next bunk.

Our first outing was for just a weekend, Friday thru Sunday. I brought my pillow and a borrowed sleeping bag for my bus bunk. When I set it up in a top bunk, I felt like I was going to summer camp - for rock stars.

I stuffed my retired school backpack with two sets of stage clothes, extra t-shirts and jeans, a makeup tote, and hair products. I was excited, nervous, cautious. Especially wary because I hadn't told my parents I was leaving. But, as soon as the guys in the band got on the bus, the chatter started, beers flowed, and music pumped out from a boombox, I didn't look back.

We played Friday and Saturday night. Three 45 minute sets each night. It was fun. It felt productive – I was advancing my music career. The out-of-town crowds were more engaged, excited, and far readier to party than in Minneapolis. They'd line up outside and pay a hefty cover charge to watch strangers, us, play live. They treated us like celebrities, asking for our autographs and telling us we're a big deal because we're from Minneapolis. I felt embarrassed giving my signature to them, yet, I obliged. I enjoyed their sincere enthusiasm. When they'd shout for their favorite cover songs, and we'd play them, they'd scream, dance and high-five us. We appeared to be the closest live music these small-town folks would get to the real deal. We sure the hell weren't Heart or Deep Purple, but these folks loved us.

We carried on for a month, playing out-of-town weekends. We crossed the Dakotas and played towns like Minot, Bismarck, Brookings, Sioux Falls, and other cities with names I struggled to pronounce. The bus was an old jalopy, but after a while, it became our home. If we weren't sleeping in it, we're partying or practicing as the miles carried on. It was not comfortable, and every bump in the road bounced us up and down like going over railroad tracks. Also, it needed a woman's touch of throw pillows, curtains, anything to soften the fact it was a renovated school bus, but I wasn't yet a woman — just a teenager. I missed my mom. I'd think how she'd make this bus cozy, but I didn't dare call her. She'd be furious I wasn't in Minneapolis.

The guys in the band treated me with respect: as a little sister. But they all drank. A lot. Especially our leader Mike, who sometimes had a hard time making it to the stage for the third set. During breaks, he would disappear with a hot chick or some fan offering blow or weed, and sometimes he'd return to the stage with garbled speech, forgetting lyrics, heavy eyelids, and missing music cues. He was embarrassing: it reminded me of my mom's alcohol binges.

At least one gig per weekend, he wouldn't turn back up at all. Considering he sang half the songs in each set; his absence was noticeable to the crowds when we'd repeat songs within the same set. It was awkward, and that pissed me off as the weeks progressed. I was also worried it would affect our reputation. I'd see the bar owner staring at us from the sound booth, with a "where the fuck is Mike" look on this face. However, I was on the outside of conversations. Still too "junior" to partake in the business discussions.

Doug was our only roadie, and he was always sober, and always made sure Mike got back to the bus after he'd gone MIA. Doug appeared oblivious to Mike's behavior, never mentioning it. Supposedly, they were longtime friends. Maybe Doug was somehow indebted to Mike? Otherwise, I couldn't figure his motive. Why be a roadie for a small-time cover band? The only conversation I tended to have with Doug was, "Hey Doug, where's Mike?" His typical answer: "He's around."

For each weekend of work, Mike floated each of us 30 to 40 dollars.

"Mike, this is hardly more than a gig in Minneapolis pays. And we played three shows this weekend. I need to pay rent back home," I complained.

"We need to play larger venues. They pay more. And the longer we stay out, we'll get bigger shows. You'll see. I got it covered, kid." He patted my back, in a dismissive way.

Mike landed more gigs. Sometimes we'd be gone for two weeks at a time, although the venues were the same size. We began playing weeknight shows, which meant smaller crowds. As we continued each month, I was catching on that the shows were not about the music. With each gig, there was less money. Instead, our reward was endless amounts of drugs offered to us backstage or on the bus. They were always rolled up in a white letter-sized envelope tied with rubber bands: cocaine, speed, weed, mushrooms, acid, white pills, brown pills, pink pills. The pills reminded me of my mom's technicolor array of meds, so I never messed with the pills, but I was curious about the white stuff, though not enough to try. Not yet at least. I was more worried about money.

Keith, Nikki, and I were eating complimentary grub at the empty, dim-lit venue we'd play later in the evening before the cigarette smoke, and stage fog would invade the air. These guys were seasoned on the road, not a rookie like me, so maybe they knew something.

"You guys, I don't get what the deal is with Mike. Why aren't we getting more money?"

"What? Come on Laurie, what did you think we'd get? Hundreds per night for each of us? This is the road. You get some cash, guaranteed bar food, free booze and free drugs," Nikki said, nodding and smiling as he noted *free drugs*.

Keith butted in. "When you add all that up, we're being paid well. Plus, being out here is better than back home with my girlfriend bitching at me all the time."

Keith's reply provoked more than the regular stomach discomfort in my struggle to eat the shitty bar food. It was the same junk offered at every gig: our choice of hamburger, pizza, hot dog, brat, cheese sticks, fish sandwich, fries, onion rings.

"Well, I didn't come along to get fucked up or play the whole show by myself when Mike disappears," I whined.

"And I didn't come to hear you bitch about it either," Keith snapped.

"Screw you! I'm just trying to figure things out. I need money!" I said.

Keith stopped eating, and tossed his pizza slice down against the paper plate. "Look, I've played with Mike a long time. Things eventually even out."

"Even out when? How? He's never around!" I said.

"Fucking whatever. I don't need this shit." Keith abruptly pushed his chair from the grungy fake wood bar table and left. The bartender looked up from washing his dishes, expressionless at the chaos.

"Man, go easy on her. She's just a kid," Nikki yelled to Keith. Keith flipped off Nikki without turning around, exiting the bar with a slammed door.

Nikki remained behind. He appeared unimpressed by Keith's departure. He leaned back in his chair, putting his hands behind his head. "Well, I hope he comes back tonight. I can't play drums, can you?" Nikki chuckled.

"No, not when I'm playing my part *and* Mike's too," I said, laughing, as well.

"Hang in there, girl. I'll cover Mike's guitar parts when I can. And you should eat all the free food *you* can. Oh, and the free pop, and beer. It'll hold you over," he said as he leaned forward, finished his pizza and wiped his hands on his shirt. "And watch out for the drugs. It can go south fast."

"No shit. The same to you, Nikki."

"Good, we'll cover each other." He held my gaze longer than usual. Our clinking Coors Light bottles cemented the deal.

Out of everyone, Nikki was the most in control of his drug and liquor use. He never got fully wasted or passed out. I felt a safety-net when he was around, and an attraction developed. As the weeks pressed on, we messed around in our bunks when the rest of the band was asleep or off getting fucked up post-show. He was 28 years old, ten years my senior, and I enjoyed his confidence. His swagger matched his impressive guitar playing. On stage, he was my partner, as we were the only guitar players when Mike was MIA and we'd lean against each other's shoulders or backs as we jammed out. Each night he was my teacher, both on and offstage. But it wasn't love. That much, I knew.

As the tour progressed so did my companionship with Nikki. My curiosity about the white stuff increased; tempted by the lure of everyone else outwardly happy on it. Also, I was bored when the show high diminished. I wanted everyone's attention again. I was especially lonely when Nikki was partying, and I wasn't.

When I did try, cocaine was amazingly fun…at first. Especially when Nikki held my long hair back for me as I snorted. I thought it was a loving gesture, but the coke still burned going up my nose and made my eyes water. But when the high kicked in, I was supremely happy and energized. The burn was a minor detail with each snort. So was the smell of a dirty rolled-up dollar bill.

I had a blast laughing and sharing stories with the band, strangers, dancing to the late-night jukebox, playing pool and just fucking off. Most bars would stay open past closing time, only for us and those we chose from the audience to stay behind. The party would continue until the sun came up and when Doug reminded us to board the bus.

By my fourth try of blow, I realized it wasn't fun anymore. It was at a post-show party somewhere in North Dakota. I got lax and combined it with a larger than usual consumption of alcohol, on an empty stomach. My mind raced and when I'd try to stand I'd fall over so I just sat there and stared at the partiers. Images of my mom and dad popped up in my head when my eyelids became heavy. I excessively shook, jaw clenched, my nose felt like fire, and I was on the verge of vomiting. As my anxiety increased, the faces of the post-gig groupies went from my best friends in the world to blurry faceless, crazed strangers. On that night, Nikki made sure I got to the bus and offered a downer and weed to calm me. I was too scared to try anything else, and I pushed it away.

"Nikki, will you just stay on the bus with me while I try to sleep?" I sniffled. A deep-seated fear of being alone was consuming me. But I couldn't be around strangers, being so fucked up.

"Okay, babe. You got it," he said as he continued his lines of coke off a bar plate on the raw wood dining table. On my bunk, I cuddled my pillow, my only piece of home. As I intensely trembled and headed off urges to vomit, I thought of my dad, my white eyelet canopy bed in Waterloo, and how when I was five I threw up for the first time from the flu. Dad had carried me to the bathroom and held my tiny head and my hair out of my face as I continued heaving into the toilet.

I still didn't have the guts to call my parents, even during this sick moment. However, in the previous days, I called the Minneapolis apartment, and Amy told me my parents had called now and then, and she'd give them excuses – I was working at Dayton's, whatever.

Cocaine lost its luster and scared the shit out of me. The high was never as good as playing live on stage. So, why do it? Most of all, the hangover–the anxiety and the depression–fuck that. I didn't want to become Mike. Or my mother. My choice was to be a musician. A healthy one.

I needed cash and food. Lots of food, because I needed to gain some weight that I had lost from cocaine use and lack of quality food. And I needed to shampoo my hair. At first, I thought my long ratty hair looked cool as hell, *rock 'n roll at its finest.* Then, it began to smell and become matted. I couldn't quite pinpoint the odor…a mix of cigarette smoke, fog machine, beer, sweat and Aqua Net? I'd usually freshen up with bathroom hand soap, but that was never enough. Once a week, we'd go to an economy road-side motel. It was a luxury to have a hot shower. Doug would park the bus out of sight of the motel office, and I'd go in solo and say I needed a room with two doubles, for my brother and me. *We're traveling to see our folks*, I'd say. I didn't feel bad about lying. I felt worse about my body order. After dark, the six of us would tip-toe into the room, like grounded teenagers. One by one we'd all get a shot at the shower, the guys always giving me the first round.

When we all looked like clean vagrants and smelled of Ivory soap, Mike would pull liquor and drugs out of his duffle bag and set up a makeshift bar on the nightstand between the two Magic Fingers bed massage machines. For a broke band, we sure had enough quarters to keep those beds vibrating, our laughter growing with each round, along with the volume of the TV, enough to summons the night manager to knock on the door and kick us out. It was rare we'd stay a whole night in any given motel.

Time on the road was wearing on me. My stomach ached, and my pockets were empty. I thought I'd be making more money and returning to Minneapolis with cash in hand and consider myself a professional musician. It had been close to two months we'd been on and off the road, and I wasn't sure if I had a job to return to or an apartment for that matter. I felt I'd lost track of life in Minneapolis and I couldn't recall the last time I'd sent money back to Paul and Amy.

At times, I feared when the next meal would come. I missed my parents. I was also scared of the horny partier who'd grab my ass when I walked off stage. Or guys who'd close in on me like a vulture, grabbing my arm, forcing me to the bar for a drink, until I resisted or Doug or my bandmates would tell the guy to get lost.

14

HAIRCLIPS

At first, the guys in the band were eager to accept road pleasures and drug bonuses. Eventually, as we finalized another multiweek stint, they got tired of Mike's bullshit and the drudgery of road life. One late night after a gig, tired, stoned on weed, and facing hunger pains, the other guys got pissed enough to take revenge.

Mike was passed out; his head lying sideways on the unpainted bus dining table, drool coming out his mouth like a kindergartener napping at his desk.

"Oh, hell, guys, Mike's out cold! Let's take his stupid hair-extensions and put 'em on the outside of the bus. Let's see how long they last after we leave," Keith said, wobbling towards Mike.

"Oh, yeah. I bet they'll last longer than *he* does on stage," Nikki said.

"He never used to get this fucked up. He thinks the clips make him look like a rock star, but they look ridic—ridicule-ridiculous," Keith stammered.

Narly pointed at Keith, acknowledging his struggle to talk and let out a high-pitched, stoner laugh, and joined the guys in gently removing the hair extensions.

Doug watched from his driver's seat in disbelief, his mouth wide open. I wasn't sure if he was about to laugh or shout. He didn't get up as the guys fastened the clips to the outside window next to the door. I sat in the seat behind Doug and didn't move either. I felt uneasy, though was enthralled by the circus show. I'd come to hate Mike, although I thought it bad making a fool of any drunk person more than they'd already made of themselves.

"Guys, be cool. Take 'em off the outside of the bus," Doug said in a calm, grandfatherly tone. He remained seated and turned away from them as if that would somehow release him from any involvement.

I let out a sarcastic laugh. "Why don't you make them, Doug?" I knew he wouldn't take the guys on.

"Shut up, Laurie." Doug sounded defeated. His head cowered.

When the evil deed finished, the guys high-fived and went to their unpainted bunks, and Doug started the drive of a couple hundred miles overnight to the next gig. We all fell asleep in our beds, as the hair clips flapped against the bus at 60 mph. I was sure a few were lost somewhere in South Dakota.

As the morning sun cracked through the windows, I was awakened by an agitated Mike, pacing up and down the aisle of the moving bus. His arms were flailing, and he was screaming.

"Where are my fucking clips, guys? What the fuck! I can't play without them!" He punched each of the guys in the legs as he passed their bunks.

"Really, man? You can't play without them? That's fucked up," replied a sleepy and annoyed Narly. He forcefully pushed Mike's hand away, almost knocking Mike backward. "Go back to sleep, dude!"

Mike continued the walk of terror, screaming profanities up and down the bus. He looked partly high and partly asleep. He passed me without a punch. He aggressively tore apart luggage and musical gear like a rabid dog looking for food.

As everyone was then awake, the prankster's soft laughter increased with each scream, but it only made Mike's rage grow. I didn't laugh. I was growing more anxious. The screaming was all too familiar.

Doug pulled the bus to the side of the road. He slowly approached Mike, hands raised either to protect himself from Mike or to jump him.

"Mike, chill, man. Just chill. Your clips are on the outside of the bus," Doug said.

"How can they be there?" pled Mike, with the innocence of a child…except for the bloodshot eyes, and cracked lips. He shoved Doug away and ran to the front of the bus. He pushed out the school bus doors. "Where? Where are they?" he screamed.

"Wow, he really doesn't remember anything?" I said. "He never does," answered Doug.

From my bunk, I watched through the windows of the now quiet bus, as Mike found his clips outside. He tenderly removed them. The five clips, he started with eight, were once twelve inches long, soft and wavy. Now they were matted and looked significantly thinner, shorter and frizzed. He came back onto the bus, unstable, struggling to keep his balance. Early morning light revealed dark black eyeliner turned to streaks down his ghostly pale face. No doubt from puking earlier last night. The guy spewed often when high. He continued to stand, barely, eyes closed, leaning against the dining table for support. Without a mirror, he attached the extensions back into his ear-length curly, brown hair. He didn't fix them up. Everyone stared at him. No one was laughing. I got down from my bunk to help him.

"Mike, do you want me to…to…clean those up for you? Put them in the right way?" I asked. The distinction between his real hair and the frizzy hair clips was significant. However, in his haze, he knew no different.

"No, no. If they're in. I'm fine, I'm fine," he stammered and stumbled to his bunk. Once he was horizontal, he instantly passed out.

At first, it was frightening to me and then entertaining: a hung-over man in yellow leopard-print pants and a beer-stained wife-beater, getting angry over hair clips. Not that he didn't deserve it, but his actions left me sickened. I didn't want anything to do with him.

We had only one more show, and I was sure we'd get through it once Mike sobered up and got his hair clips back in order. Then we'd be back in Minneapolis. I'd be bolting from this blue bus and quitting this band. I'd work at Dayton's and look for a quality band making original tunes. No drugs. No hair clips.

15

SMELL LIKE MICK JAGGER

When I got back to the Twin Cities, my plans crumbled. I learned from Paul and Amy that we had a week to vacate. "Oh shit, we're evicted? I'm sorry, guys. I'm so sorry. This is totally my fault. I know I haven't paid my share for a while," I said to Paul and Amy. I sat slumped on the living room carpet watching them pack their belongings.

"Yes, we know," Amy said. She was fluttering around the apartment continuing to pack. "And you haven't called for a long time, Laurie. Neither of us have the extra money to cover your share. I mean, I'm a little late with the rent too so I'm sorta responsible, but again, you're beyond late. Like a couple months late." For a second, she paused, and from across the room studied my matted hair and ragged clothing.

"Yeah, look, it's a bummer this is happening," Paul said, holding a box for packing. "Well, it's bigger than that. We gotta go to court to settle with the landlord. They're suing us for the back rent. I'm more worried how this affects me down the line because I paid my rent. But, whatever, it'll work out. I'm moving in with some of my buds until it settles down." He appeared more concerned with placing his vinyl collection into the box as he delicately held each record like it was bone China.

"Holy shit, we have to go to court?" I begged.

"Yup, the letter is over there with the rest of your mail." He pointed to the kitchen counter.

The eviction letter sat at the top of my small pile of mail. I didn't open it, taking Paul and Amy at their word. Behind the letter was an envelope from Dayton's, dated a month ago, which looked formal, with a stamped notice of "personal and confidential."

Oh, shit, maybe it's a paycheck! It'd been months since I'd worked for them, and I couldn't recall the last time they paid me. I did call them before my last departure with the band. I remember asking for a call-in part-time work schedule. I vaguely remembered the conversation with Human Resources. I opened the letter.

Dear Ms. Markvart:

Due to your lack of appearance for scheduled work hours on three separate occasions, and your failure to communicate promptly with Human Resources regarding your employment status, your position with Dayton's is terminated.

Sincerely,
Dayton Hudson Corporation

"Hey Paul, Amy, did Dayton's ever call here looking for me?" I called out. I tossed the rest of the junk mail in the garbage, tightly holding the eviction and termination letters to my chest as tears welled up.

"Not that I remember," Amy said. "The phone line was cut a week ago. That one is kinda my fault. I haven't paid the long-distance calls." Her face crinkled when she saw my tears. I held the termination letter up to her, unable to speak.

"Oh shit, you got fired!" She hugged me tightly, then pulled away quickly. "Laurie, what the hell! You smell like shit. Like beer and cigs and wow, literally you smell like a bar!" She laughed as she held me at arm's length, shrugged and hugged me again. I smiled and slumped into her. She didn't let go. I was thankful. She smelled like the perfume aisle of a drugstore and she's an example of the cleanliness I crave, albeit not the fashion. She's wearing a loosely fitted pink blouse tucked into white jeans imprinted with pastel flowers. Her long nails are painted pink, and her curly blond hair is pulled back with a lavender banana clip. She looks fresh off the cover of *Glamour*.

"Oh, screw it. You'll find another job. That was just part-time. Don't worry." She appeared cavalier and returned to her packing.

Paul emerged from his bedroom. "So, what is going on?"

"I got fired, Paul. I don't have Dayton's or the band. The band is done. Or I mean I'm done with the band."

"What happened?"

"It didn't work. We made no money. It was all for drugs. And I smell like a fucking bar."

"Well, yea, you've been playing bars. What should you smell like? I wouldn't expect Mick Jagger to smell like roses," he asserted with a jovial laugh. "That dude probably reeks of sex, liquor, and more sex. Ya, probably lots of sex." Paul gazed off smiling appearing to fantasize about the amount of sex Mick Jagger has.

My tears were turning to soft laughter. "Thanks, Paul. But, I'm not exactly sure what sex smells like," I said, my innocence showing.

"Neither does Paul," Amy added from the other room.

"Ha, ha. Funny, what do you know?" Paul came in closer for a whiff, leaning in. "Yup, you smell like Mick Jagger," he said. I slugged him in the arm and laughed.

"Look, I'm proud of you for trying. It took balls to go out there and play. So, it didn't work. Whatever. At least you tried." "Thanks, Paul. That means a lot. I still have dreams to make it happen."

"Well, cool. Keep trying," he said, returning to his packing.

I went to the bathroom mirror and looked at myself. Sunken eyes, matted hair reflected. I whiffed my tattered black The Cars concert t-shirt, and I did reek like a bar.

"Hey Amy, do you have shampoo?"

"Yup, I have conditioner too. I think you'll need a truckload of both," she said, appearing in the bathroom.

Paul reappeared. "So, Laurie where are you going to live?"

"Well, I sorta hooked up with the guitar player Nikki, and maybe I can stay with him until I figure it out. I don't want to call my parents yet."

"Ah, see! You do smell of sex," Paul said, roaring in laughter.

"Shut up, Paul!" Amy scolded Paul with a slap on his shoulder. "Laurie, you should probably call your parents. Your mom left a couple messages last week when the line was working."

"I know, I know. I got to get my story straight first. They don't know I left town with that band."

"You haven't talked to them?" Amy shrieked. The mere thought of talking to my mom made me cringe.

"Well, good luck with that, your dad will be pissed," Paul said. With a warm smile, he came into the bathroom and hugged me. Even though I smelled like Mick Jagger, it was a solid, brotherly hug.

"I'll miss jammin' music late at night," he said.

"Me, too."

Thinking back on it, hanging out late into the night playing guitar, drinking beers and jamming with Paul was an innocent time. Now a fond memory.

The next day, I met up with Nikki. He said I could stay at his mom's house if we kept the road relationship going in exchange. "So, we can be together? Like on the road?" he asked, as he gently caressed my breast underneath my jean jacket. "Yup, I guess so." I gradually pushed his hand down. I was less enamored with the opportunity. Also, his mom's house was in St. Paul, and I wanted to live in Minneapolis near friends. I didn't have a car or any cash, so I was stuck with him. Also, Nikki still did blow, especially if Mike from Runner offered some.

One weeknight Mike invited Nikki over to do as Mike called it, "roll an eight ball." I tagged along out of boredom. Mike was living in an upscale St. Paul high-rise apartment. I was astounded by the views from the 14th floor, but shocked Mike had no furniture. How could he afford this place, the Cocaine and not have furniture? He was equipped only with a folding card table, four folding chairs, a mattress, boom box and an acoustic guitar.

I sat with them at the card table and engaged in their conversation which strangely focused on politics. Eventually, as they rolled that eight ball, they became louder, rambling and arm wrestled like teenagers. I fled to the cement balcony, void of patio furniture, leaned against the steel railing and watched the night's twinkly lights. It was the end of summer and still warm, and I enjoyed the serenity of the perch, their voices muted by the sliding glass door. But I was lonely and frustrated I didn't have other options than that of an Owl. I returned inside, but between their loud banter, the cranked-up boom box, and their snorting, I was over it. I begged Nikki to leave.

"Oh, Laurie, don't be such a bitch. Just leave me alone," he'd say, nudging me away with his elbow. The guys stayed at the folding table under the dining room chandelier as if they were playing an intense game of Poker. Eventually, they squatted at the table, forgoing the chairs and attacked the next line of coke with the vengeance of a lion eating prey. My stomach sunk at their excess. Yet, I was relieved that in their white bliss they were oblivious to my presence.

At 4 am I fell asleep on the beige carpeted living room floor with my white jean jacket under my head like a pillow. I was satisfied the carpet smelled clean. At least this place wasn't a dump. At 6 am, Nikki curtly woke me with a light kick to my foot like I was a soccer ball, "Let's go." He was still high, and he hadn't slept.

***

It had only been two weeks since I'd been back from the road, and I wanted to pull my shit together, find a stable job, and a good band before I reported back to Mom and Dad. Until then, I got food stamps, applied for government food assistance and got coupons for free milk and cheese. I hit the local food pantry. However, I was guilt-ridden accepting a bag of canned goods, pasta, and cereal, while disheveled looking parents and their crying kids waited in line for the same food. I left the bag behind, dodging their eye contact.

To avoid the food pantry, I agonizingly visited a pawn shop. Fellow musicians told me I could get a loan for my belongings. The small store stunk of cigarettes, moldy carpet and sweat. I tightly held my black fringe cropped leather jacket to my chest before handing it over the glass counter, to the greasy, bearded, middle-aged chubby pawn guy. He held it up and ran his fat hand along the fringe, cigarette in the other hand. He smelled the jacket. "Good leather. This will sell." I cringed.

"I'm coming back for it. I want a loan. I'm not selling it," I said firmly. I shook my head in disbelief at my situation.

"Okay, fine. You'll have thirty days to pay off the loan. You need to make weekly payments, and if you don't, it's ours by default at the end of the second week. Also, there is a twenty percent interest rate, per week." My chest hardened at the circumstance.

"What else you got? I see you brought in a guitar, too?" he asked. I hesitated. I looked above him at the twenty electric and acoustic guitars hanging on the wall. It looked like an art exhibit for crushed dreams.

"How much you giving me for the leather jacket. As a loan?"

"Thirty bucks. But I'll give you fifty if you outright sell it to me."

"No, no, I'm coming back for it," I said again. His face was placid. I could tell he didn't give a shit.

"Kid, I'm busy. So, what kind of guitar you got there?" he said, as he ruthlessly tossed my jacket onto a table behind him.

I gently placed the guitar case on the counter. My hands shook as I opened each latch, revealing my Yamaha acoustic. The aroma of the wood evoked the same emotion when I opened the case for the first time when I was fourteen: giddy excitement. Without asking, he took the guitar out and played. He was good, fat fingers and all. My unease that he was playing *my* guitar like it was his brewed an immense amount of anger in me.

"Never mind, never mind. I'm keeping the guitar." I motioned with my hands for him to return it to me. He deadlocked on my eyes, still plucking, cigarette dangling off his lip.

"I'll loan you seventy-five dollars, or I'll buy it for one hundred." The air was thick, and my spirit sunk. Fretting, I looked down at the floor just in time to see a giant cockroach crawl over my white Huarache sandal. I shook it off and stomped on it. The crunch satisfied my frustration but only for a second.

"I'll do the loan. On both. I'm coming back for both. I am," I proclaimed.

He gave me the same look a school teacher gives when you turn in a paper you think will be an A, but they know you're getting an F. "All right, I'll write it up," he said.

I looked up again at the other hanging guitars. I *will* be back for this Yamaha. I walked out of the store angry but cash in pocket.

Over the next couple weeks, I donated plasma at a blood center for twenty dollars a pop. I applied for work at a local employment agency. The typical first question from a well-groomed and professionally suited man behind the desk was, "Why did you get fired from your previous job?"

"Well, I was on the road with a rock 'n roll cover band and..." No offers. Between bus fares and buying food, I was running out of time and money. The due date for the pawn loan installment was coming up, and I didn't have the cash.

I knew my next step: call my mom. The person I wanted to impress the most; the woman I ran from, was the only one I could turn to.

16

BLEW MY CHANCE

I practiced over and over what I'd say to Mom, like working on lines for a play. I had to tell her the truth. She'd sniff the guilt out of me if I lied, even over a phone line. I was nauseous with nerves when I called her from a street corner payphone-collect, of course.

"Laurie? Where the hell have you been?" she asked, sounding frantic.

"Mom, I haven't been in touch because I've been on the road with a cover band. That band Runner. I know I told you about them, right?"

"Yes, I remember, but why have you left Minneapolis? Are you still working?" Her voice still sounded high-pitched, like she sucked helium.

"Mom, I'm working. Well, I was. With Runner."

"What do you mean? Are you still at Dayton's?"

Silence overtook the phone line as I paused.

"Well, I got fired from Dayton's, Mom."

"Oh, God. Why?" Her voice shrieked.

"Well, I wasn't showing up because we were on the road. It's not a big deal. I mean, it's not like I stole something."

"What the hell does that mean? Getting fired is getting fired, Laurie."

"But, Mom, just listen. When the leader of the band said, we'd hit the touring circuit as a full-time cover band and make some money, I agreed. I need money! And, you know, I want to play music. There's a lot of money for cover bands."

"Laurie, how much are you making? Why is the number on Aldridge disconnected?" She was hitting me with questions like an assembly line.

"Uhm, well, about making money. The band really hasn't made any--not what I was promised and not enough for me to pay rent. Well, and the phone is disconnected because we're, well, we've been evicted. I'm now staying on the couch at the lead guitarists mom's house."

Silence. Dead fucking silence.

"Mom, I was too afraid to ask you or dad for the rent. I know you two are going through a lot and well, I'm sorry, Mom." My chest tightened with each word.

"Laurie, you never told us about leaving to play with this band. You didn't even ask to do it. Let alone ask for rent!"

"Mom, I didn't need to ask! I'm an adult!"

"Yes, you are, my dear, with adult problems. You're homeless!" She screamed so loud I was sure all Waterloo heard. I yanked the receiver away from my face. Frowning, I stomped my feet three times to get out my anger before returning to her.

"Mom, I really thought this band was going to do okay. I thought we'd make money and I would get better as a musician." I paused, taking a deep breath. "Look, I'm freaked out, but, I'm trying to do the right thing. I quit the band."

Silence. Again.

"I screwed up, Mom, okay? There is no money, and I had to get food stamps." The volume of my voice increased, and frustration mounted.

Pin-drop silence. Not even the sound of her husky-throated smoker's breath.

"Mom? Are you still there?" The pitch of my voice changed and started to quiver.

"Laurie, this whole time I thought you were in Minneapolis." She took a deep suck off her cigarette. "Are you using drugs? Are you drinking?" she pled with a quiver in her voice, too.

"No, Mom, I'm not. I don't like drugs. I'm scared of them. Please don't tell Dad. Please." I paused again, a deep breath to contain myself. I paced as far as the pay phone cord allowed. Street noise came and went, and my voice got louder to overcome it when needed. I yelled, "I've gotten better as a musician, though. I have."

"What? I don't care about the fucking music, Laurie!" she screamed. There was an edge of hysteria in her voice I wasn't familiar with. It incited fear and defensive anger in me.

"Mom! I want to stay in Minneapolis and find another part-time job. Live somewhere decent. I'd even move back into the Pillsbury Club." *Desperate times call for desperate measures,* I thought. "I want to find a band to make original music. I just want another chance."

"You blew your chance, Laurie. You've been fired and evicted! You're embarrassing!"

"Blew my chance?" Of all people, Mom knew how much I loved music, how much I needed it. Part of why I played was for her approval. She's the one who wanted me to be famous!

"I should tell your father because he is the one who thought you could handle moving to Minneapolis. I knew it was too soon. Goddammit, Laurie."

With the mention of my father, my heart sank to rock bottom. He did think I could handle Minneapolis. Yet her comment fueled my growing irritation at her response.

"Mom, it doesn't matter if it's Minneapolis or Madison or wherever, I'd still find a band. I just found the wrong band. Could you give me some credit? I'm trying!"

Silence.

"Oh, so what, Mom. Was I going to just stay in Waterloo after graduation? And do what? Be a drunk? Like you?" I blurted out.

Knowing my words had become weapons of my anger, I stopped. Her deep, raspy breath cracked with each inhalation. She was breathing heavier. I could imagine her lips, pursed.

"Laurie, I am coming. No, your *father* and I are coming to get you. I don't care if you're an adult. And I don't care what you think about me. I know I have a problem." She took a deep breath. "But I'll be damned if I'll let you have the same problem." Then she loudly exhaled, and I again pulled the phone away from my ear.

I was so mad, and yet, so hungry. Hearing her forced solution, I was relieved thinking of returning home to my old bed, to food, to normalcy. Even to her.

"Okay, Mom. Okay, okay. I'm sorry. I'm so sorry." I wept. My tears were not only out of sadness, more so from defeat, and embarrassment for having referred to her as a drunk. *How could I be so cruel?*

"Laurie, well, let's get you home, so there is only one of us who needs the work." She was crying now too. Her response brought resolve.

I'd miss Minneapolis and, most of all, playing live – the anticipation and excitement before the show, the cheer of the audience, the metallic taste of the microphone against my lips encouraging me to pour my guts out to onlookers. Then again, I needed to go home. I needed my mom-even my pissed off, unimpressed mom. I needed her hug. Not just any hug, but *her* hug. Besides, if she was still drinking, it couldn't be any worse than what I witnessed on the road.

Two weeks later, after a court appearance for back rent-my parents paid off the landlord-I said goodbye to Nikki. With more sadness, I said goodbye to Paul, Amy, and other good friends. As for my leather jacket and guitar, the pawnshop owned them. I didn't dare ask my parents to repurchase them. Heartbroken, I imagined my beautiful Yamaha hung on the wall with the other guitars. When packing the station wagon, Mom asked, out of Dad's earshot, where the guitar was. I told her. She frowned and shook her head. As Dad approached us, she appeared uneasy as if she didn't want to engage him and indeed not this subject. She was merciful and whispered, "Well, you can pawn an instrument, but you can't pawn talent. Just remember what you have."

17

THE MILES BETWEEN

The long 5-hour ride south on Highway 94 from Minneapolis to Waterloo was miserable. I was in the backseat as Mom drove; Dad sat shotgun, reading a book. Or he appeared to read, glancing up every few minutes to check her driving. After all, she had let the previous family car roll through a plate glass window into an ice-cream shop. Grandma had been in the front seat, my brother and me-toddlers-in the backseat. I don't remember the incident; nonetheless, it's family lore. "Mom, why are you driving?"

"Because I want to," she stated curtly. My dad didn't look up from his book.

She kept all the windows down, presumably, so her smoking wouldn't irritate my father. She was knocking off one cigarette after another. It was early September, still humid and hot. My long, ratty rocker-hair was flying uncontrollably, some of it sticking to my sweaty face.

"Mom, can we roll up the windows and put the AC on?"

"No." She glared at me through the rearview mirror. I clenched my jaw and let out an audible groan. Plumes of smoke went out my mom's window and flew right into my face. Car sickness crept in and produced a headache and queasiness. I lay on my right side. The hot black vinyl seat stuck to my face and bare legs. Oddly, I liked it.

My parents were silent, occasionally glancing at each other. I worried for them, and I wasn't sure where their dismantled relationship would leave my brother or me, but the warmth of the familiar back seat encased my body and, in my mind, for now, it melted the coldness I felt between Mom and Dad.

As I dozed, in and out of restless sleep, I was clammy, hungry, thirsty. I was incredibly sad that with each mile closer to Waterloo, I was a mile further from Minneapolis.

I gazed at the back of my dad's head, tilted forward, now apparently asleep. Perspiration was rolling down the back of his neck. My mom had two-hands on the wheel and no cigarette. *Oh, thank God, she finally ran out of them.*

"Red, I'm going to pull off for gas and cigs." *And there we go, she'd get more.*

"Yup, sure, Mary," he said, bringing his head up to full attention. "Laurie, you hungry?"

"Yes, thanks, Dad." I sat up slowly, fearing I'd tear the skin off the side of my leg stuck to the seat.

"But Mom, can you put the AC on after this?" I whined. She didn't reply and pulled the car into a truck-stop diner in Tomah, Wisconsin. My dad exited the vehicle and walked rapidly to the diner entrance. He opened the door and waited for us. I slowly exited the car, fearing the truck stop was where I'd get the impending "big talk" on all my recent fuck ups.

As Mom and I walked to Dad, she paused, turned and hugged me. She whispered in my ear, "No, I won't put the AC on because I think you need to feel the heat if you haven't already."

A swell of anger grew, and I couldn't form words. I wasn't sure if I was more annoyed with her for using that stupid analogy or because she really meant it. I pulled back from her coveted hug. Her stern expression softened as she read the frustration on my face.

"I'm sorry, Mom. I didn't mean for this to happen. Can't you cut me some slack?"

She hugged me again and rubbed my back. It's a hug that told me she wasn't as angry as she appeared. I gently wept into her sticky, smoke-reeking shoulder.

"Oh sweetheart, just calm down." She pulled away, eyes slightly red.

"But, I'm not turning on the AC. You'll have to live with it."

"Come on, ladies," Dad yelled, still holding the diner door. "I have to piss like a racehorse!" Mom and I laughed as we walked arm in arm towards him.

Hours back on the road, the smell of cow manure pierced my nose so I knew we were close to home. As we entered Waterloo, I leaned my head against the car window and wearily looked out at the familiar houses, businesses and my high school that hadn't seem to change as I had.

Our family dog, a Sheltie named Alex, whom I did miss, greeted us with barking as Mom turned into our long gravel driveway. Alex pounced on me as I bent down to him, and he licked every bit of sweat and dried tear off my face. Following directly behind was my brother. A far cry following my wretched example, he was in technical school for mechanics and close to a degree. Still bent down, I looked up at him. When he shook his head, I showed him the middle finger. He smiled. "Good to have you home, Laur."

"Sure, Dave. Sure." We shared a brief hug. We were not close. We had vastly different desires in life. He loved Waterloo and planned to stay and drive semi-trucks, be a mechanic. We may not have been similar, but we shared the same past with the same parents.

The four of us convened at the kitchen table for what felt like the last family meal. We were somber as we passed around chicken casserole and blueberry muffins. With mixed emotions, I was glad to be with my family although unhappy about the circumstances. Most of all, I was sad about my parent's divorce-now so obvious in a house filled with Dad's moving boxes.

"So, I found a house to rent in San Antonio," he announced. "I'll be leaving in a couple of weeks after I get my affairs in order here."

"So, you've settled on Texas then?" Mom asked. She appeared unmoved. She seemed to already know his plans. My brother didn't stop eating or look up; apparently, he was in on it, too.

"Yes, I like the idea of the heat as opposed to these damn winters. And there are many Air Force bases where I can bum around."

I stopped eating. *What the hell?* I had assumed, while I figured out my next move for music, I would live with him in Madison. That's where he first moved after my parents initially separated. When discussing the return to Waterloo with my parents, I thought he'd be nearby.

"Dad, can I help you move?" asked Dave. "I need to work on my long-haul driving."

"Great idea, Dave. I need to pull a U-Haul so, yes, I can use the help."

"Awesome, I can't wait to drive it!" Dave smiled, piling more food on his plate. Obviously, he's had more time to adjust to all these new plans and ideas.

Holy shit. What is happening?

I hit the table open-handed, tears welling up. "Wait! Am I the only one who knows nothing about this?" My mom and dad reacted with swift glances at each other, confusion on their faces.

"I didn't come back for you to leave me here, Dad!" I could barely eke out the words. I ran from the kitchen up to my room, slamming the door behind me. I landed face-down on my bed. The familiar scent of my pink blanket was comforting. The room was quiet, peaceful, untouched. I continued crying. I couldn't be left alone with Mom. I loved her, but I just couldn't-not here in Waterloo.

Recognizing the firm knock on my door as my father's, I wiped my face. He had been remarkably quiet on the drive back from the Twin Cities, and he had yet to address my shenanigans there.

I opened my bedroom door to a somber man. Up until that moment, I hadn't noticed how tired he looked; his shoulders slouched. I lunged to him, hugging him tightly. He reciprocated. "I'm sorry if I've hurt you, Dad. I know I've really pissed Mom off."

"Laurie, come on, let's sit down." He closed the door, and we both sat on my bed.

"Are you okay?" he asked.

"Yes, Dad, but I can't stay with Mom. You know that." My tears welled up again. "Just the idea of you not being here, and her-well, she's still not right." I fell into his arms again.

"Laurie, just calm down. Calm down. You know, you never let me finish my story of moving to Texas."

"Dad, it's just a shock. I want you to be happy. You've worked so hard for us, but I still need you around."

"Well, that's the rest of the story, Laurie. And yes, I know Mom is not healthy yet. She's working on it. But, she can't help you while she's trying to get better. So, with your mother's permission, you are welcome to live with me in San Antonio, if you'd like."

I pulled back from my dad and stared at him in disbelief, like an oasis in the desert. He held one of my hands.

"Really?"

"Yes," he responded with a curious face as if it was a no brainer.

"Oh, my God!" I screamed. I hugged him again. I'd go anywhere with him.

"Thank your mother; it was her suggestion. I want you to come, too, but she knows what you need. She's willing to let you go again if you're with me."

"I'll do much better this time, Dad. I will."

"I know you will, Laurie. You'll be under my roof and my watch." He sternly patted my hand three times and held it securely.

"What about Mom? This will be hard on her."

"Yes, but David is staying here. She'll be okay. We'll all be okay."

"What is Texas even like?"

"Hot. Flat. And a new beginning for both of us."

We sat silently. The room was warm, not stuffy. I gazed around at my youthful bedroom with red shag carpet, pink and white vertical striped walls and remnants of stuffed animals. This room that held my childish dreams now revealed the promising endeavors of a young woman.

"When do we leave?"

"In a couple weeks. It will give you time with your mom. She needs that much. Stay here at the house and enjoy each other. Laurie, she may be ill, but she loves you so much. And she's been doing good, considering we're separated. We're getting along fine. Someday we'll be friends."

"Okay, Dad. Okay. Thank you."

He left, shutting the door behind him. I moved around my room, admiring childhood knick-knacks, rubbing the dust off them. I tumbled onto the bed and looked out the window: the same window through which I'd watched when Mom would stumble home.

There was a soft knock on the door. My mom. I didn't rise to open it. As expected, she walked in. She lay on the bed next to me and whimpered in my ear, "I hope you don't think I'm pushing you off to your father, but I know you'll be safe with him. Selfishly, I want you to stay. But, if you stay here, you'll be bored. And I'm afraid for you if you're bored. And I just can't help you. I need to get better. And I feel bad about that." Big tears flowed down her soft, plump cheeks. I wiped them away. She felt warm next to me. Comforting and familiar.

"Mom, do you remember when I was little, and during the winter, you'd lie in my bed, so it would be warm when I'd come out from the bath? I'd crawl in next to you, just like this, and we'd giggle."

"Of course, Laurie." Her crying stopped. She smiled widely, and her eyes twinkled. "I loved doing that for you and David."

"Well, now I'm going somewhere so hot that I won't need that anymore. So, I guess you're off the hook. Now, you can take care of just yourself," I said with conviction.

"Oh, sweetheart. Thank you. That memory makes me happy. But honey, I want to help you." She grasped my arm firmly, head nestled on my shoulder.

"I know, Mom, and you do. Most kids can't tell their parents anything, yet I can tell you everything. Though I was scared to call you from Minneapolis. Scared to disappoint you."

"You can always call me. Day or night. Please remember that. I may not always approve of what you do, but I'd rather you call me than a friend or a pawn shop. Laur, you are the wind beneath my wings," she said. Her head remained on my shoulder.

I hated it when she uttered that because I felt like that, too, and it was a burden. However, this time, I let it leave my mind. I would not be here long, and while I hadn't missed this quiet town, I missed moments like these.

We lay silently, arms entwined. There was no question that Mom and I had a unique relationship. She was my true confidante. Sometimes, I was her only hope. She was my greatest supporter, and yet, she was my darkest secret and worst fear.

18

CULTURE SHOCK

Hot and flat-Dad was right about Texas. I'd left the land of 10,000 lakes for the land of 10,000 ranches.

Dad settled us into a newly-built, middle-class, one-story house in a planned community along a golf course in San Antonio. The house smelled like new paint, and our feet made imprints in the plush carpet like boots in fresh snow. The house felt bare compared to our place in Waterloo, but Dad was there, so it was home.

He gave me the master bedroom and private bathroom. Unprovoked, he bought me a waterbed.

"You know, it's the new thing in beds," he said. "I want you to be comfortable." I didn't have the heart to tell him I got seasick every night as I'd settle in.

Each day brought a new surprise. Lots of people in San Antonio wore cowboy boots and pressed Wrangler jeans. They found their weekend entertainment in honky-tonk bars, where people line-danced, rode mechanical bulls and wrapped their

Lone Star beer bottles in a white bar napkin. Fist fights broke out as often as slow dance songs. There was nothing wrong with any of this, although I'd been asked too often by the bar locals in their long drawls, "Where you from, sugar?" When I'd say *up north*, most responded with, "Dallas?"

I must find a rock bar.

During the first six months, Dad and I golfed, went sightseeing, visited Air Force bases, ate at Luby's Cafeteria a lot, adopted a dog, and visited family that lived nearby.

Dad kept the kitchen stocked with food he'd buy from the Air Force Commissary - a grocery store for military personnel. From chips to soda, fruits to meats, veggies to ice cream, I never went hungry again. Although the ice cream was more his nightly thing, Root Beer Floats to be exact. He'd sit back in his recliner, ankles crossed, and watch PBS shows, slurping every bit of vanilla from the glass. I was happy to see him content. Retirement from his machine shop job suited him. He was more relaxed and chattier and still played his classical music on the weekends. He even took up violin lessons. He said he needed to expand his mind and abilities as he aged. He often lamented he hated getting older.

I found a part-time administrative job as a receptionist. It was boring, answering phones, making copies, but it got me out of the house and put some cash in my pocket, none of which Dad wanted back in rent. He only asked me to pay for my clothing, personal essentials and occasionally buy him dinner. Dad often said, "I'm glad you're here, Laurie."

"Me, too," was my stock reply. I was enjoying the comforts under his roof, although lonely for friends my age.

My mom had a new man in her life, Stan. They were already living together in Waterloo. When she came to visit by herself, she appeared happy, patient and calm. Not manic, nor depressed. Her candid humor was not forefront, although it was there on occasion. I assumed she was medicated but didn't ask. Surprisingly, she also didn't ask many questions about what I was up to, though she frequently asked if I was happy.

"Yes, but bored," I'd say. "Not forever," she retorted.

My parents, then one year divorced, were friendly. My dad didn't have a new woman in his life. During mom's visit, he gave her his bed while he slept on the couch. It was just like my childhood, except she was sober, and he was untroubled.

She stayed a week. On her departure, she provided her approval: "Red, it looks like you're taking care of our daughter very well."

"Thank you, Mary." They hugged for a few seconds.

When it was my turn, I got a bear hug. "You look good, pumpkin," said Mom. "I miss you desperately. You two take care of each other."

Pumpkin. I wish she would have stayed longer.

In my search for friends and music and a way to quell my boredom, the only group I found affinity and enjoyment with were thespians-the gays and straights of a small musical theater scene.

19

ALL THE WORLD'S A STAGE

I stumbled upon the theater scene on Fort Sam Houston Army Base. Dad and I were driving around the base and discovered the Harlequin Dinner Theater. It was open to the public, though its origins were to support the troops. I could tell by the professional black and white headshots lining the lobby wall that they brought in seasoned actors. It was a reputable theater, and I would have loved to audition for a show. With only a chorus part in *Pirates of Penzance* from high school on my resume, I planned to return when I had more experience. Just the idea of auditioning for a show here made my legs shake.

I discovered other theaters around town. I attended open auditions and got a chorus role in *Funny Girl* at the San Antonio Little Theater. Contrary to the theater name, it was a 350-seat establishment with an orchestra pit and all. I was excited, if not thankful, to be back on a stage. Later I was cast as *Snow White* and

Rapunzel at San Antonio Children's Melodrama Theater. Playing both characters were fun but felt vanilla and trite. I liked to perform for little kids, as their vulnerability for suspense and action were priceless, but I was 21, and my patience was limited. I couldn't take one more five-year-old asking me how many dwarfs were in the seven dwarfs.

I ached for action, adult content, fun. The Main Theater was where I found it – an intimate 40 seat theater with a small, 2-foot-tall and 14-foot-wide stage. They were producing a run of *Vampire Lesbians of Sodom.* I had no idea what the show was about, but I wanted in, based on title alone. I auditioned and got a minor support role. I was mesmerized by the zany, intimate community of free loving, cussing, straights, gays and those who didn't give a fuck about anything but putting on a stellar show. I daydreamed during my day job, counting the hours until that night's raucous rehearsal. I felt free, expressive, and on the verge of something new, explorative for me. I didn't tell my dad the name of the show until the days preceding opening. He wasn't angry, but he chose not to attend and said he'd support me in another show.

The *Vampire* run was a turning point into adulthood. Specifically, during one show when a front row patron was casually kicked back in his chair, enjoying his cocktail and resting his feet on our stage like it was his coffee table. Our feisty lead actor stopped mid-sentence, looked the guy up and down and with Shakespearean flair, asked him, "Dear sir, do you see my dick in your drink?" The astonished man replied no but left his feet on the stage. I held my breath, and the audience went quiet, all watching the patron. Our lead retorted with the growl of a gang member, "Then get your fucking feet off my stage!" The patron's face turned four different shades of tomato, and he removed his feet as the crowd roared. Our lead turned to the three of us on stage and smiled an evil grin like a kid who just ripped off a candy store. He returned to script without a beat missed. My stomach danced in excitement at the display, and I knew then; witnessing this slightly older and more seasoned actor that the stage was a sanctuary for endless opportunities to create my own expressions if I desired.

I felt ready for more acting responsibilities, and I still had an urge to make my dad proud and comfortable. With more confidence, making my way back to the coveted Harlequin Dinner Theater I won a support role in *No Time for Sergeants,* and eventually the lead in *The Nerd.* I was thrilled to play the leading lady and Dad was enthusiastic, giving me flowers on opening night. Moreover, per my father's rules, *this* theater was an acceptable place for me to perform—with no advertised vampires and lesbians.

The great camaraderie with the various cast and crew reminded me of being in a band. Live theater was intoxicating: backstage banter; dressing room smells of makeup, hairspray; and flowers on opening night. Right before a show commenced, I loved to stand behind the curtain, breathe in the dampness of the velvet drape, and peak out into the audience. The excitement in the air left me breathless. Costume changes were the most fun, with the cast running about in a rehearsed formation; sometimes half-dressed, boobs out, wigs flying off. Also, the process of acting: perfecting the lines, staging, marking, was profoundly engrossing and satisfying. I experienced a strong sense of community with the theater companies.

Nonetheless, I missed rock 'n roll. I watched new bands like Guns n' Roses, Metallica, and REM take the national rock scene by storm. Damn, I wanted back in. However, the theater had become fulfilling, a secondary substitute, and it appeased my father.

During the second week of an eight-week run, as I was playing a lead role in *Titanic*, at Turner's All-Night Drugstore Theater, my acting came to an abrupt halt. I woke up in the morning with the right side of my face weak and droopy, like a clown's sad face. I ran out screaming, "Dad, what's wrong with my face?"

"Oh, my God, Laurie. Did you have a stroke?" He rushed me to the emergency room. I was diagnosed with Bell's Palsy, paralysis on one side of the face. I was horrified. Scared. I looked in the hospital mirror and touched my face, trying to move the dropping side up with my hand.

"It just happens," the doctor stated. "The seventh cranial nerve on the right side of the skull, behind the ear, has been cut off due to swelling. It could be a virus. It usually happens to the elderly. It's strange; you're so young. Well, you should make a full recovery within four to six weeks." He sent me away with pain meds, anti-inflammatories, and the phone number of a local physical therapist.

I had to quit *Titanic* but went out with a bang. Instead of exiting stage left, embarrassed and with my tail between my legs, I did my final show with stage makeup only on the functioning left side of my face. It was strangely odd when I saw my reflection. I looked grotesque, yet I felt powerful. Before the show, I told the audience I was only capable of giving them half a performance, and it was true. I gave them the most enormous smile I could, revealing my dysfunctional, distorted face. The small, intimate audience quietly clapped, the look on *their* faces a mix of horror and curiosity. The show itself, a dark comedy, was fitting for my departure from acting. Problem was, I didn't want to depart quite yet.

I did not make a full recovery within four to six weeks, as the doctor predicted. The right side of my face remained paralyzed for four agonizing months. The pain behind my ear was a persistent throbbing like I'd been clubbed against the head. I wore an eyepatch at night to keep my eyelid closed. There were times when I was overcome with hopelessness and despair but found it impossible to cry when my eyelid wouldn't close. I carried a bottle of eye drops with me to lubricate my eye, which was every few minutes.

I would never unconsciously take the act of smiling for granted again. I spent the first four months as a hermit. Every day I looked in the mirror, on the hour, for a change. Eating was messy. At times, in private with my dad at home, we'd joke about my eating--he bought me a baby bib. Mom called often and begged me to come home so she could take care of me. I entertained the idea.

Outside of a part-time day job, I was embarrassed in public. I was distracting to other people and often they stared. I wore big sunglasses to hide my disfigurement. I'd tape my eye closed with medical tape when wearing the sunglasses. Sometimes I just went out…fuck it…this is who I am now, and I'm not going to succumb to embarrassment. Yet I just wanted my face back. My smile.

At month five, spasms in the facial muscles appeared and little jolts of what felt like static electricity tickled my face. I could muster up a faint smile on the Bell's side. We visited a neurologist.

"You should have recovered sufficiently by now," the doctor said, his glasses sliding down his greasy nose as he examined me. "I'm sorry to say you have some residual effects. It's called Synkinesis. The nerves growing back are cross-wired. It's uncommon but it happens." I looked in the mirror, and he was right. I hadn't noticed before. When I blinked, my mouth also twitched. When I attempted to smile, my eyelid closed.

"What can we do about it?" pleaded my father.

"I'm afraid nothing," the doctor said flatly. He didn't look up from his clipboard. He checked his watch.

"That's not an option," I said, turning to him. The doctor stood up and shuffled his feet into a casual stance. His head was down. He pushed his glasses back up his slippery nose as he walked to the door, partially turned to us and said over his shoulder, "Be happy you have nerve growth. I have patients here with Cerebral Palsy, Muscular Dystrophy. Your case is minor. In comparison, you're normal." He left the room.

"What an ass! Okay, I hear what he's saying about his other patients. But this isn't normal!" I said, pointing to my face. "I actually use my face!" I slumped into the exam-room chair.

My dad stared at the closed door, his face hardened and red. "Oh, that sounded so stupid. Everyone uses their face," I said.

"But I need my face to work for acting, for music, for everything. If I can't show expression, how can I work? It's like rowing a boat with one arm."

Dad remained quiet. His face became redder, and his breathing louder. He made fists with his hands. "Laurie, you're a pretty young woman, and you still have a lot going for you. We'll figure this out. But I didn't like his Goddamn attitude. I'm going to talk to him." He steadily moved for the door. My dad rarely cussed so I knew he was pissed.

"No, Dad. Don't. He was rude, but he's right." I sat quietly, and my dad waited. He let out a deep breath and sat back down. He gently stroked my hand.

"I guess this is my new normal," I said. "Let's go."

My smile would never be symmetrical; my eyebrow would never raise with expression. My face would always contort when I smiled. But I had activity. Nerves were coming back. I'd work with that. I'd figure out a way to smile, to look as normal as possible. I would make something out of the shit I'd been dealt. I decided to use the hermit cave to my advantage. Since acting was off the table, I'd work on my musical abilities. I'd dedicate my time to singing, playing guitar and piano.

At the two-year mark of my arrival to Texas, and the year of the Bell's Palsy diagnosis, I ignored any residual facial malfunction, and fantasized, plotting my way back to rock 'n roll.

20

FIND A GOOD MAN

I was exploring San Antonio's music scene at Sneakers rock bar-looking for musicians, not love--when I met Patrick, a drummer the same age as me. He was there alone, and I was too. After our eyes met through the crowd, we started a conversation with a simple hello—no pick-up lines.

Patrick had a thick Southern drawl, was shy and soft-spoken. It was hard to hear him over the loud live music pumping from the stage speakers. At first, Patrick's shyness was challenging, but he became chattier and louder as the night continued. Plus, I liked his shaggy shoulder-length brown hair. He was handsome, fit, and had defined biceps that popped from his sleeveless Iron Maiden t-shirt.

Once I got the nerve up, I mentioned my Bell's Palsy. He said he didn't notice. Either he was lying or being kind. Or both. But his response did encourage me along as he was the first guy I flirted with after the Bell's came around.

That night at Sneakers, when we could hear each other over the music, we fell deep into conversation about our favorite bands, styles of music, different passions and hobbies, and everything else in between. I loved that he was sweet and kind and not looking for just a hookup. We watched the local live bands on stage, and we both commented how we'd like to play Sneakers in our own bands. But the talk about our music dreams dropped when he asked me to slow dance to Whitesnake's "Is This Love" that played over the sound system between live bands. I was smitten.

We ended the night making out in his old white Nissan 300ZX that looked like it was past its prime, and yet Patrick said it was his passion project to fix up. He said he was still living with his parents, and of course, I was living with Dad, so we didn't have many options for fun except to use that 300ZX interior.

We started dating immediately after that night. Patrick was excited to find a band, too, and he spoke of his interest in moving to Austin. He had spent his youth growing up near Houston before recently moving to San Antonio with his family, and to him, Austin was where musicians went to "make it." I agreed.

After a few months of dating, Patrick and I finally had his parent's house to ourselves. They went out of town to visit family, and Patrick and I settled in for a long summer weekend. Of course, the first thing Patrick wanted was to play his drums for me. Up until now, I hadn't heard him play.

His drums were set up in the lower-level den of the family home. He crawled behind his kit like he was getting behind the wheel of his 300ZX. He was all smiling.

I settled in on the couch a few feet away with a cold bottle of beer. I was excited but cautious to see what Patrick could do. Maybe he'd be another "skin beater," as we call them - one of those drummers who could hit hard but could not keep a beat. I hoped he was better than that because I didn't know if I could be honest with him if he sucked.

I took one drink of my beer, and he started. I didn't take another sip. I couldn't do anything but stare at him in awe. Patrick was a vibrant, hard-hitting, tempo-driven rock drummer. He had a large kit in jet black with two kick drums, and he played double bass, as I'd never heard before. His shyness disappeared the second he stepped behind the kit. Patrick hit the snare with such thrust and strength that I felt each hit vibrate my body like a shock wave, and it rattled the glass windows. It reminded me of my first Rush concert! Wow! I wanted to be in a band with this guy! But dang, we're dating. I was perplexed. What do I do?

After he was done, I questioned him, "Why are you not in a touring band? Why are you not in *any* band? Holy shit, you are incredible!" He smiled but didn't reply, except he asked for the tape I brought with of me singing "Boy oh Boy" that I recorded in Minneapolis. Now I was concerned. What if he thought *I* sucked?

I nervously chugged the rest of my beer as he listened to the song. He kept his finger on the cassette deck play button of the boom box. I was nervous he would hit the stop button at any moment and not listen to the whole song. But he never moved his finger, and he listened the entire three minutes and twenty-nine seconds. After, he took a swig of his beer, and he appeared perplexed. He didn't look at me but tapped his drum sticks on his thighs like he was deep in thought. He finally spoke.

"I like your style. Your raspy vocals. You're different." He had a frown on his face, and he struggled to look at me. He continued, "I wish we could play together, but that's not a good idea, is it? To join a band together?" We finally made eye contact.

I was stunned. Most guys wanted the traditional male singer, yet Patrick didn't care. I couldn't believe this was happening. To me, he was a dream drummer! And he wanted a female singer!

I was tempted to tell him we'd stop dating and start a band together as friends. But, instead, I replied, "You're right; it's not a good idea to be in a band together." I liked him enough; I'd rather be his girlfriend than his singer. Many times, down the line, I would regret that decision.

A month later, I sat down to dinner, and I broke it to Dad.

"Dad, I need to find a band again. Austin is where it's at. I've driven up there a couple of times to check out bands and the music scene is huge! I must go."

"You *must* go?" he asked, as he ate his favorite, corned beef and cabbage. I didn't stop eating either—it was also my favorite meal—but I did continue to look at his flustered face.

"Well, I knew I couldn't keep you forever. I've loved having you here, though this last year has been hard for you. I know you've been going to these rock bars, so I figured you're up to something."

"Well, I'm not getting into trouble. You know that much, right?"

"Yes, Laur, I know. But this Patrick guy. He's a nice young man, and I can tell he's into the rock music, too, just by his shaggy hair." Dad stopped eating.

Sitting quietly, I didn't reply.

"Well, you're 23 and not a kid anymore. Have you talked to your mom about it?"

"Yes. She asked me again why I can't stay with you longer or just come back to Wisconsin and find music there. But, I can't go back."

"Well, your mother will always want you at home or with me. She's a mom. Especially after the Bell's Palsy. She's getting better, although she's still an ill woman. And you two will fight if you went back." He took a drink of root beer, setting it down with pause. He appeared drawn into his thoughts.

"Well, I don't know about fighting, Dad." I put my fork down. Indigestion danced in my stomach at the mention of her illness. He's right. My need for her approval and her need for attention was always the base of our quarrels.

My hunger gone, I continued, "So, after some back and forth, Mom finally gave in and said, 'Go for it, kiddo, just keep your ass out of trouble.'"

"That sounds about right," he said with a huge smile that made an audible squeak. "I can't agree with her more. How about a job? Also, what about this Patrick guy?"

"Yes, Patrick is going too. We may live together," I said with caution.

"What, Laurie? Live together? No, no, no. Go together but live with someone else, a female roommate." He pushed back from the table and brought his half-eaten plate to the kitchen counter and set it down forcefully.

"Dad, I thought you'd be happy he's going. I won't be alone, and you like him, right?" I squealed.

"Yes, but you don't need to live together. You're not married," he said sternly.

He sprayed the kitchen faucet at full force over dirty plates in the sink, clanging and rearranging them as he went. His face frowning. I waited until he stopped running the water.

"Dad, it's sorta set. Honestly, we can't afford to live there alone. It's too expensive."

"When are you going?" he asked after a long silence. "Next month."

"Oh, hell. Well, do what you're going to do. You will anyway. What about work?" His eyes locked on mine.

"I'll find a temp agency and do admin work like I have here. It's my fallback, Dad. I'm not worried about a day job. I'm more worried about finding the right band."

"Of course, you are," he said with a sarcastic tone. He sat back down and stared at me; arms crossed. He held his breath as if he was about to deliver grave news and then let out a deep sigh.

"Laurie, why can't you just be a normal young woman and get a nice job, find a good man, a doctor, a professional, who will take care of you, and plan a lovely future?"

His words stung. I could sense his disappointment in me. I looked away. I never felt trapped living with him until now. He's never understood me. Besides, it's hard to find a good man when you're not looking for one. I was looking for a good band.

"Dad, I am planning a lovely future. In music," I said, looking him square in the eye. He unfolded his arms and just before he could move another muscle, our white cat jumped into his arms. Dad shrieked, "Oh, Jesus Christ!" and then sighed, petting the cat.

The only sound between us was Whitey's gentle purring. "Laur, do what you must do. I wish it were different, but I'll always be here for you."

Frustrated by his lack of approval but realizing this is about as good as it gets, I went to his side of the table. I hugged him from behind and kissed the top of his oily, bald head. Whitey jumped down, swirling between my legs. Dad moved his hand to my hand on his shoulder and briefly held me to him.

21

BAND WANTED

Patrick and I moved into a small second-floor studio apartment that appeared stuck in the late '70s with Formica countertops and laminated white cabinets. The brown stained carpet was at least a decade old and slightly musty, but we were excited to have our own place within walking distance to Austin's main rock bar, the Back Room.

After moving in, and stacking his drum cases up against the wall, we laughed as there was only room for a twin bed, TV and a folding chair. We used his tom-tom case as a coffee table and the bass drum case as a dining table.

Within a month, Patrick found an auto mechanic job and I landed a day job as the assistant to the Operations Director at the local newspaper, *Austin American-Statesman*. A few months into the position, my boss told me the job offer was between another woman and me. He said he probably would have hired her because she had more experience, but when he watched her leave the building from his office window, he saw her light up a cigarette. He knew then he didn't want her. He said cigarette smokers take too many smoke breaks. He hoped I didn't smoke and took a risk offering the job to me with less experience. And he was happy when he noticed I stayed at my desk, and I didn't, as he'd say, "smell like an ashtray." Of course his comment made me think of Mom and her endless smoking, but I pushed the thought out of my head.

I was proud of the position at the newspaper, and strangely, I was good at administrative work. It was the last thing I wanted to do, but it came easily to me: answering phones, printing reports, making copies, and the newspaper had a liberal vibe. Better than working at a bank! And I was pleased I had money coming in. Dad was satisfied, and I didn't want to be the starving artist I was in Minneapolis. Besides, I needed money to buy a microphone and rent rehearsal space. Being a musician wasn't cheap.

Patrick and I got along effortlessly, at first, even though we were different people. He was a homebody, and at the most, he loved to go hiking on the weekends. I liked to go out to bars, hang out in the music scene. So, when we caught bands at the Back Room, I was the talker; Patrick was the watcher. I chatted up with other patrons and bands, trying to find a way into the music scene while Patrick stood to the side. He was the nicest and sweetest guy, and the people who got to know him liked him. But his shyness kept him in the background. But we both loved rock 'n roll, so I went with the relationship. Besides, he was handsome, very good to me, and we were in Austin. And Austin was to Texas as Minneapolis was to Minnesota. A mecca of music. The city itself, Austin, was picturesque, with the rolling hills of the "hill country" to the west and the majestic state capital anchoring the downtown skyline. The vibe of the town was laid-back and liberal. There was a blend of diverse folks, University of Texas students, hippies, professionals, and lots and lots of musicians.

People appeared to get along very well while out and about and were welcoming to anyone. This was unique to Austin. Not so much all of Texas, unfortunately. In Austin, you could find hippies drinking beer with 10-gallon hat wearin' cowboys and eclectic musicians with tattoos and piercings working professional day jobs. In 1991, at most professional or corporate jobs, tattoos and piercings were acceptable. With rules. For a while at my new job, I covered my nose piercing with a band-aid. I had to "disguise it" as it didn't fit their professional appearance policy, but they finally gave up.

Times were changing. At any company, under long-sleeved shirts of young men and women were beautiful and funky tattoos. The "beautiful expressions" were covered up based on their company rules. But we all knew if someone in corporate saw the tattoos, they wouldn't get fired. There was a "knowing" in Austin that Austin was simply weird, ahead of the times, and like nowhere else. And I liked Austin a lot. I could be anyone here.

Sixth Street was the main drag for music venues hosting live music every night of the week: blues, rock, country, hillbilly, Tejano, metal, jazz, cover bands. In addition to Sixth Street, in other parts of Austin, other venues enticed me, too: Antone's, Liberty Lunch, The Hole in the Wall, The Continental Club,

Saxon Pub. However, the Back Room was where I set my sights to start.

Patrick and I began searching for separate bands, having decided it was still in our best interest to keep our personal life separate from our music. I tacked a "band wanted" notice on bulletin boards at local music stores and rehearsal spaces around town. I also placed an ad in the local free newsweekly *The Austin Chronicle* which read: **Experienced singer looking for original hard rock or metal band. No cover bands. No drugs. No bullshit.** I was nervous to mention I was female, afraid most rockers would focus on my gender and not give me a shot.

Not many original hard rock bands had female singers, and certainly not the metal bands I loved: Scorpions, Metallica, Black Sabbath, Judas Priest, Guns N' Roses. Imagine them with a female lead? That intrigued me. I wanted to be unique. I wanted to front a metal band. It didn't matter that I may have been shooting high; I wanted it.

Within days after posting my first ad, I was fielding calls. Some guys were straight-out uninterested in a female singer. One even said, "You're a chick. How can you sing metal?" *Next*!

This would not be my last experience with sexism against women fronting a metal band. Women were mostly seen fronting alternative or mainstream rock bands. They were accepted as the artsy musician or the sexy rock chick but not metal.

For a female to front a heavy metal band and write her own songs was not acceptable by many men in the bands, especially those promoting it. Male booking agents especially. Eventually, the booking manager at Austin's Back Room told me how to dress on stage. He never told the guys in the band how to dress, but one day he called me after one of our shows and critiqued the jean shorts I wore over black tights. He said, "You can't wear that if you want to attract a crowd. You're a pretty girl; you should show it off. Look, guys come to *hear* the guys in the band, but they come to *see* you. So, make it worth it." I was floored. I knew that my voice, my stage presence was what I wanted to show off. Not my legs and tits. Fuck him. But privately, I was worried that we wouldn't get better gigs if I didn't show a bit more. I bet none of the male singers in other Austin metal bands worried about how much skin they were showing.

So, booking managers, security guards, ticket office staff...all were wary of me or any female wanting to crack into metal. When entering backstage before a show, some security guards would ask who I was with in the band. They assumed I was "with" the band, not "in" it.

Music society said metal music was for the boys the rebellious, pissed, testosterone-driving male was to front a metal band, and the female was to show her tits and support her man when he got off stage. I had way more to offer than that. Plus, I was pissed off too. I wasn't sure at what, but I knew I was.

After weeks, and off the same ad, I found some guys worthy of a jam. A guitarist, drummer and bass player. We met up at a dingy rehearsal studio in a timeworn retail strip mall that was refurbished into rehearsal rooms. Twenty-five bucks for three hours for a room with a PA and carpeted walls to dampen the sound. We split the cost and jammed on some covers and got a taste of our abilities together.

I was slightly nervous. It had been over two years since I'd jammed with other musicians. I was distracted and worried they'd notice my Bell's Palsy. They didn't appear to, and soon enough, I was having so much fun, I forgot about it. It was invigorating, having a microphone in my hands again.

They were all excellent players, although I only felt a musical connection with the guitar player, Bobby. He was in his early twenties too, with long, straight, black hair past his shoulders, and he was skinny as all hell. He played a smoking lead guitar; up and down the fretboard with speed and precision. And he was friendly, with an air of confidence.

"Hey y'all, would it be cool to bring in another guitar player to thicken up the sound? I've heard around about this guy Levi. That he's a solid player. Should I call him?" inquired Ruben, the bass player. We all agreed, yes. A week later we were back at the rehearsal space to jam with Levi.

The first moment I saw him, I walked right by, not knowing it was him. He was sitting on the edge of a stained, hand-me-down couch in the rehearsal complex lobby, his guitar case and half-stack amp at this side. His frizzy hair was pulled back into a short ponytail. He was wearing loose jeans full of huge holes, and I wasn't sure how he was keeping those pants on with all the missing pieces. He appeared a few years younger than me. His warm smile was magnetic; I was drawn to say hello to the stranger. But I was eager to get to the rehearsal room, so I kept walking.

The drummer Joel, and Ruben were in position by their instruments, Bobby too in front of his Marshall half-stack, ready to jam when I entered the rehearsal room.

"Hi, Laurie. So, the guitarist Levi is here. I'll get him," Ruben said.

"Cool," I replied, as I set up my microphone and adjusted the floor monitor.

Ruben walked back in with the holes-in-his-pants guy from the lobby. Well, I'll be damned.

Introducing himself, Levi nodded to me with a big grin. I nodded and smiled in return. He set up his gear, and within minutes he was ready to play.

"Let's begin with *Kickstart my Heart*," Bobby said.

Mötley Crüe was not my favorite; however, it's a quick way to tell if a musician could play rhythm guitar or not, and it was a cover all rock guitarists knew. Bobby fired up the lead riff--it sounded like a car revving its engine. Levi followed and added the rhythm. He was solid. More than that, he was skilled and talented. I was now happy to join in and sing the lead. We played the whole song without a hitch.

"Wow, I like the way you play, man," said Bobby after we finished. He shook Levi's hand.

"Thanks, man. You, too." Levi looked at me again as if he knew I was about to say something.

"So, what type of music you into?" I asked Levi.

"I like metal, like hard, hard rock. Not glam though. Crüe is not my thing. What are you guys trying to play?"

"Hard rock or metal," I said quickly, not giving the others a chance to talk first.

"Yeah, but not heavy, heavy metal," Bobby inserted.

I shot a look at Bobby, realizing we differed in our interests. I was glad Levi was into metal. I totally dug this guy's style and energy: positive, lighthearted and silly and yet serious about the music. Interrupting my thoughts, the drummer Joel added. "I'm not into the metal stuff either. I like straight up rock."

"And I'm more of a rock guy, too," Ruben added, looking to Joel for support.

"Yeah, I think we both like it just solid rock," said Joel. "Okay, that's cool. I'm not sure we all agree on music, but do you guys want to jam some more now? You know, since we're here?" Levi asserted. Everyone looked around and nodded. We jammed out covers. It was fun, not electrifying.

After the jam, Ruben and Joel talked amongst themselves. I made my way over to Bobby and Levi.

"Hey, Bobby, Levi, this was cool. Are you guys into trying some heavier music? Something more metal? These guys are good players but I'm not into what they want to do."

"Yes, the heavier, the better. That would be fucking awesome," Levi brimmed a broad smile and put his hand out to shake mine. There was a great sense of humor behind those twinkly eyes. I felt a connection, a synchronicity.

Bobby's face remained placid and unchanged until he spoke; his face hardened as he bagged his gear. He paused before he responded. "Well, it depends how heavy you guys are talking. I'm interested in trying. I like what you're both doing. I mean, man, you are solid on guitar, Levi. And Laurie, you sing from the gut. You put a hell of a lot of emotion into it."

"I agree, Laurie, wow. You're different that is for sure," Levi said. "And Bobby, man, you shred. So, this could be cool. I know of another bass player, Will, he's badass, and I know he'll play heavy. I don't know about a drummer though."

"Cool, I'd like to see the other bass player," Bobby said.

I got quiet for an instant, thinking of Patrick. How we had agreed not to join a band together. But I knew he'd like these two guitar players, and they'd like him. A lot. Damn, there I went.

"I know a drummer. Well, he's my boyfriend, and we don't want to play together. I mean, we don't want to complicate things. But, he's damn good. Do you care if we're together?"

"Nah, shit. If he's good, it's worth it! Metal drummers are hard to find," Levi said. "I mean, I get why you're hesitant. We can at least jam with him, right? Why not at least try that? And I'll call Will the bassist."

Ruben opened the rehearsal room door, and cool air rushed in from the hallway, refreshing the dense warmth of the space. Neither Ruben or Joel appeared to care we were making our next plans.

"Cool. I'm game. Wait, Laurie, you and your boyfriend are cool and all, right?" inquired Bobby.

"Yes, we're cool. We get along. I don't know about in a band; generally, we do." I tried to hold back a chuckle but failed. Maybe I was nervous?

"Okay, let's give it a go," Bobby said with a shrug.

The next week, the five of us met in the same space. Bobby and Levi on electric guitars, Will on electric bass, Patrick on drums and me with a microphone grasped in my hand like it was my lifeline. I immediately felt a high-octane vibe in the room, upbeat and exhilarating. I paced the rehearsal room, excited to get going. Will, the new bass player, and Patrick appeared to get along fine, which was crucial since they'd keep the rhythm section going. Patrick was talkative, even though he stayed seated behind his kit. He was being reserved, as expected. I didn't blame him.

Will had a bounce in his full step as he walked around the room, offering a firm handshake to each of us. He was the opposite of Patrick. He was opinionated, talked loudly, if not bordering on obnoxious, and he was dramatic, speaking with flailing arms. He came across as confident and in control. I liked his attitude and his vibe. He was tall, good-looking, mid-length hair and tattooed. He had a natural leadership quality, which usually belongs to the lead guitarist or singer but when I discovered he was the oldest of us, I wasn't surprised when he took charge of the jam with directions.

"Hey, guys, let's just jam something original," said Will. "You know, fuck doing a cover. Patrick and I will just throw down a groove, and you guys come in when you want. Let's see what happens."

Before Patrick took his first hit, he twirled his drumstick in one hand like Tommy Lee famously would. I hadn't seen Patrick do this before and it was cool. Patrick started by playing a standard eighth-note drumbeat that's heard in most rock or pop songs. Michael Jackson's *Billie Jean* beat, but Patrick's was heavy as hell. He hit the snare with rhythmic force, driving the energy forward, and eventually he added in a second kick drum. Man, he could play double kick with fierceness.

Bobby's mouth dropped open at Patrick's strong presence. Levi also stared at Patrick with a smile. I knew Patrick was really good, but his effort gave me chills. Will gave a thumb's up, then dropped in on his bass to support the beat. He ran up his fretboard, dancing out a melody. He used his fingers on his right hand to play the strings instead of using a plastic pic. *Man, he is badass. Thank, God.* I had no doubts about this guy as a band member. Levi joined in on the jam, then Bobby.

It was my turn to add a vocal on top of the loudness. They were throwing down some massive metal grooves, and I was so excited by the intensity, all I could do was scream random lyrics on top. I bounced in one place and banged my head to their intensity. When Bell's Palsy popped into my mind, it was quickly extinguished by euphoria. For the next three hours, we jammed and jammed, all original sounds. It was magic. My ears were ringing, my throat hurt, my hair was stuck to my face and I was back to rock 'n roll.

We were all covered in sweat when we finished, with huge smiles like we just had the best sex ever. Patrick and I beamed at each other. He winked, and I knew then that our life as a couple changed. This band would become more important than us. But I couldn't stop smiling. I had found my place, home, purpose. It appeared we all felt the same. The five of us stood quietly, catching our breath, and observing each other. The cigarette smoke from Will and Levi lingered near the ceiling, echoing how none of us wanted to leave.

22

DREAM BAND

Album Notes:
Patrick –drummer
Will –bass player
Levi –guitarist
Bobby –guitarist

Over the next three months, we cranked out original songs like an assembly line. They came easy during rehearsals. Either Levi or Bobby came in with guitar chords they'd been working on together or separately, and the rest of us would add our parts. Or I would come in with lyrics or a melody, and the guys built the song around that. Usually, just by jammin' it out, we'd create a song. If we played a cover, it was an unexpected artist, and we'd throw a metal twist to it: Janis Joplin's *Piece of My Heart*, Jimi Hendrix's *Purple Haze*, James Taylor's *Fire and Rain*.

We recorded a three-song demo of original songs in the fall of 1991. Compared to the Minneapolis studio experience, which felt like losing my virginity to studio time, this occurrence felt like experienced sex. I not only knew how to approach the microphone in the isolation booth, but I also sang into it like there was a cord from my heart, through my throat into the mixing board. I pushed my lips up to the spit guard in front of the microphone like it was my lover. I giggled when the earphones tangled in my long red hair when I listened to the engineer guide me to the next punch-in, which I anticipated and treasured, knowing measure by music measure we were creating a song.

But, by the beginning of 1992, Bobby's desires and musical tastes became at odds with the rest of ours. We wanted more metal. He didn't. Arguments dominated our practices about music styles, song choices.

We parted ways with Bobby and it wasn't smooth. Bobby was pissed claiming it was his band too, but we knew the remaining four of us – Levi, Will, Patrick, and I wanted success our way, and we moved forward without him and without looking back.

Over the next year, we played every show we could: from small biker bars, college bars, and rock venues between Austin, Corpus Christi, Dallas, San Antonio, and Houston. We even managed to get shows at the San Antonio rock bar Sneakers, where Patrick and I met. The first time being on that stage was deeply fulfilling. Singing to the audience who was smiling back and gazing at us like rock stars, just as Patrick and I had done a few years back.

At most venues, the audiences were small at first. Twenty or so people. Then slowly increased to fifty or more and kept going.

I loved every part of the shows: the equipment setup, soundcheck, putting makeup on in the pickup truck visor mirror, or a ladies' room stall if there was no backstage dressing room. But, most of all, I loved the live show, the fans, their screaming, my screaming. And above all, I loved the band.

As a band, we had the youthful energy to play a show at 11 pm in Houston and drive sweaty and happy, packed with our friends into two small pickup trucks like smelly sardines, weed and cigarette smoke streaming out the windows, back to Austin the same night. Each weekend was a new, exciting adventure.

When we were in Austin, our Saturday late nights were dedicated to appearing on CapZeyeZ public access television show. The creator and sometimes host was, perhaps singlehandedly, the person behind the early success of the band. He was deeply respected in the music community, and his music show was the most popular on late-night Austin access TV. We were one of the lucky acts he repeatedly interviewed, and he let us play live in his studio.

As our momentum and popularity grew on the music scene, we were approached by a genuine and enthusiastic band manager, Bruce, who saw us on CapZeyeZ. He was smart about the business and thoroughly understood the Texas music scene. He knew how to talk to each of us, to appeal to our individual needs, without it being at the band's expense. That was a talent. And Bruce proved, many times over, he knew, when it was called for, how to tell a promoter or bar owner, "Go, fuck yourself." He became our manager, part of our inner circle, a friend, family.

23

CLOUD NINE WITHOUT A SILVER LINING

I was on cloud nine, growing more deeply in love with the band, even though the Grunge revolution was taking over the national music scene. It was forcing us to examine our straightforward metal style. But our new songs were getting airplay on local stations ZRock & KLBJ, so we stayed dedicated to our original sound. Besides, we were still having a killer time on stage. I certainly was. On stage, I was in my zone. I was confident and deeply present. And I controlled my life. I'd cuss like a sailor, act like a queen, or completely lose my mind if I wanted. I was safe losing my shit on stage. It was part of the show. I'd spend many songs crouched down, on my knees, mic cord wrapped around my neck, thrashing my body up and down like I was having a seizure. The whole time I was screaming complex lyrics on top of the roaring music. One time, I squirted my water bottle on one of the male fans pressed right up against the stage, and asked him over the mic, "How does it feel to have a chick cum in your face?" His smile was huge and he high-fived me. I experienced euphoria while performing that I found nowhere else.

Though I could usually turn that persona off, sometimes once I left the stage, in the first hour after a performance I would get a raging headache and an urge to throw up. It was a clear signal my adrenaline or blood sugar had crashed. I would be forced to go home and lay down until it passed. The feeling brought waves of anxiety. I was out of control of my body, and my mind would race at the loss of control. Although, these episodes never stopped me from going all out at the next show.

After we'd been together three years, our fan base was increasing. But the hustle and grind to keep our band moving ever forward was tiring. Even with a manager, we still promoted the group as much and as often as we could in the bars. And I was not good at it. On stage, I was loud, aggressive, fearless. It was an act, a performance, and I was at my absolute most comfortable. Though I was an outgoing person offstage, I was surprisingly bashful when it came to promote the band to strangers. I was nervous at the rejection if someone turned me down while I handed them a show flyer. I was overcome with nervous tension so much so, I leaned on Will and Levi to do it. They were gregarious, strong-willed promoters. It was part of their character. There was not a lick of shyness in any of them.

But another complication was brewing, and it was my feelings about Patrick. We managed to keep our relationship private, and to the public, we were just bandmates. But secretly, I was struggling. Patrick and I were with each other constantly, and this wore on me. If there was a band disagreement, and we didn't have a lot of them, but if we did, I felt I had to take Patrick's side. How could we disagree in the band and then go home and sleep together yet alone be loving? Or if I was frustrated with him in the relationship but how could I not let that carry over into the band? Plus, we all hung out a lot together. We'd hit movies, parties, restaurants, bars, anything, and everything together. It was a dream come true to have my best friends be my bandmates. I knew it was unusual to find such friendships and be in a situation that most musicians coveted. I tried to stay positive. But after a while, I didn't want to do anything alone with Patrick. We'd already been together too much. I assumed he felt the same as he often disappeared to go hiking. The only thing we had in common *was* the band. But I figured we'd work it out somehow. We had to for us and the band. And I loved him. I thought that would minimally be enough, but it felt like we were fading. I wasn't sure I was in love with him anymore.

My mom came to visit after months of my agonizing. I had confided my frustration to her, and she came when I was at an emotional low.

When I picked her up at the Austin airport, the sight of her immediately comforted me. I fell into her arms. I had her all to myself, and she was healthy and sober.

Her first weekend in town, the band had a live show in Austin and Mom convinced my dad to drive to Austin and attend the show with her. She even made him wear a band t-shirt. I asked her after how she got him to wear it, and she said, "I just told him, put the damn thing on and support our daughter." She still had a way with him I didn't comprehend, but I was grateful.

I was deeply impressed Dad was willing to enter a loud rock bar and wear an all-black rock-n-roll t-shirt. Afterward, he patted me on the back, hugged me and smiled. He had no words, but his hug was enough. He and Mom didn't linger but the satisfaction of seeing them together, supporting me, was moving.

Our next show, the following night, was at the rock bar Dallas City Limits. Mom made the trek up I-35 to Dallas, with the band in two pickup trucks full of equipment. She and Patrick were cordial to each other, but Mom engaged Levi and Will in humorous banter. She kept them in stitches, one dirty joke after another.

"Your mom is kooky, Laurie! She's a blast!" Will said backstage as we got ready before the show. *Kooky?* He should have just called her crazy. I've heard all the names over the years: kooky, nuts, nut job, crazy, mad, ill, sick, mental, troubled, off.

"I bet she was fun growing up," Will continued. I didn't reply. He didn't know. And I knew he liked her a lot so it wasn't a slam and yet it was. It wasn't his fault. It was my youth that was at fault so I put his comment out of my mind.

After the show, Mom hung out with us in the small dingy dressing room behind the stage. The room was filled with plastic folding chairs, a warped floor-length acrylic mirror, and a worn in black fake leather couch that assumingly saw lots of backstage sex. But there was one old-school white vanity makeup table with the round lights around the glass mirror. A classic setup that made me feel like we were a big-time act if I ignored the graffiti engravings in the wood.

Mom wore our band t-shirt again and mingled with fans as they'd come and go. She was a better promoter than me, encouraging fans to buy our cassette tape. Minus the endless dirty jokes, her sobriety made her manageable, and enjoyable.

As the guys left for the bar and everyone else cleared out, I asked her to stay behind and tell me her thoughts on the show. She laid her jacket down to cover the couch cushions before taking a seat. I sat next to her with no concern for the sex and drug remnants on the couch.

"Well, is not my type of music. I can't understand a thing you're singing. But I love how excited you are on stage. You're happy, Laur, and it shows. And you are truly captivating. You are. The audience loves you, and I've had so much fun watching. I'm happy it's better than that Minneapolis crap." The mention evokes slight irritation, but I let it go.

"Well, thanks, Mom. Did I embarrass you when I mentioned you were in the audience?"

"Oh hell, no! That was fun! And you know what? After you said that, a fan asked if I would autograph their t-shirt." Her eyes were wide and sparkling as she giggled.

"Wow, did you?"

"Hell, yes! I signed it *Laurie's Mom.*" "Oh, Mom! That's fucking awesome!"

"It was fucking awesome. I'm a celebrity!" "Oh, jeez!" I poked her arm, smiling.

"Well, I don't experience this in Waterloo. I'm glad I can be here for you. Now, what is going on with Patrick?"

I went on to explain the feelings I'd already shared with her on many phone calls: I loved him, but I wasn't *in love* with him. If anything, I was in love with the band. I didn't know what to do.

She told me she thought Patrick was a nice kid. Although she felt from the start, he wasn't for me.

"Why didn't you say so?" I was perplexed.

"You wouldn't listen to me if I told you that. You're so damn stubborn; you would have stayed with him anyway." She took out a cigarette, lit up and took a hard puff.

"I'm not sure about that, Mom. And I don't want the band to break up over this."

"I'm not sure why you keep mixing relationships with music," she said. "Why do you think you need a man all the time? You should be alone and just have fun."

This comment hit me in the gut because I knew she was right.

"I guess I don't want to be alone."

There was silence in the dressing room except for the far-off-resonating sound of the DJ music in the bar.

"And now I'm stuck in a relationship going nowhere."

"Does he know how you feel?" With each puff, the orange and red color on the end of her cigarette got brighter, her exhalation more noticeable. I wanted to move away from the smoke, not her.

"Well, sorta. I think he knows I'm not happy. But we don't talk about us. We don't talk much anymore. If we do, it's about the band. I think we're only together because of the band."

She put out her spent cigarette and lit another, a plum of fresh smoke rising above her like a Midwest storm cloud.

"Well, Patrick is sweet. He's probably just comfortable and content. Men get that way, Laurie. But, he's not even a man yet. He's only 23. You're both so young. I don't think Patrick will ever leave you, though. You'll have to do it. Just go easy on him, honey."

"What the hell does that mean?" I snapped. I was obviously stressed by the topic.

"I know you. Once you make your mind up, you move on to the next thing, and you don't look back. Just don't go onto another guy." Raising her eyebrow at me, she finished her diet Pepsi. "I can't guarantee that, Mom. That's kind of what I do." I popped open a beer from the complimentary backstage stash cooler.

"Well, stop it, if you can. The only time you're happy is when you're on stage. And that's not enough time for you or anyone. You must be happy with the rest of your life, too." She paused and watched me take a drink of beer. "I know you're scared, Laur."

"I am beyond scared. I'm afraid of losing the band in all this shit. That just shows you where my heart sits: I'm more worried about that than losing Patrick!"

"I hope that doesn't happen, but if it does, you'll find music somewhere else. I know you, my dear, you're destined to make it somehow."

I took a longer swig off my beer. The cold, refreshing bubbles soothed my dry throat.

"How many beers have you had since the end of the show?" "Me? Really, Mom? This is the second one. So, I've only had one and a quarter." I moved away from her and sat on an uncomfortable folding chair. I could only take her smoking when she was helping me or had something funny to say.

"Well, just watch your liquor. Especially during these times." "What the hell? That's your issue, not mine," I said, irritated.

Her face fell. Her cigarette burned closer to her finger. She didn't put it out or take a drag. She stared at me.

"Oh, Mom. I'm sorry," I said. I moved to sit close again and hug her. She put her cigarette out in the plastic tray and hugged me back.

"Well, I deserve that one, kiddo. I do. Just remember, it's in the genes."

24

PLEASE WAKE UP

I was distant with my mom for the rest of her visit to Texas. Her comment backstage --"It's in the genes," put me at arm's length. When she left back to Wisconsin, I was relieved. Until a few days later when I received a call from my brother.

"Laurie, Mom is sick." Dave was breathless as he spoke, his asthma getting the best of him.

"What do you mean, sick?"

"Well, she came down with a headache. She's confused and just not right. We've taken her to the hospital. You should come home right away."

"What's wrong with her?"

"They don't know yet. Just get here. She's like, life-threatening sick." His voice was quivering.

She was fine just four days ago, here with me, I thought. She was more than fine. She had been the best: sober, relaxed, playful, loving, healthy. Annoying with her smoking, but healthy.

In tears and shock, I took the next flight to Madison. Waiting for the connecting flight in Chicago, I called my brother. He told me they had a diagnosis: Bacterial Meningitis. I was in agony, with two-and-a-half hours before I could get to her. I must tell her I love her. *Please let me say that to her.*

After I arrived, I joined her new husband Stan at her bedside in the ICU. My brother David and his wife were there. Mom had a breathing tube in her mouth. Her eyes were sunken and, she was pale.

"David, what the hell happened?" I pleaded.

"When she came back from Texas, she said she had an earache," he said. "Like pressure in her ear, from flying maybe. She didn't know for sure. It turned into a massive headache. She said it was unbearable."

Stan added, "She also became agitated. She didn't know what time of day it was. She was dizzy and said she felt like throwing up. She was incredibly confused."

My brother was glassy-eyed. He leaned against the wall, gazing at her. "Well, that's not new," he said, shaking his head and chuckling.

"David!" his wife yelped. I laughed softly, agreeing he was right. I appreciated his dark humor. I took a deep breath and let out a sigh of relief that I made it.

"Is she sleeping? I want to talk to her," I begged, holding her hand, which was cold and damp. My sister-in-law held my mom's other hand and quietly wept. David placed a hand on his wife's shoulder. My mother and my brother's wife were close. Mom was close to many people. Even though she was wacky and unstable, she was devoted and loving and had many friends who adored her. "No, Laurie. She's not sleeping," Stan said. "They have her in an induced coma. They think the Meningitis came from an inner ear infection." He stood at the foot of her bed, stoic with arms crossed, staring at her. I didn't know Stan well, but I liked him. He was tall, had a beard, and he wore a flannel shirt that made him look like a park ranger.

We sat in silence. I watched her chest move up and down at a steady pace.

"Why the induced coma?" I asked.

"Her brain is swelling. They're trying everything they can to reduce it," Stan said.

The urge to ask a hundred more questions increased when the doctor entered. I greeted him without letting go of my mom's hand.

"We need to put a shunt in her skull to release the pressure off her brain," said the tall, also bearded, stoic doctor. "Of course, there are always risks entering the skull." He pointed to the right top of her forehead, just at her hairline. "We'll need to go in here."

"What are the risks?" examined Stan.

"If we don't release the pressure, she will die. If we relieve the pressure, she has a good chance of recovery. However, the risk of the shunt is a stroke. We won't know what other adverse reactions the infection has caused until we wake her. I'm sorry, the shunt is necessary."

"Do it. Do the shunt," I blurted out.

"Hold up, Laurie," said David. "When do you plan to do this? The shunt?" he asked the doctor. "As soon as possible."

"Can you wake her before you, do it?" I asked.

"That is not advisable. We need time for the antibiotics to kill off the infection, and we'll need to keep her in this induced state for at least five to seven days. We need her body and brain at minimal function for her immune system to fight this infection," he said, his voice soft and gentle.

"I want her to know I'm here." I sobbed. My brother came and hugged me.

"Laurie, she knows," said David. "We told her before they put her under that you were coming. She was terrified of everything, but she knows you're here." His hug was reassuring.

The shunt was placed. The doctor said the initial results were promising, although he wouldn't know the outcome until he woke her. Hours turned to days, and Mom remained sedated. A touch of color appeared on her cheeks, and I talked to her as if she could hear. I didn't speak of my boyfriend issues or the band; both were far from my mind. Instead, I told her how much I needed her. How much I loved her. How funny she was and loving and kind. How so many people in Waterloo missed her. I told her the roses in her garden were blooming, and she needed to wake up to see all the colors. To see life. It wasn't over for her yet. Her mental health was better now. She must wake up.

I bought a small stuffed mouse wearing a floral dress from the hospital gift shop and placed it in her hand. She loved garden mice. She thought they were adorable, even though they ate everything. When I wasn't around, I wanted her to hold the mouse to know she wasn't alone.

Dad arrived from Texas. He waited with the rest of us. He and Stan appeared at ease with each other. They even grabbed a coffee together. I knew they both loved this incredibly complicated, zany, demanding, emotional woman.

On day six, dawn broke outside her single inoperable window. The doctors reduced the coma-inducing medications and began the slow process of waking her. By mid-afternoon, they removed the ventilator, and she quietly breathed on her own. Now off smoking for two weeks, her breathing was tranquil. By late afternoon, she appeared asleep but began moving her legs, blinking her eyes. I didn't leave. None of us did. The beige painted walls, uncomfortable hospital chairs and the solo framed Ansel Adams Yosemite picture on the wall above her bed, had become our familiarity. And why does that Yosemite rock look so strong and my mom so frail?

She continued to fall back asleep. In the evening, her movement increased, and she opened her eyes fully. She was serene as she looked around the room at all five of us. We encouraged her to talk. However, she was silent. She fell in and out of short naps. During that time, her face was placid, other times she grimaced. She remained that way until late into the evening. Finally, she woke, at 11:15 pm, scanned the room again, and smiled. "Well, it's a party," she said in a soft, hoarse voice. I tightened my grip on her right hand, she equally responded. I cried and folded my head into her arm. *It's her! It's her! She's... her!*

Everyone laughed and moved in to hug her. Mom continued to smile.

"Well, what the hell have I missed?" asked Mom as she blinked her eyes and looked puzzled.

"Mom, you've been very, very sick," said David. "With Meningitis."

Her face crinkled and her eyebrows folded. "Where the hell am I?"

"You're in the hospital, Mary. In Madison," confirmed Stan. "Madison? The last thing I remember was being with you in Texas," she said, looking at me with glassy eyes. "When did you get here, Laurie? And you too, Red?" Dad smiled at her, his eyes glossy, too.

"I've been here for a week, Mom. It's all okay."

"No, it's not okay. I don't understand what's going on!" Her face grimaced. She tried to reach my brother with her left hand. It didn't move. "Why can't I move my arm?" She gasped. Her voice was still hoarse.

"Well, maybe it's all the tubes, Mom," David replied, his furrowed brow matched my thoughts. My dad pressed the nurse call button without saying a word.

My mom suffered a stroke from the shunt. The left side of her body impacted. She could move with assistance, but her left arm and leg were weak, and she had minimal sensation on the left side of her body. Her left-hand formed into a fist. Her cognitive abilities were affected. She was easily confused when discussing complex subjects and became overwhelmed and tearful over difficult physical tasks or questions. She would need rehab, and we were told she'd never gain full physical or cognitive ability. Nevertheless, she was still…her. Her overall memory and humor were there. However, she'd changed. My life had changed. And I was furious that this woman who had already dealt with enough had to take on more.

25

LIBERTY LUNCH

I returned to Texas from Wisconsin with a heavy heart. I encouraged the band to play as many shows as possible and to record new songs. I needed to sing to get lost, to find my high.

After a month of rehearsals, we had our first live show.

It was Saturday night. I knew the minute I walked in the stage door at Liberty Lunch that it would be *one of those gigs* I wouldn't ever forget. The intense energy of the crowd engulfed me even before I saw them. The show was hosted by local radio station Z Rock and the audience was large. I planned to hit the stage with wild abandon, forgetting my mom's health or any problems with Patrick. For an hour, I'd forget everything. That is where the performance high puts any drug to shame.

I got some cooler air outside before we started. Levi and his girlfriend Anne were sitting on the cement loading dock, smoking, drinking beers and talking with our friend and helper, Luke, an excellent guitarist himself. He was the heart of our band: he'd been with us since the beginning as a guitar tech.

"Hi guys, how's everyone doing?" I inquired, as I neared the others.

"I'm fucking pumped. The crowd sounds loud as hell," burst Levi as he gave me a hug upon arrival.

"Yeah, this should be a good show. You ready, Laurie? And how's your mom?" Luke asked, providing a similar brotherly hug.

The humid air and the question made me pause as I sat on the dock next to Anne.

"She's struggling. But damn, she's a strong woman. So, we'll see." Anne hugged me. I felt no need for tears at the disclosure, but it was not our typical pre-show talk. "Hey, I'm always ready to play, though," I said, pumping my fist in the air.

We're interrupted by the DJ inside working the crowd, his voice spilling outside. "How you guys doing tonight, Liberty Lunch? This is a good-looking crowd! I see there are some nice breasts in the audience! I like this! Thanks so much for coming out!" The audience of a couple hundred roared.

Luke said shocked but also with excitement, "Yikes? I'm glad there are some nice breasts in the crowd?"

"Maybe you should go in early and do a boob count," I said, pushing Luke towards the venue. He playfully pushed me back.

"Sick bastards," Levi said, laughing.

"We have lots of great music coming up," the DJ continued.

The crowd erupted with enthusiasm.

"Now that's what I like to hear," Levi said.

"Oh, hell yes," Luke said. "And you're getting great radio coverage right now on Z Rock. Even though you're not Pearl Jam or Soundgarden."

"True, but I like them," I said. "We just have to be who we are."

"Let's just fucking play," Levi said. "That's what I came to do. Besides, the best shows are in Austin." He took a long puff off his cig and popped me a cold beer from the venue-supplied cooler.

I accepted the bottle of slippery condensation, although I wasn't much for drinking before a show. I'd now have a beer on stage but used it more as a prop.

"Where's Will?" I asked.

"He's inside. Probably talking to the sound guy. Making sure shit is ready. Or Will's taking a shit. You know him. He can't start a show without a shit," said Levi. Levi and Luke clink their beer bottles, chuckling.

"He's not the only one," I replied. My bowels had been gurgling with pre-show uneasiness.

Bruce, our manager, strutted out the stage door. His 6'5" frame gave him a presence of authority for a band manager. A Liberty Lunch employee behind him pointed at us and said, "You're on."

Bruce motioned the guy off. Shaking his head, he looked at us. "Do what you need. Take your time," he said, returning into the venue. I adored Bruce. He knew when to push industry people away or when to welcome them.

Suddenly from behind us, "Hold up, fuckers! Don't go in, yet!" It was Don, another very close band friend. His high-octane energy was magnetic. This is the guy who rides a bicycle with no brakes down a 5-story circular parking ramp. Drunk.

"Hell, yes, get over here!" I screamed. Don made me happy. He always arrived with a big smile, a six-pack of Grolsch, and contagious enthusiasm. Whether he's doing grunt work or loading gear, he's part of our group.

Will stomped outside to us. He grabbed Patrick around the shoulder and squeezed him like a brother. Patrick had been talking to other friends near the stage door.

"Guys, let's go! Come the fuck on!" Will said, smiling and high-fiving us. Patrick joined in with fist-pumps, then we fell together into a pre-show hug. All of us. The band, Anne, Luke, Don. *Family.*

"I love you guys," said Will. "Let's have a kick ass show." "The same from me, guys, same from me," Levi said, patting backs.

"Yee-haw!" Don screamed, holding two beer bottles high in the air.

I couldn't find words, but I held each person on my side close. I loved these people, through everything, I loved them. Patrick was direct across from me. Our eyes met. He winked with a cocky smile. His confidence always appeared before a gig. And I knew how much he loved this band too.

"Let's do this!" Will screamed. "Yes! Fucking awesome!" I yelled.

We broke our hug, all clapping. I quietly walked behind everyone, I briefly held my hands in prayer mode at my heart, thankful for this band, this music, this chance to sing.

As I entered the semi-dark stage, only a spotlight illuminating the DJ, I watched the crowd. They noticed our faint profiles and acknowledged our arrival with a sudden increase of cheering and screams.

Thump, thump, thump. The audience pounded their fists on the stage as they cheered and shouted. Like us, they're eager.

The smell of spilled beer, weed and cigarette smoke overtook me. I smiled. I loved the aroma of a rock bar. Sweat was dripping from my forehead to my upper lip; Texas heat and nerves, the cause. I didn't dare wipe it away; it would smear my makeup. It tasted of salt and Maybelline as it entered my mouth. I enjoyed the flavor. I knew it meant I was on stage.

I lingered in the shadows, close to the drum riser, partially out of their view. But I saw grinning faces in the front row, pressed against the stage.

Thump, thump, thump. Their impatience sent chills down my neck to my lower back, like an electric bolt. I shook out my legs to release it. *Oh, God. I may shit myself. I won't, I never have. Maybe this time I will?*

I was surging with anticipation to start. I bounced up and down in answer to the energy. I was at the starting gate, and it hadn't opened yet. In my mind I could hear my mother say, "Hold your horses, Laurie. Hold your horses."

The DJ had been out there for five minutes pumping up this crowd. Throwing out t-shirts, cups. *Just shut up, man! Get off the stage!* The more time he took, the more time my mind could muster up anxiety over my mom, my feelings about Patrick. I just wanted to sing. Once I took the microphone, all thoughts would disappear, along with the urge to shit. *Hurry up, give me the mic, give me the fucking mic.*

The DJ's face turned red as a siren as he motioned to me and screamed with a huge smile, "Let's Go!"

The stage-lights fired up as the houselights went down. The crowd roared. We were fully exposed. I felt the welcome, scorching heat of the stage lights bury deep into my body, like a warm fireplace, a hot bath, my mother's hug. I opened my eyes to the brightness and squinted to see the many screaming faces. A lurch in my stomach made its way to my throat, but it turned into a smile. I was familiar with it. I longed for it. I moved to meet the DJ at center stage. In an instant, as many other announcers had done before, he handed me the microphone. Now it was my stage, my show.

Facing the shrieking admirers, I closed my eyes, wrapped my hands tightly around the mic and bent slightly at the waist. I forgot everything that came before this moment, with no thought of what was to come next.

The gate was open.

Deep from my core, I let out an earsplitting, guttural metal scream. It was show time, and I was mentally higher than a fucking kite.

26

DESTRUCTION

In the weeks after the Liberty Lunch performance, we had a lull in shows. My stage high waned. I was restless. Dealing with my relationship with Patrick became the task at hand, but how? I was confused. I didn't know how to talk about it with him.

As a romantic couple, we'd separated months ago. We didn't do dates or have much alone time together. And as friends, we just didn't talk anymore. Except about the band. So, to bring up "us" made me super nervous because I wasn't sure what to say! Patrick wasn't a bad guy to me. He was a good guy! So why did I want out? Maybe I was the problem? I felt guilt and confusion that I was not familiar with. Patrick was my first major relationship, and I didn't know how to handle it under the pressure of being in a band with him too. So, at first, I thought it would be best just to stick it out. I wondered, is this what unhappy couples with children do? The ones who stick it out for the children. I felt like the band was our kid. But now, I was frustrated, angry, and felt like the circumstance controlled and restrained me.

At one of our after-show parties in which Patrick didn't attend, a stranger caught my eye. His long curly blond hair that looked like a lion's mane, twinkling dark brown eyes, enticed me. He was vibrant, outgoing, funny, smart as a whip, and his attention to me was consuming. A few years older than me, Dean was an artist on various levels and working odd jobs. I knew my dad wouldn't like him, as the guy appeared too hard to pin down to any career, but I was intrigued with his stories and upbeat energy. More than anything, that he wasn't in the band.

Out of sight of other partiers, after slamming three rounds of Tequila shots chased with Shiner Bock beer, Dean and I were making out behind a tree in the host's backyard. I knew it was wrong and yet I felt free, finally free of all responsibilities to Patrick. And also, to the band and the expectations of Patrick and me *in* the band. I just wanted to be the singer without the heavy weight of also being the drummer's girlfriend. But was this the way to do it? Quite frankly I didn't know what the hell I was doing that night, but it felt right. It felt like freedom.

By the end of the night, somewhere around 4:00 am, I finally had the nerve to end my relationship with Patrick. I'd met someone else I wanted to hang out with--now I had a definitive reason. As messed up as it was, it made sense to me. I needed a reason. I couldn't be with Patrick if I were interested in someone else. I didn't two-time. And it wasn't fair to Patrick. So, there's my reason. Sorry, Mom, guess I won't be single just yet.

I went home to Patrick, crawled into our quiet bed inches from him, convinced I smelled of another. Patrick didn't move. I assumed he was asleep. Maybe he already knew? Perhaps he had someone else? An instant later, his breathing deepened, and I knew he was asleep. My heart ached for us. Sure, Dean had piqued my interest but was I doing the right thing? I had been sure of it up until now. No, I had to do it. The risk was huge, but I was done. I lay awake, knowing I'd soon deliver the news. This was the last night I would sleep with this man.

Late the next morning, moving about in our tiny kitchen, somewhere between closing the refrigerator door and stepping to the stove with eggs, I casually broke the news.

"Patrick, I think things have shifted for us and we've drifted apart. I can't do it anymore."

Patrick looked up from a magazine laying on our thrift-store dining table with an expressionless face. "Huh?" he said.

"I'm not happy anymore," I rasped. Watching him, I paused. His face and body were rigid. "I met someone else. I need to move on." I looked away and cracked two eggs into the frying pan, not looking at him until the last egg was in. "I hope we can keep the band together," I muttered. I was nauseous.

When I looked, his face was still frozen in a *what the fuck?* look.

Patrick scoffed. "Shifted for us?" He lurched up from the table and approached, arms folded stiffly across his chest. I left the eggs alone to sizzle. I turned and crossed my arms. I was immobile.

"What the fuck is going on? Are you crazy?" he yelled as spit came out of his mouth. His hands came down and turned into fists. His face reddened.

Crazy? I felt adrenaline surge up my stomach. It was different than performing adrenaline. I felt like I was about to jump off a building. "Patrick, you haven't been around at all. You don't want to do anything with me anymore." I paused and noticed my shaking hands. "I thought you were done with us, too."

"Laurie, just cause I don't want to party or be all up and crazy and shit like y'all, doesn't mean I'm not into us." He moved back to the table and buried his head in his hands.

"Well, fuck. Could have fooled me, Patrick." I turned off the stove. The eggs burned. The apartment filled with smoke.

"Oh, so is this my fault somehow?" said Patrick, fuming. "And you've already met someone else? So, just, just like that? I don't get a say? Nothing?" Removing his hands from his face, his eyes were bloodshot.

"No, it's not your fault. But I can't handle you, the band, all of it, all the fucking time. I must cut something, and I can't cut the band."

"So, you're cutting me, that's it? But I'm *in* the band!"

"I know!" my voice squeaked. I stood silent, trying to find the right words, and realizing that I may be doing the wrong thing but not knowing what to do. This was all me. Or was it? Aren't relationships 50/50?

"Patrick, at times I feel like I'm protecting you. You're shy and quiet, and sometimes there's a huge wedge between you and the other guys. I don't think you get along with them as I do, but I can't always speak for you. I'm tired."

"Thanks, Laurie. Thanks. Yeah, I may not speak up all the time, but hell, sometimes it's hard to be in this band with all the big mouths. The rest of you pretty much run things."

"Patrick, we have to figure out how to keep the band together, while we're not together." I remained in the kitchen, leaning against the warm stove.

"Well, fucking good luck. I don't see how that's going to work, Laurie. If there is anyone who will go, it's me. Do Will and Levi know?"

"No, they don't." I stared down at the linoleum.

My mind was swirling, and I felt dizzy. Oh, that's right. I hate confrontation.

"Patrick, I thought…I swore that you had the same feelings as me. I'm surprised. As for Will and Levi, I assumed we'd tell them together."

"Why the hell would we do that? This isn't our decision. It's yours."

"Patrick, where have you been? We don't have sex anymore. We don't hang out. We don't do anything but the band!"

"Well shit, Laurie. I don't know why! Sometimes I'm tired, too, but I wasn't ready to walk."

Sadness overcame me as I realized Patrick was genuinely hurt. His head was back in trembling hands. Quiet. He looked up but didn't make eye contact. He stared at the band posters and show tickets that we had proudly taped to our living room wall over the past three years. This apartment--our second, and larger--had held many pre-show gatherings, post-show parties, band meetings, and celebrations. Now the room held doubt and anger, and I felt like I was holding a cannonball in my arms.

Patrick removed the hairband that was holding his hair in a long ponytail. He slingshot the hair band across the room, and it snapped like a whip against one of the band posters.

"No, Laurie. I don't feel the same," he said with a croak in his voice. "This is messed up. I don't want to lose the band either, but I'm, I don't know. I was okay with things the way they were. I wasn't thinking about it."

"How can you not think about the obvious?"

"Oh, Laurie. Never mind. Fuck this. You're on your own. You can tell Levi and Will yourself. You know what? This sucks. And whoever the new guy is, he can fuck off."

Patrick stormed out the front door, leaving it open. He stomped down the wood stairs outside our second-floor apartment. I closed the door, leaning against it for support. Tears formed, and my head throbbed. I needed to let him go, but that was abrupt and far more painful than expected. He had shown more intensity in the last few minutes than I'd ever seen. He's right: this sucked. But what did I expect? My mind fell into a state of anxiety, fear, sadness and strangely…euphoria. What the hell did I just do? I must call Mom.

27

THREE STRIKES

In the days following our break-up, Patrick moved in temporarily with Will, who didn't appear surprised, nor did he take sides. Levi didn't seem fazed either. Both were more concerned with the health of the band.

"If we keep the band together, that's all that matters and that you guys are okay," Levi said.

Two weeks later, after a pause, and with few words shared between us, Patrick and I forged on with the band. But at times, I was unsure I did the right thing breaking up with him. I kept having panic attacks and shortness of breath. I hated what I did to Patrick, and I was consumed with worry if I messed up my future. But I knew there was no going back to what we had. By this point, I'm sure he thought I was the worst girl on the planet. The way I was acting, I wasn't a woman yet.

As for Dean, he did serve a purpose for me: freedom from the pressures of being in a relationship with someone from the band. And I easily caved to his attention.

Dean mingled into our band life, attending all shows. I willingly, albeit with a surprising lack of sensitivity for Patrick, brought Dean along to radio interviews and band events. Dean got along fine with Will and Levi, but they treated him like just another person along for the ride. They had fun with him, hung out. However, he was not *family*. Despite Dean's presence adding to the discomfort and stress between Patrick and me, I continued to include him. Patrick and Dean would share barely a word.

The band had been invited to play a music conference in Detroit, and we accepted. We planned to load up Will & Patrick's pickup trucks with our equipment, like any out-of-town gig, and just the four of us make the drive to Detroit. However, two weeks before the Detroit show, Patrick was involved in a five-car collision on I-35 on his way to our Austin show. His small blue pickup truck and all his drums in the back were totaled. Patrick walked away from the accident, unharmed but shaken. He lost everything. He had insurance on the truck, not the drums. Like any struggling musician, he didn't have money to replace the thousands of dollars of equipment.

That night's Austin show was canceled.

My heart ached for him and the band. Without Patrick, we couldn't go to Detroit. However, Dean had an idea: He had a pick-up truck, and he knew lots of bands near Chicago and Detroit. He could borrow drums on Patrick's behalf. Surprisingly, Patrick accepted, even if this meant Dean came too. And it *was* a *long* ride: 1,400 miles, rotating five drivers, non-stop, in two mid-size pick-up trucks loaded with equipment and lots of tension.

As promised, Dean's friends set Patrick up with a kit. They even offered our band an opening slot at their local show a few days later. We had great shows, and everyone was grateful to Dean, but the whole experience was exhausting and confusing to me.

On stage, I sometimes thought Patrick and I were still together. I'd get lost in the performance high like the early days. We shared warm glances and jammed out together. By the end of the set, reality crashed in. The crowd moved away from the stage, and we had to break down equipment. Glances became glares. Post-show gatherings were filled with lots of alcohol to ease the strain between us. However, I had a new appreciation for Patrick. For him to stick it out, under those circumstances, took balls.

Back in Austin, I asked Dean to move more to the background, to not show up to as many gigs. I wanted to show more consideration for Patrick. Dean tried, but he was now becoming friends with Will and Levi, and it became complicated to keep him away. Maybe my mom was right: Don't go from one guy to another. Perhaps I had just traded dramas.

The band moved forward, albeit strained. Patrick borrowed drums from other bands as he saved money for new equipment. When we had band meetings, it was forced and uncomfortable. Patrick and I barely shared glances or words. Our breakup put Levi and Will in a precarious situation, and it was growing harder for Patrick and me to act pleasant around each other. Then we suffered another bizarre occurrence.

Hours before our next Austin show, Levi cut the tip of his left index finger on a piece of kitchen equipment at his fast-food job. His finger was deeply slashed, and it was impossible for him to play guitar. In the past, any fingertip crack or cut would be filled with superglue to get through a show, but not this time. Again, we had to cancel that night's show. The band was on hold for two weeks while Levi's finger healed.

I was regretting the breakup. Not because I thought Patrick and I should be together, but it felt like the band was deteriorating. And so was I. Without live shows or rehearsals, I was depressive and confused. I struggled to stay focused at my day job, but I knew my main focus had to be on upcoming scheduled gigs. Keeping the band together became my priority.

After a couple of weeks, Levi was healed enough for a rehearsal for our next show in San Antonio. The weeks apart appeared to help Patrick and me. There was a lighter air to the practices, and I was so excited to be rehearsing that I did my best to communicate with Patrick directly. He, in return, was friendly if cautious. Maybe we'd make this band work after all.

And then a third strike. Four days before the San Antonio gig, Will was out with Dean. In a drunken, macho display at a local bar, Will broke his wrist. He *won* a game against a boxing robot sparring-machine.

Will was out of commission for six weeks. San Antonio canceled. I felt life canceled on me. We decided to wait it out while Will healed. Will encouraged us to practice without him, but Patrick stopped returning anyone's phone calls. He went

MIA. The wait for him to surface became tortuous. We'd heard rumors he was jamming with other bands, but we couldn't confirm.

Will, Levi, and I met early in the evening on a weeknight at the Back Room. A few regulars, twenty or so, sat around the bar side of the venue listening to the jukebox and playing Pool, not giving much attention to us but occasional thumbs up acknowledging we're the band. Over a pitcher of beer, Will, Levi and I sat tucked away at a corner table and quietly toyed with the idea of replacing Patrick. But with the mention of another drummer, the conversation deteriorated to silence. We agreed it wouldn't be the same with someone else. As the beer in the pitcher decreased, the frustration of whys, should've and maybes increased and swirled in my brain like a Texas tornado.

Maybe if we had a record deal, he'd come back, or it would be worth replacing him? Maybe if we had a tour offered? Maybe if we had chosen another drummer originally? No, nothing was worth replacing him and we had chosen the best drummer, Patrick.

After four years as the band, and six months after Patrick and I broke up, on one of the saddest days of my life, Will, Levi and I officially decided to surrender. My dream band was over. Will and Levi left the bar together. I watched them walk out with the swagger of seasoned musicians. Both, their hair now long, down the middle of their backs but no length could hide their slumped shoulders. The last glance I caught, Will was putting his arm around Levi's shoulder. I remained at the table and nursed the remains of my beer.

A new Pearl Jam song played out the jukebox. I closed my eyes. Pearl Jam played here at the Back Room, just like we did in 1991.

I didn't want to leave, fantasizing that Will and Levi would return, Patrick included, and this was all a nightmare. I was startled by the crack of a new game of Pool near me, and I knocked my empty plastic beer cup over. I left it, got up, steadied my legs, and walked out alone.

28

ECSTASY

The demise of the band sent me further into depression. I stopped caring about what I ate: Whataburger or Sonic became my go-to meal. I didn't exercise. I considered sleep boring. A six-pack of Shiner Bock frequented an otherwise empty fridge. I didn't pick up the guitar or write. Dean was still hanging around; although we were on and off again and we didn't live together. He was useless at providing emotional support, but occasionally he filled the loneliness gap, and we'd hit bars together and knock off casual, loveless sex.

Even though I was not a 9-5 girl, my regular day job at the *Austin American-Statesman* was my only source of getting out of the house. I retreated into that world. Once again I traded rock n' roll boots for corporate heals. It offered a distraction. I didn't want to do it, but it provided the daily satisfaction that at least I was doing something right. Even if it was for someone else. Although with each day I made one more photocopy or printed one more report, it ate at my musical spirit and devoured my creativity like maggots on roadkill.

Lonely, bored, anxious, angry and depressed, I found no restraint to turn down the Ecstasy offered while out drinking with colleagues from my job.

After I swore off drugs in Minneapolis and refrained from all drugs offered during the previous four years of the metal band, Ecstasy swirled into my life. It took my hand and whisked me off to an euphoric wonderland: a trendy EDM rave bar in Austin called *Ohms*. This 1995 scene was the total opposite of the loud and aggressive sound and vibe of rock bars; EDM was mesmerizing in its fluid, dreamy and repetitive beats. And it was welcome to my mind and spirit.

When I danced at *Ohms*, I swore I was floating across the dance floor while I slithered off other's sweaty bodies. We all equally appeared to enjoy each other's sweat and touches, encouraging each other to get closer with smiles and gentle tugs. I willingly got lost in the crowd of hundreds who were following the same rhythm, surge, and then the beat drop: orgasmic. But it was so much more than the music. It was the feeling, the taste, and the joy in being totally at ease and lost in another world.

For a solid month, every weekend I dropped E and escaped into the intense, happy-high of velvety touches, glow sticks, soft wet kisses, and constant expressions of chemical love for fake friends and rave strangers. Even women. If I ever desired a woman before this time, it was now confirmed by my sensual touch of their soft breasts while kissing, lounged on a club couch sipping grapefruit juice to sustain our high. There were many times in my teenage and young adult life that I found girls attractive, usually the pretty ones with beautiful silky long hair, curves, and nice cleavage. But I never acted on my desires. It was a fantasy, or so I thought. But now, kissing a beautiful woman while fucked up on E was far more sensual than kissing a guy, but not enough to continue it further. I liked guys more.

I'd found the answer to my depressed state: I didn't need a band, I only needed Ecstasy. This shit blew my mind; but not for long. The comedown and my depleted mental post-high state were as intense as the rise, and far worse than cocaine. It left me more depressed and anchored to my couch than when I'd started. My life felt profoundly out of control.

When I was crashing, I was paranoid, nervous and anxious. I wondered why bits of memories were blank. What did I do last night? Who was I with? What the fuck was I doing? Oh, my God, what if I'm losing my mind like my mother?

I asked my friend who set me up with the E if she was having problems, too.

"Yes, but I just bump it with a hit of Prozac, and I'm better." "But, why is this stuff so intense? It's just Ecstasy, right?" "Yeah, well, no. Those little brown flecks in the pill, I was told that's heroin, but I don't do heroin, so I don't believe that."

Her answer did not satisfy me. I talked around, and sure enough, the brown flecks were heroin. *Fuck.* No wonder the first time I did it I puked my guts out before the high hit.

I was 27, massively depressed, scared as hell I was losing my mind, severely missing my band, and no longer self-identified as a musician. Instead, I was a weekend druggy. One night, soaking in my bathtub, the bathroom was lit only by a night light air freshener that had long lost its scent. I let the hot water go cold as I contemplated how I'd kill myself. While shivers overtook, I thought how easy it would be to get a bunch of downers from someone and go to sleep in the bath. Like a capsized boat, I'd sink. Forever. Images of my mom and dad flooded my mind. Especially my dad. He'd already been through too much.

My shivers turned to intense shaking. I wanted to get out to warm myself and yet I hated myself. An internal voice said three times, "You'll be okay." I didn't know who it was, but it was steady and convincing. I reached for a towel. I knew it wasn't my time, but I wasn't sure how much time I had.

Dean noticed my depression and suggested I try LSD. "You need a good trip, babe. Something that will make all your negative shit go away." Despondent, I agreed. On a Saturday afternoon, I slipped an innocuous little piece of paper under my tongue and waited with Dean on the couch for all my negative shit to go away.

It was just the two of us. To ease my concerns, he reminded me he was a professional at it--"I've done it a dozen or so times." I assumed he'd walk me through it, but he didn't. When his buzz set in, his only movement was from the couch to the porch and back. Over and over. He didn't speak. He was on his trip, and I wasn't a part of it.

Mine was spent lying sideways on the kitchen linoleum floor, the same kitchen where Patrick and I broke up. I now envisioned fluid, molten waves of white-light through the crack of the partially-closed bathroom door down the hall. I was burning up; certain I was bathing on a sun-soaked beach. I seized the plastic ice tray from the freezer and brought it to the floor. Captivated by the profound temperature change, I stroked the cubes across my hot face and chest. The ice melted gracefully down my belly into my jeans. With great relief, I felt it pool in my underwear before it puddled on the floor below me. I could smell the ice. Does ice smell? I was fucked up. I didn't like it. But wait, am I resisting this? Should I just let go and experience this? Except I didn't know what I was experiencing.

I called Levi from the band, who was still one of my closest friends. I hoped he or his girlfriend Anne would walk me through it, and they did. They got Dean and me out of the apartment and nursed me through a twelve-hour trip from hell. They drove us around Austin to sightsee. They took us to Sonic Drive-In to sample icy drinks, and they humorously questioned my ability to define taste. They encouraged me to swim in my apartment complex pool, wanting me to at least enjoy some of the sensory overload.

The black tank top and white boxer shorts I wore to swim in felt like silk slithering across my body an inch at a time. The water was smooth, luscious, like melted chocolate, and I wanted to drink it, but my friends reminded me I couldn't. I floated on my back, ogling at the stars, wishing I could connect them.

Eventually, Levi and Anne sat me in front of the TV with *The Simpsons* show. Before they left, they assured: "You'll be fine tomorrow. Try to get some sleep." I took their suggestion.

Dean fell asleep spread-eagle on the living room floor, with his fake black Ray-Ban Wayfarers over his eyes. I was on the bed with a blanket over my head in a desperate attempt to squash any light that would make me wander down another mythical trip in my head. But my body overheated, and I was forced to remove the blanket. I fell asleep with my hand over my eyes, smelling every single touch I made in the previous twelve hours.

I recovered the next day but not entirely. Odd sensations would come in waves. One second I'd feel normal, the following I could taste the sky and see my thoughts. I wasn't sure what was real but as the days wore on and the LSD hangover decreased, my anxiety amplified.

29

STRIP CLUB

A week later, Tom, a friend of Dean's called and said he and his girlfriend had a fight and he needed our help. He wanted to go out and get blitzed. I was down for it. I needed to get out too. Holing up in the apartment on a Saturday night with Dean, especially after the failed acid trip, was not the best idea, so the three of us went out. We started at the Back Room with beers and shots and at midnight Dean suggested we hit a topless bar to help Tom beat his blues. I hadn't been in one since St. Paul. I was curious and twitchy for fun.

We arrived, sloshed but upright, at the moderately upscale Sugar's Strip Club. It looked like a Vegas hotel bar with fancier lighting and fake velvet drapes here and there, but it still smelled like a damn bar. And I bet the men here were paying three times for that beer than the boys down the road at the local pub. But of course, pretty women were dancing naked on stages. This place was many steps up in class and style from that St. Paul nude bar, but in the end, it felt the same: Women – physically glorified.

We secured a table, away from the stage, at my urging. I lazily drank a gin and tonic and lounged back in my leather bar chair as Dean and Tom stood close to the main stage, enthralled by a pole dancer. The club was pitch black except for the dim candles on tiny round tables, strobe stage lights, neon reflective strips on stairways, and exit lights.

I liked sitting in the dark. Serenity and relaxation came to me for the first time in a while. However, the cigarette smoke and stage fog were dense and dried my contacts. I blindly fumbled around in my purse for my small plastic bottle of rewetting solution, eager for relief. I squeezed a dollop on my right eye and my eye dried up like frozen sand, burned, as if I touched it with a hot pepper seed, and the unmistakable smell of glue pierced my nose. With horror, I realized I was holding my bottle of glue for my fake nails. Covering my eye with my hand, I bolted to Dean and Tom, avoiding all the dudes gazing at the stage with dollar bills held above their heads. I tugged Dean by the arm, and I screamed over the loud dance music.

"I fucked up my eye! We need to go now!" "What?" he screamed back.

I clasped my right hand over my right eye like a pirate. I screamed the same message, but he shrugged, appeared confused. The dancer on stage saw me. She motioned to a male security guard and next thing I knew I was backstage in a brightly lit dressing room, rinsing my eye out in a sink, surrounded by topless women coaching me through.

"You got it, honey, get as much water in there as you can," the one in hot red stilettos said. From my point of view bent over the sink, all I could see with my good eye, was stilettos, G-strings, and boobs.

"Girl, you put nail glue in your eye?" the one in a turquoise bikini bottom said as she rubbed my back in a motherly way. "You better see an ophthalmologist right now!"

"Gail, there is no eye doctor open this time of night. What the hell you thinking?" said another dancer in a cheetah print robe. The burning subsided but my eye lid felt sticky, and the smell of glue persisted.

"Honey, you need to get to the ER," said cheetah print. With the mention of the ER, I bawled out loud at the circumstance and the resolution of where I'd arrived. I was drunk, in a strip joint and had nail glue in my eye. Five strippers surrounded and hugged me, like football players surrounding their quarterback. One gently helped clean makeup off my messed-up eye. They sat me on a pristine fluffy white couch, layered with zebra print tasseled throw pillows. I had never seen such an immaculate backstage. Part of me didn't want to leave. They gave me a glass of water and talked me down as I sobered up and complained of boyfriend problems and the heartache of missing my band. One girl, Julie, swore she had seen one of the band's shows.

"I thought you looked familiar. How exciting! My boyfriend was into you guys. You're awesome!" Julie said, squeezing my hand and giving me a hug--bare boobs and all. Her potent perfume smelled like wildflowers and musk, and for a moment the smell of glue diminished.

"Well, tell your boyfriend I'm sorry the band broke up." I cried again and the tears most likely helped my eye, but my vision was blurry, and my pride gone.

"Oh, don't you worry, girl. You'll sing again. You have a strong voice," Julie said with such conviction that I assumed she knew more about singing than stripping.

I asked one girl to tell Dean to meet me at the exit. Before I left, I thanked the women for their help. Being in their backstage sanctuary of bosoms and pretty pillows brought me a sense of sisterhood I didn't think I needed. However, we always need sisters. And sisters always need their mom. I wish I could call mine right now.

Dean, Tom, and I walked to my little two-door red Toyota Tercel parked in the club lot. "I'll drive since you can't really see," Dean offered with a vigorous laugh as he hugged me.

"You need to take me to the ER, Dean."

"It's three in the morning! Your eye doesn't look that bad?" he said as he pulled back from me and adjusted his sloppy stance and sleepy eyes to look at mine. "Oh, shit, yeah, your eye is red." "Are you okay to drive?" I begged, holding him upright. He adjusted his pose as if to prove he could and just then Tom bent over and puked behind my car.

"Tom" I screamed, reaching for him. Tom held up his hand, still bent over, motioning me to step back. "I'm good. I'm good," he said.

"Well, he isn't driving, so yeah, I got this," Dean replied, giggling again but he took on a more serious tone as he helped Tom into the backseat of the car. Tom apologized and passed out, head leaning up against the car interior wall. Dean and I got in. I became more anxious as my eye ached, and my stomach roared of nerves, but at least I felt sober. I put my head back against the seat rest and closed my eyes. The hospital was only twenty minutes away. I'll be okay; we'll all be okay. I kept repeating to myself.

Dean reversed, drove 30 feet ahead to exit the gravel parking lot and I felt the car make a sudden, hard crash that jerked my head forward.

"Oh, shit!" Dean yelped. The car stalled. Dean drove the vehicle into a four-foot-high bright yellow round steel pole that marked the exit of the parking lot.

We both jumped out--it felt in slow motion--to look at the damage. The passenger side bumper, headlight and hood were smashed. Yellow paint was scratched into my red car, and my car's red paint likewise scratched into the yellow pole among many other colors of past vehicles achieving a similar late-night mishap. "No! Dean, what the fuck?" I screamed. Now my aching eye turned into a headache.

Dean tried to settle my words by attempting to hug me and repeating over and over in slurred speech, "I'm sorry babe, I'm sorry. Why'd they put that pole there?"

"Get in the fucking car, Dean! I'll drive!" I yelled as I pushed him towards the passenger door and I made my way to the driver side.

"But you only have one eye!" he said with a dash of arrogance. He remained outside the passenger door, uneasy to enter, his hands holding his long blond hair above his head and away from his crinkled face.

"It's better than your two! Get in!" I replied, slamming my driver door shut so hard it woke Tom.

"What's going on?" Tom mumbled and then promptly leaned his head back against the headrest. He's out again. Dean obliged my demand and got in the car.

One eye or not, I was driving myself to the ER. The car started on the third try, and I was thankful no one in the parking lot took notice of our shenanigans. I gingerly drove away. Within minutes Dean was passed out too.

30

CRAZY

I drove under the speed limit, tightly gripping the steering wheel with my left hand, covering my right eye with a tissue in my right hand that Gail had given me. I was frightened the police may pull me over with one headlight. I couldn't imagine what I'd say. The idea of it only increased my anxiety and unsettled stomach. Holy shit, I think I'm losing my mind. Maybe the doctor can help with that too.

I made it to the ER. I left the guys, asleep, in my smashed Tercel. By the time I walked into the emergency room, I was convinced I was having a mental breakdown. I had paranoid thoughts of the police chasing me like on the *COPS* tv show. My mind twisted with anger and frustration about my car, and how my dad would be greatly disappointed. I must look like a drunk loser. Then again, at 3 am, I'm with counterparts in the ER.

Once I made it to an exam bed, even in its sterile, clinical form, it was appealing to my exhausted body. I immediately laid down. As I rested my head on the thin, foam pillow, I thought of my mom. *I want my mom. If I'm going to lose my mind, I want my mom.*

The doctor arrived and before he could address my eye, I hysterically yelped about my fear of going crazy. He reassured me with a steady, calm voice: "Laurie, I'm Dr. Jones. You're safe and you're not having a breakdown, okay?" He slowly closed the thin blue exam curtain behind him. "You're having a panic attack because of what just happened. A minor car crash, and the super glue in your eye, well, you dodged a bullet on both counts."

"It wasn't super glue. It was nail glue," I stubbornly replied. "Same thing. But your eye will be okay, and I want you to follow up with an ophthalmologist. But you're not having a breakdown," he said, listening to my heartbeat with a stethoscope.

Really?" I gulped, embarrassed but still not convinced.

"Yes. But, since you're concerned, let's talk more about the drug use you mentioned on the intake form," he replied while reviewing my chart. "And by the way, thank you for your honesty. Most people lie about drugs. Your honesty shows me you're okay. You want to get better, right?"

"Okay," I nodded, sitting up and no longer covering my eye with my hand. Instead, I cuddled the coarse white hospital blanket. "Yes, I'm freaking out here. Are you sure I'm not losing it?"

"No, you're not losing it. You've simply done too many street drugs. Ecstasy, Acid, not good. Some people have different thresholds. You've reached yours." I nodded as he spat out the bullet-points. He handed me a prescription for Alprazolam. I knew of it. My mom used it. It's generic for Xanax.

"I'm only giving you a few pills. This will help your anxiety for now. I suggest you see your general physician and address your overall mental health, okay?" He made his way to pull back the curtain to leave. Terrified at the mere mention of *my* mental health, and being alone, he can't send me away.

"Doctor Jones, please stay!" I squealed.

He returned and casually sat next to me on the exam table. He appeared only a few years older than me. Collegiate haircut, pleasant features. With a gentle voice he stated, "You've had a hell of a night. Just get home and rest. And look, this *is* Austin. I get lots of college kids and musicians just like you every night. I've seen a lot worse. You'll be okay." My all black tight clothing, high-heeled black Dr. Martens, pierced nose, and messy hair must have given away my musician identity. He patted my hand and walked out. I didn't call him back. But, Doctor Jones didn't convince me. I walked out of the hospital with anxiety and paranoia. I swore everyone was looking at me like I had a sticker on my forehead that said CRAZY.

After I dropped the awake but hungover guys at home, I went to the pharmacy. I kept my head down as I bought the pills. My paranoia told me the pharmacist was judging me.

Shut up, Laurie. Like this pharmacist guy gives a shit you're getting anxiety pills?

Once home, I took the first pill. I was blown away at how quickly the Alprazolam calmed me down. I had a bodily warmth and a sensation of head to toe relaxation. The chatter in my mind slowed. I felt like I drank a couple of beers, but my mind wasn't fuzzy. The intense, onslaught of concerns and worries evaporated. Did I just trade street drugs for real drugs? I could get used to this. But I knew from my mom's use of pills, one is never enough. I'd have to find another way to beat this. I needed my mom more than ever. I just hoped she was well enough to handle me.

I called her after I got some sleep.

"Hey, Mom, how's things at home? How are you feeling?" I said as I twiddled the rope trim of my couch throw pillow between my fingers.

"Well, you know, not much happening here, except I can't put my goddamn pants on, or take them off, for that matter. Thank God, Stan is here. He knows how to get in my pants." She bellowed with a robust laugh, sounding higher than even I'd been.

"Oh, Christ, Mom! Really? Are those good pain pills you're on?"

"Oh, Laurie. Why not laugh about it? Shit, I read the *Waterloo Courier* three times to make sure I understood what the hell I'd just read. Oh well. The rehab people said I'll get better."

"You sound good to me, Mom. Your humor is, well, even better. I think if you ever had a filter, which I don't think you did, it's now gone for sure." I chuckled softly but had no more energy.

"Laurie, what's wrong?"

"What do you mean? I haven't said anything." "You don't need to. Your voice sounds different."

"Well, you know, the band broke up. That's taken a toll. Of course, the breakup with Patrick which you called correctly, has been hard. But, it's worse. I'm worse."

"What's going on?"

"I'm not sure, Mom." I hesitated to tell the truth. Dammit, I felt like a nineteen-year-old in Minneapolis, set for a good telling off. Worse yet, abandoned with a problem I should have been able to handle on my own by this age.

"Laurie, you still there?"

"Mom, I've dabbled in some drugs, and I'm scared. Don't worry. I still have my day job. I'm just scared. I'm not sure who I am anymore, and the drugs have left me paranoid, suicidal even. I need help."

"Suicidal? Oh, dear God, not you. Not you!" She shrieked and began to sob.

"Mom, please, if this is too much for you, tell me." "Have you talked to your dad?" She said through tears. "No, I'm afraid it will freak him out."

There was a pause on the line as I heard her rearrange herself in her squeaky dining table chair.

"Are you still using drugs?"

"No, definitely not anymore."

"Is your new boyfriend still around? Cause if he is, get rid of his ass and go to your dad. He's the only man you need right now." Her sobbing stopped. She sounded renewed, stronger.

She was right. He was the level head. "Um, okay, but I'm afraid."

"Of course, you are! I'm afraid for you. I can't lose you. I'm the sick one, not you! Not you!" She was crying again. "If I could be there, I would. Just get to your dad, and you get better. Get yourself back on stage, Laur. That's what you're missing. And I need to see you on stage again. It makes me happy."

"Yes, you're right, Mom. You're right. I love you."

There was a lingering pause. She then coughed heavily into the phone. After, her breathing was slow, crackling. She must have been smoking a lot.

"Sweetheart, I need to go. This upsets me, what's happening with you, but also, there's a physical therapist here helping me."

"Okay, okay."

She let out a soft chuckle. Her mood sounded lifted.

"They have me working on a puzzle. They say it's to help my mind. It's a puzzle of a fluffy, white cat. I'm sneezing just looking at the goddam thing. You know I don't like cats."

"Yes, I know, but it's not real."

"But, I hate fucking cats!" Her voice was loud. She was instantly angry.

"Okay, Mom. Okay. I'm sorry to push you."

"Oh, dear. I'm sorry." She wept again. "I'm so sorry. It just happens. This damn illness, the stroke, the meds I'm on. I'm sorry. I jump from one emotion to another."

"Mom, hang in there. Screw the cat puzzle. Ask for a puzzle of dogs or flowers."

"Or how about a penis? A puzzle with a penis on it. Just like my fiftieth birthday cake. Do you remember how that cake had a balloon in it and it exploded when I cut it?"

I laughed. "Yes, I remember." I blushed at the memory.

"Good, I got you to laugh. I needed that, too. Call me soon to tell me how you're doing."

"I will, Mom."

I hung up the phone and sobbed. In one conversation, I felt loved by her, sad for her, embarrassed for me, embarrassed for her, entertained by her, and then, pushed away by her. She was incapable of helping. It rang familiar and true.

31

TRAILER PARK
CONFESSIONS

I visited my dad at the trailer park where he'd temporarily set up his cream colored fifth-wheel RV. He'd become nomadic, driving around the country, picking his destinations on a whim. As he said, "I'm free to go where I want when I want." This time, I was thankful he was parked in north Texas for a month.

His RV was luxury on wheels, including a full kitchen. A pullout, he called it, extended his living and dining room to include a TV, full-sized couch and four-person dining table. There was a small bathroom with a shower and toilet and even a built-in washer and dryer. The décor in soft blues with masculine wood trimmings was impressive. It was an extravagant tour bus - for seniors.

We sat outside at a weathered wood picnic table in the afternoon, amongst young juniper trees and gravel roads that made up the RV grounds. The park was serene except for the occasional seniors who'd pass with their barking labs, retrievers or poodles and offer a hello. My dad's dachshund, Mitch, would bark in return.

"What happened to your car, Laur?" he said, motioning with his thumb to the smashed Tercel. Humbly, I told Dad everything. He listened patiently. He handled me like a military man: "You're better than this, Laurie. Clean up and set yourself straight," he said, his face serious.

Instead of asking me to fall into formation, he got up and gave me a long, steady and unfaltering hug. Longer than he'd ever embraced me before. When he pulled back, his nose was red like he'd been crying.

"You know, your mom put me through hell, and I couldn't help her. Laurie, I can't really help you, either, except you need to learn how to help yourself," he said, slowly sitting back down. I wiped a tear away as I waited for more.

"You need to find out how to do it alone. Stay away from the drugs. You've already seen what a mess they are. If you do that, you'll be okay." He stopped, closing his eyes, apparently to take in a welcome breeze passing through. It was playing with the light filtered through a few trees. We both took deep breaths.

"I struggle to say this," he went on, "because I don't understand your music and I've always imagined a different future for you. But if there was ever a time you need to make music, it's now. Get singing again. It's the only thing that makes you, *you*. If you do, you'll feel a lot better."

"Dad, that is the best help I could ask for. I was afraid you wouldn't see me through this," I whimpered.

"Laurie, you're my daughter. I don't agree with everything you do, but I'll be damned, I'll help how I can. If you need to go to a hospital, a doctor, tell me, and I'll bring you."

"I hate to admit it, but I think I need therapy." Saying the word alone evoked repulsion and additional tears to flow.

"Why do you hate to admit it?"

"Because I've seen mom so ill. I don't want to be like her." My tears stopped, and I gripped the bench, digging my nails into the flaking wood.

"Laurie, there's a big difference between you and her. She was sick from the start. It's in her DNA. You're just sick from drugs. You can stop this. She, well, can't stop herself."

His words of wisdom made sense, but a deep sadness loomed in my belly.

"But Dad, I have her DNA."

His eyes narrowed, and he appeared frustrated. His hands were now formed into fists, resting on the table.

"Yes, and you have mine, too. We'd know by now if there was something wrong with you." He looked away from me. He shifted his shoulders back to a rigid posture and then he released them. He slumped forward.

"Dad?"

"Look, my side of the family may not have mental issues like your mom, but we have addictions. Every other person in my family drank heavily when I was growing up. That's why I don't drink a lot. So, you shouldn't drink or sure as hell do drugs either." His brow furrowed, and he appeared bothered. "Well, our side of the family is a bunch of alcoholics."

I knew this already. I'd been to Markvart family reunions. Alcohol flowed like fish down the gullets of pelicans when the Markvart men gathered around a table. However, to me, it just looked like men having fun. Nothing I worried about as a child. My dad always appeared in control.

"Dad, what's the difference between mom and alcoholics? I mean, Mom drank like crazy too," I said. He looked relaxed now, a secret freed. He released his hands.

"Laurie, I don't know, but your mom is different. You may not know this, but your mom knew, even before she met me, that she was ill. She'd been mentally ill since she was a child."

I felt like I took a punch in the gut. I was despondent to think she had suffered so long, but I was also confused and heartbroken for my father.

"Then why did you marry her?"

Dad stared at the wood table for a few seconds, and afterward he warmly smiled, like a beautiful memory crossed his mind. He looked up at me.

"Because there is more to her than her mental illness. And I loved her. She is one hell of a woman. Plus, she has great legs."

It caught me off guard. "Wow, Dad!"

"Well, she does. The day I met her was the day that changed my life." He didn't flinch as he stared at me. "She is an extraordinary woman, Laurie."

I stared at my father. His face had become flush and serious. His candor struck me.

"I needed a housecleaner, and a co-worker knew of a single mother who needed work. I thought, a single mother? Her husband must have passed. But no, she turned out single by choice. As you already know, your mother had your brother David five months before she met me. She had chosen not to marry the father. It was the sixties; I was curious about her independence. I also figured she must need the job."

I never heard this story from my father's point of view. I always assumed this was a delicate topic.

His eyes danced as he continued. "The day I showed up at my house to meet my new cleaning lady, I walked in the kitchen door to the backside of this beautiful broad in a floral day dress, standing on a stepping stool. She was cleaning out the top kitchen cabinet above the sink. Her legs were long and lean, and she had a thin waist and shapely hips."

After my father finished his goddess-like description of my mother, he went on to tell me he faintly heard what sounded like his cat bellowing. It was as if my mother read his mind, turning around to smile at him. She said, "Sorry, I hate cats and I left the damn thing in one of the kitchen cabinets."

He laughed out loud as he finished his story, and I grasped his hands. His eyes became teary, and his smile looked like a man who just met the woman with whom he'd fallen in love.

"Laurie, at that moment, I already knew I loved her. We moved fast, you know. Married within months. I immediately adopted David. Within a year, we had you. So, yes, that day changed my life. *She* changed my life."

We sat in comfortable silence. The light was softening as the sun moved across the sky. Birds chirped in the distance as they readied themselves for night. It smelled like fall: campfires and damp leaves.

"But she also wore me down," he added, squeezing my hands. "And I know she wears on you, too."

I quickly retracted my hands at the mention of this. "Yes, you're right on all counts. I love her no matter what, but she drives me crazy." I teared up again.

"But not the kind of crazy you should worry about. You'll be okay, Laur."

He reached for my hands again, and I returned mine to him after dabbing my eyes with my hoodie sleeve. His hands were callused and warm. He held mine securely against the top of the plank table. I loved it when he'd hold my hands. "Dad, can I stay here with you for a couple weeks?"

"Absolutely. My home is always your home." He paused as he observed me like a parent examining their child-with love and curiosity. I smiled at him in relief.

He continued, "But you can't take long showers, and when you use the crapper, make sure to push the correct pedal on the toilet to dump the shit. Or the shit comes right back up," he said without laughing. He was deadpan. I couldn't tell if he was joking until he smiled. "Remember that in general for life. Always push the correct pedal. If you do, you'll be fine."

I stayed with Dad for two weeks. I wrote in my journal, composed music and read. I watched the other seniors take their daily dog walks and engage my father in chats of the weather and politics. Sometimes I'd join dad and his friends in the community center for Friday night BBQ. Mostly, I slept. My dad let me use the one and only bedroom in his trailer which had a full-sized, firm, ten-inch mattress of a bed. The only separation between us was an accordion-styled, thin plastic door. He insisted on taking the couch at night. "Of all the shit-holes I've slept in during my military service, this couch is a luxury. Also, I want you to have privacy."

Every night I felt comfort and safety lying in his bed, listening to crickets and knowing he was close. The night was remarkably quiet, my ears ached; a stark contrast to loud rock or pumping EDM. Knowing my dad was a few feet away brought immense peace. But I couldn't hide at the RV park forever.

The day I left Dad to return to Austin, I drove off in my banged-up Tercel with pride, peace, and a bit of anxiety. But I was thankful for my dad. I looked in the rearview mirror as my car created a mini dust tornado on the gravel road. Dad was smiling and waving me off, his dog, Mitch barking at my exit. One of Dad's neighbors joined Dad and waved too. I paused at the gated exit of the park, not wanting to leave the tranquility and yet yearning to go. I drove on to Hwy 933 knowing my future was in my hands and I was okay with it.

When I returned to Austin, I visited a medical doctor to make sure I was physically healthy. He advised me to stay on the

Alprazolam for a few more months but warned me he wouldn't refill the prescription. "You need to find your own solutions to deal with your anxiety--like go to a therapist, exercise, and meditate." He offered a prescription for Prozac. "This is a very low dose. It will help you." I reluctantly took the paper. As I stared at the prescription, I was tempted to tell him that people took Prozac recreationally, but I figured he knew. But I also knew I didn't want the pills.

I handed the paper back to him.

"I don't want to take any more pills. My mom is bi-polar and well, I don't want to be like her."

"Ah, even more reason for you to take it." He handed the paper right back to me like we were playing a card game. I accepted it, folded it up, and stuck it deep in my purse. I didn't ask him what that comment meant. I just wanted out of his office. But I eventually started taking the damn green and white pill.

I saw a therapist weekly to discuss the remnant anxiety, how I missed performing, and the previous thoughts of suicide. I asked the therapist why I was able to talk myself out of suicide when some people can't. Why did that voice come to me while in the bathtub? Who was the voice? And why did my mom survive her attempts?

Softly, the therapist spoke as she gave vague answers to my questions. They ranged from inner strength, guilt, and survival instinct to faith and God. But then she dove a bit deeper, "Laurie, some people are so sick, there is no off switch to their pain. The illness is stronger than their ability to stifle it."

My heart ached as I listened intently, thinking of those who'd succumb. It didn't seem fair.

She finalized, "And of course, it's about getting help. Some never seek it. They're too afraid, can't afford it, or even know where to start. Most of all, they're embarrassed. They'll go to the doctor to fix their broken leg, but not their broken brain." She became visibly agitated, gripped her notebook and pen tighter, and then sighed before she continued. "Society has caused that problem. But most of the time, their illness is so dark, the illness keeps them from help."

I pulled the pillow on the therapist's sofa closer to my chest to bring myself some comfort.

"So, it's like the car you need to take to the mechanic to get fixed is so broken it won't start?" I said.

She blankly stared at me before she replied, "Something like that. Or more like, the person doesn't even know the car is broke."

***

Over the next few months, the fog, depression, darkness slowly lifted. But as the fog lifted, I was left emotionally flat from the Prozac. I wasn't low anymore, but I also couldn't feel joy. It was the strangest sensation, like going to a comedy show and understanding the joke but not being able to laugh. I couldn't access happy feelings. After a couple months on the Prozac, I went cold turkey. Not a great idea as it caused more anxiety, but I had the Alprazolam for that.

I received a small box in the mail from Mom. It was the little stuffed garden mouse I gave her in the hospital when she had meningitis. Included was a note in her pretty handwriting, unaffected by the stroke:

> *I think you need the mouse more than me,*
> *Sweetheart. Love, Mom.*

I held the mouse to my chest, overcome with her warmth and love. For the first time since quitting Prozac, I felt joy, and I cried happy tears.

I continued my day job at the Austin newspaper, found a roommate, and, for the first time in a long time, I was single. My Alprazolam prescription ran out, but the doctor was correct about exercise. I began running around Town Lake four times a week, six miles, which reduced my anxiety. With each step on the gravel path, I crushed invasive negative thoughts. As I'd run I'd ponder why it's called Town Lake. It's actually the Colorado River that separates downtown Austin from South Austin. It's a wide river, probably 400 feet or more and medium-sized boats and pontoons, rowers and canoes are as much of the scenery as the people running its trails. Sometimes when there's too much rain, the brown waterway overflows into Zilker Park, and the park becomes a lake. Nonetheless, I enjoyed running the path and being around other folks whom I assumed were running off their own troubles, body weight or aiming for the same runner's high I was getting.

My creativity returned. Had I stayed on the Prozac, it would have crushed my imagination. The recent pain and anger were my inspiration, and it flowed into words and music against love, marriage, union, drugs, pain. The lyrics were harsh, but I wanted and needed to sing them.

32

IMPOSTER

I looked at band-wanted ads, called old music business friends, and showed up at clubs. I had been out of the music scene for over six months, and I wondered how I'd get back in.

I was healthy-minded but being back in the corporate world meant I was also bored. I showed up each day like an imposter in someone else's dream. Working at the newspaper was still an excellent job, with some wonderful people. However, the corporate world of alabaster-colored walls and wood office desks was *their* life, dreams, hopes, and passions--not mine. I agonizingly went about the job while searching for other music options.

Bruce, the dream band manager, returned my call. I told him I was looking for a gig, and he thought he had the perfect project. An investor he knew was starting an Austin indie label. They were looking for a singer to mold and form into an artist for their first release. Luckily, with Bruce's continued interest in my career, and the investor's familiarity with the band, I was signed as their first artist. I treated this new opportunity as a blessing and was ever indebted to Bruce and his faith in me.

My solo career began in winter 1996 on Plazma Records. I used the stage name Laurie Marks, an earlier suggestion of my San Antonio talent agent. She had thought Markvart was too complicated for people to remember. I disagreed, but obliged.

As the project started, I was encouraged by the label's interest in me. Enough so I quit my day job at the *Austin American-Statesman* to fully commit to the project. I figured I'd pick up temporary admin jobs if I needed extra money and fall back on my small 401k if things got desperate. It was scary to leave the job after five years, but I was ready to go full time with this unique opportunity. However, I had waves of doubt about my musical direction.

I didn't want to make metal music anymore. I wanted to experiment and expand my voice in new ways. Besides, I was done screaming, but I wanted to keep the same stage energy. I leaned towards alt-rock, but I needed time to solidify my sound. However, the label pressed forward quickly, hiring a producer, suggesting songs I could cover. Their reason to push? They were excited, which was great. But I felt rushed.

Along the way in making the record, I found it easier to let the label and producer drive the project. They picked the studio musicians, engineer, and photographers. I didn't fight unless something really annoyed me creatively. I was eager to please everyone and to play again. I agreed to just about everything.

Except for one thing: I insisted on bringing a hot new guitarist on the scene, Aaron, on to the project. I had met him at his show at the Back Room. Fixated on his technique on the guitar; I hadn't even noticed the rest of the band. His playing was confident and distinct, attacking the strings of his Les Paul with long, down pic strokes. He entranced me, if not slightly intimidated me. I knew I was in the presence of someone special and I wanted to work with him. It was the same feeling I'd had when meeting Levi from the metal band. After Aaron's show, I swallowed my guts and introduced myself to the 21-year-old. We connected effortlessly and began writing songs together the following week. It was dreamlike. I was no longer alone on my journey.

The label wanted the album to focus on bluesy rock songs, but when they listened to the alternative rock songs Aaron and I co-wrote, they agreed to add them, and Aaron, too.

Aaron became my next musical brother. We're both Libras. We shared a mischievous sense of humor, we liked the same style of music, and we were in-sync songwriting partners. Aaron was thrilled with the paying gig, and I was happy to find a player who suited my style.

Selfish released with ten songs in Spring 1997. While I wasn't in control of the creation of the album, I enjoyed the recording process. I always loved studio work. The CD had high-quality production, excellent performances, and a top-notch recording but it didn't feel like *mine*. I wasn't even on the front cover. Instead, it was an image of a young girl holding a real anatomical heart. Conceptually it fit, and it was a badass photo, but it wasn't me or a picture I would have chosen. Mostly, the music failed to represent me. The CD lacked a cohesive thread; it was a hodgepodge of bluesy and alternative rock. Weak sales and dismal reviews met its release. One critic gave it 1.5 stars out of 4 and stated, "There's a reason they don't make albums like this anymore, and *Selfish* is it." I took the harsh review to heart. If I had full creative control, it might have been different. Nonetheless it was an unfair review.

Selfish was a successful failure: it brought me back into music, but I was disappointed and pissed at the reviews. Thankfully, the label still wanted live shows to support the CD. I agreed with one caveat: I pick the live band and control the set list. On stage was where I got my high-no one would fuck with that. They agreed. Aaron and I put together a tight-as-hell live band and eventually dropped all the bluesy songs and brought in our newer originals. My confidence in myself, and my music grew with each live show. Plazma Records wanted me to do a follow-up album with the songs Aaron and I wrote under their label's publishing--songs we didn't use on *Selfish* but were playing live. Despite my frustrations over the first CD, I was thankful to do the second album. However, the second one had to be *my* way.

When they again pressured me to conform to their concept of what my record should be, I wasn't having it. I wanted our songs back and I wanted to record them my way. I stalled the recording with the label. By the end of 1997, the songs came back to Aaron and me. The label and I parted ways.

I was musically independent, and it was a relief. It also meant the money to keep the live show musicians or studio time was gone, as well as any income for me. I found a temporary admin job but knew it wouldn't be enough to support me *and* a recording project. Still, I had a yearning to record those songs.

I turned to a close friend. She had always been supportive of my music and had the financial ability to help. She agreed to loan me money to cover recording costs. I was elated and enormously grateful.

I booked time at Hamstein Studios in Austin, with Aaron producing. I fully trusted him, but I remained in control of the writing, song choices, and styling of the CD. When I entered Studio A, I paused. I felt a tingle up my spine. This was my fifth time in a studio, but it always felt like the first in an exciting way. I walked to the 24-track Neve mixing board and touched its nobs and buttons. It was like shaking a wrapped gift under the Christmas tree, eliciting curiosity and excitement. That studio, with two isolation booths and state-of-the-art equipment, was ours for the next week.

We only left the dimly lit studio-cave for sleep, fast food, or beer and cigarettes for the players. An assortment of the best Austin musicians and friends came to play on the songs. The process was so joyful I put any worry about the financial or critical success into the back of my mind. Come what may, though I knew I must pay my friend back.

When Aaron and I finished the six-song EP called *Intro*, it mirrored my re-introduction back into music the way I wanted. I released it independently under my real name, Laurie Markvart, and with my photo on the front! I was ecstatic with the final product.

Aaron went on to other creative projects and, while I missed our partnership, I played local acoustic shows to support the release. I enjoyed playing the coffeehouses and small bars; but solo gigs, on my acoustic guitar, didn't carry the same rush as playing with a full band. Also, I was lonely. It was more fun to play with others. But I pushed forward.

I put my songs on mp3.com. A lot of independent musicians used it for promoting their work. Maybe I'd get picked up by some stations to get airplay and gain some notoriety. Pushing the record was difficult without a label. I couldn't keep it all going and work my temp day job at a local TV station. Once again, I was good at administrative work and they offered me a full-time position. I accepted. It was keeping a roof over my head and providing the ability to pay back my friend. Still, I tried to keep my foot in the creative waters. My previous San Antonio theater agent sent me out on top-shelf auditions: a Janis Joplin biopic, and a singing part for a major film director's new internet site featuring artists and musicians.

The film director's audition was remarkable. To perform for him, albeit for two minutes, in a large conference room in a generic corporate building, was an honor but it's what happened before I got in the room that proved noteworthy. Apparently, after her audition, a very naïve teen reached over "the other side of the table" in which the film director was sitting and attempted to shake his hand. I'm sure she was denied.

When she returned to the waiting area, she was promptly ridiculed by the casting director in front of everyone that her actions were inappropriate in an audition setting. The young girl burst into tears, and I felt horrible that someone had not prepared her for the "no touch" or "wait until you're directed" policy. It's Auditioning 101. This is the first rule I learned in my days of theater auditioning in San Antonio. So, when I entered the room, I went straight to the X on the floor and waited for instruction. When I left, I walked directly to the door and didn't glance at the big-time director behind the table.

Notable auditions and all, I got no offers. Waiting for callbacks that never came, that was the worst of it. But sometimes, unexpected and appreciated calls came out of nowhere.

33

PLAYBILLS AND WORN HEELS

"Laurie, this is Lewis in New York. Your Aunt Nan's agent. I understand you're quite the singer and you've done some acting, too? I have something you might be interested in. Can we chat?"

Aunt Nan called immediately after I hung up with Lewis. "Hello, my sweet Laurie, I'm sorry if Lewis' call put you on the spot, but when he mentioned this opportunity, I had to remind him about you. This is very exciting! What do you think?"

"Hi, Aunt Nan! But, what do I think of auditioning for Broadway?" Sitting on the couch at home, I took a breath before I continued. "I'm flattered he'd take you at your word about me." "Honey, I'm one of his longest-held clients. He trusts me, and I know you're very talented. Just remember, this business is harsh, so stay strong. I love you and break a leg!"

214

Unfortunately, I already knew quite well how harsh this business was. I assumed I knew what Aunt Nan meant, but, as it turned out, I didn't.

I didn't think it was crazy to ask for a couple days off from my new full-time job, fly from Austin to New York City, do an audition for *RENT* the same day, then fly back to Austin the next. I was thrilled for the opportunity. Why would I let logistics, or my day job interfere? Plus, this was New York City! My childhood dream!

After Lewis's initial call, a long call to Mom giving her every detail and temper her excitement as she'd scream over and over: *Broadway! Laurie, Broadway?* I barely had three days to pull together a flight, prepare my audition song, and make my way to New York. I was given specific details to arrive by 2:00 pm on Thursday at a rehearsal studio in midtown Manhattan.

I had my song ready, *Guilty*, a blues number by Randy Newman. It was the last song on my *Selfish* album. I knew I had only one shot at the gig, but I had no idea what to expect at my first Broadway audition. The stakes were high. When I asked Lewis what to expect, he simply said, "Kid, show up on time and sing your ass off."

I arrived in good time at the location, but nervous energy was consuming me. My legs trembled as I approached the mid-century, inconspicuous corporate building that looked like any office building among the bustling sidewalks of New York. I was not expecting a colossal neon *RENT* sign hanging above the door, as one might expect at The Nederlander Theater, the show's

Broadway venue. Yet, I was struck by how ordinary this building appeared. I wondered if people walking down the street even knew this was where actors auditioned for *RENT*. It's the hottest show on Broadway. I hadn't seen the show yet but I knew this much!

After ringing the call button, the loud buzz of the lock release sounded. The glass door popped open a few inches, threatening to close immediately if the door wasn't held open. I grabbed the door, but it was heavy. I stuck my foot in. With a thud, my boot held the door open. Although I winced slightly in pain, I smiled that I literally got my foot in the door.

As I entered the well-lit, small lobby, I was drawn to the letter-sized framed tenant directory, hung on the mirrored wall to the right of the elevator. The building had no doorman or security guard. As I skimmed the directory, most names listed were either casting or production offices. My palms started to sweat, and a brief dizziness came over me. *What song am I singing again?*

I pulled out my compact mirror on the way up. After the long trip from Texas, I needed to make sure my eyeliner was still around my eyes and not down my cheeks. Everything about me from lips to eyes looked in place but was this the reflection of a Broadway actress? Is this who Mom promised I'd be when I was a little girl? I was still looking at my compact mirror when the doors opened, and there was a waiting room, instead of an antici-pated corridor. A production office occupied the entire floor, decorated with framed playbills and photos of Broadway shows. The room was silent, warm. I was met with curious looks from two apparent auditionees, seated on cushioned benches on opposite sides of the room. A man and a woman appeared stoic, hiding their tension, headshots in hands. I wondered what roles they were there for, and if their palms were as clammy as mine. I felt my mouth dry up in anxiety with the mere thought I was about to join them.

Across the room, a stylish woman in her mid-thirties and all chic black sat behind a tidy metal desk. She acknowledged me with a nod and stated my name for confirmation. I nodded back and offered a friendly smile. She halfway returned the smile while motioning for me to take a seat. I glided onto an open bench but got distracted by the *RENT* playbill on the wall and stood up again.

The cast photos confirmed my perfect wardrobe choice for this audition: Black, torn fishnets with funky worn-in high-heeled boots; a fitted, black satin mini-dress. It was buttoned only halfway up the front to expose a colorful purple paisley tank. Two thin, multi-colored scarves draped across my back and chest; they highlighted multiple necklaces and large-hoop earrings. With my airplane-traveled, tousled hair and inadvertent chipped nail polish, I'll be damned if I didn't look the Bohemian part.

The door to an audition room suddenly opened and out walked a dashingly handsome, hip actor. I couldn't take my eyes off him. His exit was smooth, but persistent, as he made his way to the elevator, never once turning around. He had a coolness and confidence that made me feel inadequate in his presence.

"Laurie, you're up," a female voice said from the audition room. I couldn't look in her direction; I was too mesmerized by hot actor-guy. As he entered the elevator and spun around, he caught my eye. He smiled and winked just as the door closed. For a fleeting moment, it boosted my confidence.

"Yes, I'm Laurie," I said, turning to the direction of the voice.

Oh shit, here we go.

The large-windowed, wooden-floored rehearsal room doubled as a dance studio. It was lit like a classroom and was stuffy. A faint scent of cigarette and coffee lingered in the air.

"Do you have sheet music?" the friendly man sitting behind the upright black piano inquired.

"Yes. I'm also ready to sing *a cappella*," I said. He nodded but didn't ask for the music.

From the other side of the room, the woman who had escorted me in took a seat behind a rectangular folding table. "Do you have your résumé, please?" I assumed she was the casting assistant and was proven correct. Two piles of résumés sat in front of her on the table, headshots facing down. My hands were trembling as I passed mine over. She looked up and smiled, but it was all business.

At the same time, I sensed the watchful, keen eye of the casting director sitting to her left. I briefly glanced at him, too nervous to make full eye contact, but I could tell his eyes were on me. He was smartly dressed, small glasses, wiry hair, poised and quiet. I sensed a genuine interest from him. I felt honored in this position, yet nerves were setting in deeper. I realized the importance of my delivery was not only for my sake but also for my agent's reputation.

I walked back to the piano, wishing I could lean on it to support my weak legs. There was no X on the floor for me to stand on. Waiting for my cue, I loosened my locked hands to let them naturally fall to my side. I looked to the woman for more direction, but she was taking her time reviewing my résumé, making notes on her pad. What could she be writing? I kept my eyes on the table and tried to relax. At the same time, I let out a soft sigh and looked to the pianist for support. He was reading his notes. This was just another day's work for him. For me, it was the rest of my life.

Surprisingly, it was so quiet; no New York City street noise from below. The room must have been sound-proofed: I heard nothing but my pounding heart.

Although I was impatient and nervous, I felt respected from the three in the room, even though they'd barely said a word to me. They were treating me as if I deserved their time. If I was in that room, it meant I had a reputable agent; and that meant I had recognizable talent. It also meant I would not be wasting their time. I dare not let anyone down. I need to bring something of quality.

As I had been preparing in the days before, I had reoccurring visions the audition would be dramatic like from *Chorus Line*-being forced to stand center stage, pouring out my personal drama in song and monologues. This was different. We weren't even in a theater. I wished we were. At least then I'd have had more physical distance to buffer my mental strain between that table and me.

"Laurie, please go ahead and sing a few bars of your song a cappella," said the casting assistant. Her voice was pleasant, yet I was caught off guard because I needed to perform. Fuck. The room was so damn quiet. I needed to take the worries and silence and turn them into performance. *Oh, what the hell: Just sing*, I thought.

Slowly, but powerfully I eased into the song. I gave it as much energy, soul, and feeling as I could. *Guilty* has a slow start and a strong, ballsy chorus.

With my eyes closed, I began. As I gained my strength, I opened my eyes slightly to make brief connection with the two behind the table. My fists clenched as I reached a strong peak of emotion in the song. My knees locked, my nerves swerved back in. Soon, I naturally relaxed as the song took over. I stepped a bit to the side to regain my posture and show movement. Then, it was almost as if I moved to the passenger seat and was watching myself steer. My instinct, endless practice and natural ability were driving the performance. I didn't think of the next lyric or note; it just rolled off my tongue like a metal Slinky going downstairs.

I barely finished the twelfth bar when the accompanist interrupted. "Excuse me, can you pull out the sheet music and give it a try?"

The casting director didn't blink an eye at the request.

"Of course." As I went to grab the sheet music, my internal dialogue kicked in: I hope this is a good sign he wants to hear more. On the other hand, I need to sing the song in the same key as the sheet music and it better sound just like my *a cappella* version!

The accompanist took the sheet and spread it out on the piano.

"Key of E?" he asked. "Yes, E."

"All right then, let's have another go at it," he stated, never glancing away from the music.

I faced the table again and stepped three feet away from the piano. From the first note he played, I knew it was the same key as when I sang *a cappella*. *Whew*!

Damn, he played as if he'd known the song all his life. Once I heard my cue, I didn't have time to think or react: only to sing. It gave me comfort to have someone else representing the song with me. Now relaxed, I sang with heart and guts.

After completing the first chorus, the woman at the table put her hand up ever so delicately, slightly raised from the table, like she was playing Blackjack and waved off a hit, smiling warmly. "Thank you," she said. She nodded at the pianist.

"Can you run scales, please?" he asked. "Absolutely, yes."

I'd worked scales before. I knew it was used to determine vocal range and pitch. I gladly stepped closer to the piano and ran a few scales. I took joy in the activity. I felt that sense of fulfillment and recognition that I was doing something right. The whole process up until then had probably taken five minutes--far longer than I had expected.

After I finished singing through a final scale, he stopped playing and kindly said, "Thank you for your time." He handed me the sheet music. I smiled and turned to the two at the table. They both smiled.

"Thank you for coming, Laurie," said the assistant. The casting director never uttered a word. He also never looked away and maintained eye contact. His gaze was pleasant and strictly professional.

"Thank you." I grabbed my bag, and just like that, I was done. I walked to the door and felt the heat of their gaze on my back.

I hoped the backside of my dress wasn't stuck up my ass crack or that my worn-down boot heels didn't look too scrappy. I knew the nails appeared through the plastic on the heel. I hadn't noticed the clicking on the floor when I entered. When I left in dead silence, the worn heels sounded like a metronome as I walked. I probably looked perfectly in character. Besides, there was nothing else I could do but leave.

Walking through the waiting room, I understood why the handsome hip actor before me was so driven and purposeful when he left. When you've done well, that high sets in, a sense of accomplishment and euphoria. That, and the need to get the hell out of the hot zone and go somewhere to cool down and process. I avoided eye contact with others and held my breath to the elevator. By the time I exited the building, my euphoria turned into an explosion of tears. I felt satisfied at how it went, but also bewilderment, adrenaline, excitement and fear--all cooked up into one big crying cocktail with a touch of nausea to top it off.

I stood a few feet from the building's entrance, boots hovering over the street curb. I didn't know where to go next. My tears grew into simple sobs. I didn't want anyone from the audition to see me. I gathered my breath and hoped my body would stop trembling.

With my scarf, I sloppily wiped away the remaining wetness from my cheek.

The fresh air and sound of car horns was welcoming and grounded me. I walked back in the direction I had come from—catching my breath before calling Lewis.

My agent's voice was blazing with energy and interest. "Kid, how'd it go?"

"Well, after I sang *a cappella*, and then to the sheet music, they asked me to sing scales." My voice squeaked like a teenager.

"Fantastic! That's great! Come uptown to 52nd and 9th for a margarita at El Azteca. Have Nan meet us, too. I want to hear all about it. See you soon, kiddo!" His animated voice sounded like an afternoon TV cartoon announcer.

Before I headed uptown, I stopped and leaned against a building. I needed to call my mom, but I had to call my aunt first.

"Hi, Aunt Nan. I'm done," I said. "Oh, darling. How do you feel?"

It's interesting she asked how I felt instead of how the audition went. I sighed and said, "I feel like my heart is in my throat and my stomach at my feet."

She sighed in return. "Sounds just about right, dear. Where are you now?"

"I'm at the subway stop near the audition. I'm heading up to some Mexican restaurant on 52nd to meet Lewis. He asked if you'd meet us."

"Ah, El Azteca. Okay, I'll leave now. Just remember I walk a bit slower now."

"I know Aunt Nan. Thank you for coming out. It means a lot to me."

I walked a few blocks to the next subway entrance and called my mom along the way. The walk stabilized my wobbly legs, but not my worn-down boots.

Sadly, I got my mom's voice mail. Hearing her recorded voice wasn't enough to satisfy my need of her.

34

HELL'S KITCHEN
MARGARITA

Lewis sat at the bar near the entrance, beaming, with a margarita in front of him and arms open wide to welcome me. He gave me a long hug and a firm pat on the back. It was Aunt Nan: "Look in the bar for the tall, handsome, mustached man with sophisticated glasses wearing a fabulous purple button-up."

The minute I took a seat next to Lewis, the bartender swiftly placed a margarita in front of me. I liked this place, and Lewis. He was my mom's age and paternal. I gave Lewis the blow-by-blow as he listened, wide-eyed.

"Well, it all sounds good. Kid, congratulations on your first Broadway audition. Cheers!" We clinked glasses, and both took a hefty drink.

"Thanks, Lewis. I'm a bit overwhelmed by it all. I think they liked me, but how do I know if I got it?"

"Ah, you never know when you know what you'll know from these shows until…you know." He did not appear confused when he said this.

"Look, Laurie, they're trying to get this touring cast in place soon, so I would suspect we'll hear something in the coming weeks."

I checked my phone, hoping Mom called.

Aunt Nan arrived 30 minutes later, out of breath, beads of sweat dotting her forehead. After long hugs for both of us, she sat next to me at the bar, leaving me in the middle of her and Lewis. The bartender greeted her with a kiss on her outstretched hand.

"How are you doing, sweet Nan?" He placed a glass of white wine in front of her.

"Fine. Thank you, Bob. And you?" "Better now that you are here." He smiled.

Nan and Lewis appeared to be regulars at this Hell's Kitchen joint, which made me feel more comfortable.

"Oh, I do love the service here," Aunt Nan said. Looking at both of us, "And to meet you both here? Splendid!"

I sat quietly and enjoyed listening to Nan and Lewis catching up. I took a few more sips of the margarita, sending warmth to my stomach and cheeks.

"Darling, I am so very, very proud of you," said Aunt Nan. "It takes a lot of gumption to handle your first big audition. Also, to come from out of state." She gave me another hug.

"Thank you, Aunt Nan." I tried to hold back unwanted tears.

Aunt Nan noticed, patted my knee in acknowledgment.

"Eventually, all auditions will become just another notch in your belt. You won't be so worked up over it *or* the outcome," she said. I nodded, knocking back more margarita.

After a pause and another sip of wine, she added, "I hope your skin is thick enough for this business. Can you handle the ups and downs? The rejections? Or even the successes, for that matter?" She swigged another drink of her wine. An invasion of noisy car horns rang out when a patron opened the nearby front door.

"I worry about you getting into this business, Laurie. With your family history of alcoholism and your mom's illness, well, this business is hard," she said once the door closed, and we regained a sense of quiet.

"I've been in this business. In music," I stated with confidence. I sat up straighter on my stool.

"Oh, but nothing is like Broadway, darling."

Lewis noticed my confused reaction as I perched, speechless. "Oh, she'll be just fine, Nan. I've seen far worse nerves on those who *are* experienced."

Dumbfounded by her acknowledgment of my mom's illness, I stared at my margarita in the frosty glass. I'd lost my taste for it. My shoulders slumped.

"What did my mom tell you?" I said as I sheepishly looked at my aunt.

"Oh, honey. It's not what she told me, it's, well, I've known for years of her struggles." She gently touched my cheek with the outside of her hand. Her hand smelled of cigarettes, but I leaned into it. It was a loving gesture. "But this business will bring anyone to drink," she said.

"Oh, hell, Nan," Lewis injected. "Every business brings people to drink. Accountants drink. Doctors drink. Lord knows, lawyers drink." Lewis placed his hand on my shoulder. "Laurie, don't worry. You're doing fine. Besides, some of the best damn actors I know are drunks," he proclaimed, dramatically waving his other hand in the air as if to swat a fly.

Astounded and now amused by the contradictory conversation I sat between, I grabbed my margarita in both hands and took a satisfying swig.

"Well, you could be right, Lewis," said Nan, "But some of them are just plain drunks. Look, I'm an old woman. I've been bruised many times in this industry. And, I don't want you to … to get your hopes up, Laurie. Or worst of all, turn out like me." Her brown eyes locked on mine. There was an emptiness in her eyes I didn't want to stare into.

I glanced away from her and looked down at the mosaic tiled floor. Lewis and Nan fell quiet, the only sounds came from other patrons' chatter until Aunt Nan slowly got up from her stool.

"Have you spoken to your mother yet?" asked Aunt Nan. "No, I left her a message. I'm anxious to talk to her."

"I'm sure she can't wait to hear the details. It's very exciting. Well, I'm going out for a cigarette. I wish these damn restaurants still allowed smoking. What the hell was this city thinking? Bars and cigarettes go together. Next thing you know, they'll take alcohol away from bars." She kissed my balmy cheek before departing out into the loud city scene.

"Okay, Nan, we'll see you in a few." Lewis turned to me and smiled like he was holding a secret. As soon as she was outside and out of earshot, Lewis said, "Don't worry, kid. It's all part of the game. Taking criticism from family. Or strangers. Oh hell, everyone." He motioned to the bartender. "Bob, can you pour us another?"

My posture sunk. The wood stool was hard under me, and the room grew stifling, and the other conversations overwhelmingly loud. I was dizzy from my aunt's words. A new frosty green glass was placed in front of me. I put the cold salted rim to my lips. The taste of tequila stopped my internal world from spinning.

***

A few days later, I was back in Austin. Initially, I couldn't shake my aunt's comments. When I spoke to my mother, her adoration and fascination with the audition details built me back up. Then Lewis called.

"Kid, they liked you," he said. "They want to see you again. In four days. Can you come back? They want you to read and sing for a specific part."

Speechless, I was thrilled but nauseated at the same time, like how you feel on a roller coaster as it climbs the first hill.

"Kid, you still there? Laurie?"

"Yes, sorry, Lewis. Hell yes, I'll come back."

Lewis faxed me the side of dialogue and two pages of music for the character Maureen.

For the next three days, I studied my ass off. I put everything else on hold for the biggest audition of my life. I tried to find out more about *RENT* and the characters but, there were only reviews on Netscape, Lycos, and Yahoo.

I took the same early morning flight to Newark on a Thursday. The same one-hour bus ride to Port Authority, and the same subway. All of it included the same stomach somersaults, except this time, I had more hopeful internal thoughts: *Could it change everything for my career? Will I go on tour? Do I need to move?*

Once inside the waiting room, I sat instead of reading the playbills on the wall. The room was roasting hot, and some women visibly perspired, blouses damp. My legs trembled, beads of sweat invaded my powdered forehead. The room was crammed with twenty or so women who looked like me: white, in our twenties with long, dark hair, dressed in a funky bohemian style.

Lewis advised me to wear the same outfit as the first audition-worn-down boot heels and all. The casting director wanted to see the same person from the first audition.

Ten minutes after arriving, an unfamiliar woman in her twenties beckoned me. Following her lead, I entered the same audition room. The familiar faces of the casting assistant, casting director, and accompanist sat behind the table. Thankfully, the room was much cooler than the waiting room.

"Hello, Laurie. Welcome back. Please wait there by the door until we're ready," said the casting assistant. She looked at the headshots on the table and spoke quietly with the others. What could they be saying? Behind them, next to a video camera on a stand, stood a young man with nerdy glasses and his arms casually folded over his chest. I focused my gaze on him to camouflage my over-active tension. My legs shook. I jiggled each one out like a runner about to start a race. The accompanist rose from behind the table and approached me.

"Hi, Laurie. Yes, thank you for coming back. You can place your bag on the floor by the door. He smiled but did not offer to shake hands, as he waited for my response.

"Ah, yes. Okay. Thank you," I said. I placed my grey satchel down.

"Okay," he continued. "We're going to have you start with the monologue that opens the song. Then we'll run lines off the sides if we desire. I need you to stand on the large white X, and if you choose to move in character, which we recommend, please stay within the four small white x marks on the floor that create a square. Those keep you in camera frame." He pointed at the floor before moving to the piano a few feet away. I walked to the square and looked straight at the camera. The young guy behind it had his finger on the button, ready to roll. A jolt of stomach acid crept up my throat. I closed my eyes and used a moment of silence to take a breath and think about the song I was about to perform, *Over the Moon*. It began with a speaking bit--a funny, charismatic monologue with a cappella singing.

Out of nowhere, thoughts of Bell's Palsy entered my mind. When I sing, I can close my eyes to disguise my non-symmetrical face, but not for a monologue. Opening my eyes, I looked at the camera, but the light was not on. I'd had no direction yet. *Oh, fuck. What was I thinking?* How can I do a monologue without full expression? I must leave. *Hold your damn horses, Laurie, my mom whispered.*

My breath left my body, but it rushed back as I heard the casting assistant say, "Start, please." The camera light turned red. *Shit!*

Beginning the monologue, I delivered the words effectively, emotionally and with timed humor. I gestured and made small steps when I felt warranted for the character. I made eye contact with the casting director, but he didn't return any expression. The casting assistant was making notes, not looking up. Words were rolling off my tongue as if I was forcing some of the dialogue instead of enjoying it, but it felt spot on. A minute into the monologue, the accompanist abruptly interrupted me by raising his hand above his shoulder.

"Thank you, Laurie. Now, please follow me to sing."

He pointed his finger in the air to conduct me, and he immediately played. I let out a breath, my head feeling like I was on a Tilt-A-Whirl ride. On cue, I sang. Thank God, I rehearsed so much because I knew the exact spot to start. I performed from memory with no sheet music. After about twenty seconds, he again raised his hand in the air to signal me to stop.

"That is all." He patiently smiled. He turned to the others and nodded. Was that a yes or no nod? There was no other body language to suggest anything. The red light on the camera went dark. The camera-guy folded his arms and returned his gaze to the floor.

Behind the table, their responses were, once again, swift: a nod of acknowledgment and an audible, but not loud, utter of thank you. Within a flash of starting, I had finished.

I exited the room with a familiar urgency to get to the elevator. The waiting room, even warmer than before, was full of more women. The emotional intensity nearly overcame me, and the smell of cosmetics tightened my chest. My steps quickened, as I gazed at the floor and noticed a slight rut, a straight path, was worn into the wood varnish from the audition room to the elevator.

When I reached the street, a massive sense of relief came over me like I'd conquered something. The fresh air was again a welcome rush to my face. My chest loosened, and I breathed normally. I stood on the curb and rejoiced now: I completed another round. Damn, I flew three-thousand miles for a one-minute audition. Except I was curious why they did not ask me to run lines. Instead of calling Lewis or Aunt Nan, I strolled the streets and took in the city and my accomplishment. I figured I'd call my mom later when I was calmed down. Right now, she'd be *too* needy for all the details. She'd always say, "Tell me everything that happened just as if I was there." Sometimes I needed that. But this time, I didn't want the stress of detailing every single fucking second for my mom's enjoyment. Her need to live through my adventures could be exhausting.

I returned to Austin the next day with guidance from Lewis that if there was another call-back, he would know soon. When I asked how many more times they might ask me to come back to New York, he said, "As many damn times as they want, kid!"

I jumped back into life in Austin, working at the TV station and playing live music at coffeehouses. Days turned into weeks with no call-backs. Both Lewis and I reached the same conclusion: the show had made other choices. Now my choice was to worry about it or let it go. So, I let it go until four months after that audition, when I got an out-of-the-blue call from Lewis. The *RENT* touring company was coming through Austin and would I be interested in going in front of them again? I was stumped. I wasn't that interested anymore but maybe? Like when you never want to speak to a guy who broke your heart…but he calls a few months later and you're curious enough to take his call.

Auditions were held at a local theater, and far more laid back for my third time. I didn't recognize any faces behind the table: three twenty-something women, sipping take out coffee, slouched in their chairs, and had headshots clumsily spread across their table. Unfortunately, their attitude rubbed off on me.

Once the audition started, and I was directed to sing the same part of Maureen…I sang. I did the basics. I don't think it was the same performance or showmanship I presented in New York, but I performed.

RENT never contacted me again.

I was proud of the experience and the opportunity. Also, thankful to have top-level representation with Lewis. Yet, I was growing tired of the hustle, the grind of the business. Fame and success was elusive. Maybe it was best to give up, throw in the cards. Possibly, my mom was wrong all those years back when I was a kid: *Someday you'll be famous like Elton John, Laurie*! What the hell was she thinking?

I was on the verge of turning 30. I began to value the rewards that came with my day job: a decent place to live, functional car, dinners out, nicer clothes, and predictability. Predictability looked good to me. And so did the handsome man named Neil in the news department at my TV station job.

35

DOMESTICATION

I first caught a glance of Neil in the elevator, when the door closed behind me as I entered. It was just the two of us facing each other. His hazel eyes met mine. He smiled but quickly turned to face the door. I smiled in return but was sure he didn't notice. Frozen, staring at him, I was nervous in his presence. Feeling a girly tickle in my tummy, I wished he'd seen me smile. I turned to face the door, too. He side-glanced me.

He was tall and markedly handsome, with a chiseled chin and mid-length sideburns. I liked how his light-brown wavy hair touched the collar of his button up work shirt. It clung tightly to broad shoulders but fell loose against his lean waist in belted jeans. I spotted a sexy beaded choker just under his collar.

I wish I had something to say, but it felt awkward. He tapped his foot on the elevator carpet in brown Doc Martens. When we reached his floor, he turned to say something just as the door closed. I reached for the open button, eager to hear him, but was too late. The opportunity was gone.

Our chance encounters occurred more frequently. He often walked past my tiny windowless office that felt like a storage closet, and he'd lean against the door frame as if to say something; then he'd say *never mind* and walk off. Anxiously, I was left twirling my hair.

As the weeks passed to a couple of months, our conversations at work grew from hellos to how are you? But that was it. I casually dated others but always wondered about Neil. Eventually, we had discussions about music, TV, art, and Austin, but none of them led to his asking me out. I assumed he was nervous. I told him about my music, and he asked if he could listen to the *Selfish* CD.

With caution, figuring it wasn't his style of music, I gave him a copy. A week later in passing, he said he liked it. Yet, still no date. So, I invited him to a work event at a local bar. It would be an easy out for him if he needed it, but before I finished the question, he answered, "Yes, absolutely." He smiled warmly, and my tummy tickled again.

A few days later, I was thrilled when we met up at the work event. Our conversation flowed with more ease after we kicked back a beer. We lasted twenty minutes, bored by our co-workers, then bailed to a rock bar to watch live music.

Our tastes in music were as vastly different as our upbringings. He came from a large religious family; his parents were still married. Differences aside, we sealed the first kiss in the rock bar parking lot. I was love-struck.

We spent every day together after work grabbing beers, or hiking, and listening to live music. He was creative, moral, respectable, stable, and I quivered every time he looked at me. I was falling in love with Neil. Within months of dating he asked me to be his girlfriend during a weekend of hiking at Enchanted Rock.

We told our parents. Both sides were accepting and happy, especially my dad. He remarked, "Neil is an educated, church going gentleman with a good job. Well done, Laurie. I'm proud." I wish he'd felt that way about my music, but I was happy he was satisfied.

Mom, on the other hand, had questions: Will you continue with music? Do you really need a boyfriend? Well, maybe it's time you settle down. Are you going to get married? Are you sure you want to give up chasing your dream? I ignored her confusing jabber. However, she insisted on flying to Austin to meet Neil in person.

I had to tell Neil about her illness before she arrived. It seemed a silly thought, but I knew judgment and stigma went along with mental illness.

I'd already met Neil's parents over a hospitable dinner at their quiet middle-class home. They were soft-spoken, polite and each greeted me with a gentle hug like the one you would give a neighbor. Neil's mom was pretty with elegant facial features. She carried herself with poise, that of a delicate beauty queen. A small gold cross pendant fell just above the top button of her long-sleeve pink blouse loosely tucked in a long jean skirt. Neil's father was handsome, modestly attired in a dress shirt with no button left open. When I looked at Neil and his father together, it was like seeing twins born decades apart. Except the younger one was less rigid.

Neil warned me to not cuss around them: *they fly by a stricter moral standard than most.* I removed my nose piercing in anticipation. When I met them, their sincere hospitality of baked cookies and tea upon meeting, made me comfortable and yet uncomfortable. I didn't want to disappoint them. I spoke only of the studio album, not the metal band, when they asked what type of music I played. It felt odd faking a part of me, but they appeared too modest to understand my prior night life. Yet, their normalcy made me desire Neil that much more. With Neil came reliability, something I'd never known. While I was on my best behavior when I met them, I wondered if my mother would be on hers?

A month later, Mom flew to Texas to assess my new relationship and meet Neil's parents. Neil and my mom got along fine upon their first meeting. Mom was nervous and needed to smoke a lot, which meant she spent most of her initial time sitting outside. Neil was not a big conversation guy, and she dominated their talks anyway and kept him on his toes with funny jokes. When I asked Neil what he thought of her, he replied, "Laurie, she's a lovely woman. Goodhearted and with a great sense of humor. You remind me of her."

"What!" I screamed.

"In a good way. Laurie, she's your mom. You can't get around that. She's jittery, sure, but, don't worry about it."

When we arrived at Neil's parents' home for dinner, they welcomed my mom with a hug and said, "Our home is yours." Conversation flowed cordially, but I wondered if they noticed the way my mom rambled on in nonsensical chatter, fidgeted or sometimes didn't make eye contact. Politely, my mom held off going outside to smoke, although, she often looked at the clock on the wall and reached into her purse to touch her cigarettes.

During dinner, Mom was as polite as I'd seen her during previous semi-formal social gatherings. She was brought up with strict manners, but I was more concerned with her vulgar tongue and propensity for raunchy jokes. I was impressed she remained proper thus far. That was, until the table conversation took on a more casual tone over dessert and coffee. My mom must have assumed that after a few hours around these generous people she was on safe ground to let her guard down. Without smoking, I could only imagine she was internally fretful, so she went for a joke. She courteously asked if she could. I held my breath.

"Of course, Mary. We love funny jokes," Neil's mom said. "Oh, good. This is about a priest, a monk, and a Jew," she said. Off she went, telling a bawdy joke to a Norman Rockwell family. I never took my eyes off her. No one did. The laughs were thin, and Neil's parents acted unmoved, assuming their best manners. They quickly cleared the plates as she departed the house for her smoke. I joined her outside on the sidewalk near the street.

"Mom, why did you have to tell *that* joke?" "Did I embarrass you, honey?"

"Yes! But, well, no. It was a funny joke, but because of his parents, it just felt wrong. Mom, I don't want to mess anything up."

"Sweetie, if me telling a joke over dinner ruins something with Neil, then he's not for you. Neil is wonderful, and they're lovely people, but a bit square. I just had to spice it up a bit."

"But in *their* home?"

"Yes, honey. I always say, leave people with something they'll remember you by."

My mom was right. Her joke wasn't about to ruin anything.

But now his family knew: She's a wildcard.

My typical way in the past had been to rush into things with guys, but Neil and I didn't move in together for a year, and my dad approved when we did. Dad must've finally given up on his idea of how things should be.

Our house in North Austin, a small mid-century traditional, was all Neil and I needed. Neil and I'd frequently entertain friends and I felt like a grown-up when we rented and eventually bought the house. Neil and I spent many hours together gardening, decorating, domesticating, and bonding. Even my mom became more accepting of our relationship although I had a sneaky feeling she wasn't always honest about her opinion, her desire for my fame I assumed was still on her mind. Her stock reply became: "If you're happy."

Our domestic life was good. I enjoyed my day job, although by no means was it a dream job. Maybe my dream job of being a rock star at thirty-two was unrealistic? The emergence of Lilith Fair on the national scene, of young women songwriter/musicians like Fiona Apple, made me feel old. I was ten years older and thought I had missed the boat. My gut told me to still try, but I received more requests to sing *Ave Maria* at weddings than to perform at live music venues. I spent so long trying to be relevant as a professional musician, a rising star, and now I felt irrelevant.

To me, pursuing a music career was always black or white. You live it fully, or you leave it. I discovered that being in a romantic relationship wasn't part of living it. Now, could I be a part-time musician? To live it without the hustle, the grind, *and* be in a relationship? Others had done it, but they were few compared to all those who'd broken up over music. Mostly, when I ran into musician peers still going at it, I was embarrassed to admit I wasn't playing live, but I also noticed most were divorced, childless, and broke. I convinced myself I wasn't giving up music, just puttin' it on the back burner, to chase a new dream of domestic bliss that seemed a better bet.

One morning before work, I sat on the backyard step having my coffee. Neil was close by doing the daily plant watering, an attempt to make our parched Texas garden grow. He looked at me and softly smiled. With the water hose in one hand, a coffee cup in the other and asked, "Do you want to get married?"

After two and a half years together, it wasn't a question out of left field. We had talked about it here and there - usually while at

Home Depot, the grocery store or when friends and family asked us what our future plans were. The pressure was mounting at our age of thirty-two. As well, in intimate moments we'd talk of what our desires were for our future.

I admired the unanticipated setting he'd chosen - how the morning sun illuminated his handsome face, while he squinted at me while awaiting an answer. He put his tin coffee cup and the hose down, water still running, and got down on one knee. He presented a gold ring out of his pajama pocket. I didn't get up from the step but stayed at his level. Smiling, I said, "Yes, absolutely."

I was excited to plan a wedding. Fleeting concerns of becoming *too* domesticated appeared now and then as I was increasingly interested in reading bridal magazines. However, Neil was the first guy to provide a future and I was enchanted by building a life with him. Neil was offered his dream job in Los Angeles, so I didn't hesitate to accept marriage *and* the move when he asked. As well, once settled into marriage, I figured Los Angeles was a city with an endless supply of opportunities for my stalled music career. I'd start over. But a wedding came first.

Attended only by our immediate family and close friends at a small, idyllic church, lit only by candlelight, in rural New Braunfels, Texas, we wed. The church aisles were decorated with wild flowers picked by our family from the adjoining fields. The weather was still warm in October, but the night was breezy. I wore a cream-colored, sleeveless *Jessica McClintock* long sheath dress, with a short lace train I decorated with rhinestones and beads. I chose a shoulder length poufy veil that allowed my waist-long auburn hair in tight curls to flow beyond it. I was excited, thrilled and very happy the day had come.

Before beginning the pageantry inside the church, my dad and I had our last private moment. He gave me a nervous smile and jokingly asked the stock question, "Do you want to make a run for it?"

The I-35 freeway buzzed in the far-off distance but there was no temptation. I kissed his dewy cheek and giggled. "Let's do this," I said. As I wove my arm through his, I clasped his black tuxedo arm. He patted my hand. We lingered a second. Eager to enter the church, yet I was in no rush to leave the calm of this delicate private moment, the last bit of dusk, or the sweetness of the man who was my father. I was a branch to his giant oak. A soft breeze carried the familiar scent of his cologne. I turned and hugged him, caught up in the splendor. He hugged back and whispered, "Laurie, he's waiting."

During the ceremony, my mom teared up a lot and appeared unsteady when she stood, I assumed from her anxiety or pain pills-or both. Dad had told me the day before not to worry about her. He would never leave her side except to walk me down the aisle. And he did just that. He always had his hand on mom's elbow to steady her. At times during the ceremony, I was embarrassed by her predictable sloshy antics, yet considering Mom lost her second husband, Stan, to a heart attack a mere four months earlier, I thought she was holding up well. Well enough with pain pills that is. Although, I was worried about her. Pain pills can't take away all pain. Mom and Stan's relationship had been topsy-turvy after her stroke, and she was stunned by Stan's sudden death. He was a good man, and their relationship did last close to ten years; however, I couldn't let her grief and grogginess overtake my wedding, as I was happy for the first time in a long time. At least, what I thought was happiness.

36

THE CITY OF ANGELS

Leaving Austin was hard, but not as challenging as adapting to Los Angeles. I quickly found out, as I searched for musicians, that L.A. players wanted a paycheck. All the ads I scanned online or in industry trades stated *paying gigs only*. I figured it out: it was expensive as hell to live in L.A. and musicians couldn't afford to play for the love of it.

I didn't regret moving; though I longed for my dad, and I was a little homesick. And I missed my other close friends. I also yearned for the quaintness of Austin. However, this was Los Angeles. All musicians dream about playing here! Anyway, that's what I told myself while scouring music ads, or while driving the countless freeways one had to drive to get anywhere.

One highway particularly interested me: IH-10. Starting in Santa Monica, it went all the way to Florida and passed through San Antonio. Just point the car east, and I'd be back in Texas.

While looking for musicians, I also applied to an entertainment employment agency for administrative work. I was offered a temporary job as a broadcast traffic coordinator for the KNBC sales department on the NBC lot in Burbank. I landed in the building adjacent to *The Tonight Show* set. *What a great gig!* A portion of my job was to hand carry Beta SP tapes of TV commercials between my department and *The Tonight Show.*

There was an electrifying ambiance the first time I entered the NBC Studio building at the corner of Alameda and Olive Avenue. I was wide-eyed. Framed show posters of *Friends, The Tonight Show, Seinfeld, Frazier,* adorned the walls.

The first time I went to *The Tonight Show* set, I felt like I was going to Disney World. I was super excited. This *was* the big time. An experienced co-worker walked me down two internal flights of stairs from our corporate KNBC offices to the bustling soundstage housing *The Tonight Show, Entertainment Tonight* and *Days of Our Lives.* The main hallway of the soundstage connecting each set was at least three-cars wide by four-stories tall. It was abuzz with production staff hustling about, actors, and forklifts moving set designs. There were two entrances to *The Tonight Show* set: one, down a standard hallway and through two ordinary, metal doors. The second, through the two floor-to-ceiling wood set sliding doors that when opened exposed the backside of the actual *The Tonight Show* stage. These doors were opened to load equipment and sets. Not far from these vast wood doors was a loading dock where *The Tonight Show* guests and bands would enter from the main entrance of the NBC lot.

My co-worker guided me down the standard hallway, through the ordinary doors to another hall where a box sat on a table to drop off the tapes or pick them up. Simple enough. The set security guard was welcoming to me with a handshake and smile when my co-worker introduced me as the "tape person." A matter of fact, everyone was friendly. In the oddest way, it reminded me of Waterloo: a tight little community where everyone knew each other and said hello.

After a few months on the job, I was star struck the first-time Jay Leno walked past me in the main hall. He casually mumbled hello as he walked by very fast. I barely had time to blurt a response. The massive stack of tapes in my hands were the only thing keeping my jaw from hitting the floor.

One day I was departing the studio commissary, a separate building on the NBC lot, to find a seat outside to eat. The wind caught my paper napkins, and they blew off my tray onto the ground. As I awkwardly bent down in my corporate high-heels, trying to balance my tray, a familiar voice said, "You might need these." I stood up to Dick Clark holding my napkins. He handed them to me, smiled warmly, and said, "There you go."

"Thank you!" I said, smiling, sweating bullets at the sight of him. In a flash, he was off. As soon as I sat down at an outdoor patio table, weak in the knees, I called Mom. She answered on one ring.

"Mable's Whorehouse. Mable speaking." She caught me off guard, as usual.

"Oh my God! That is funny!" I shrieked. She laughed. I continued the joke.

"Madam, is Mary Ann in?"

"Let me check," she said and then screamed out loud, "Mary Ann?! Are you available?" I continued laughing, and then Mom came back to the phone in a calm tone with a childlike giggle in her voice.

"Hello, this is Mary Ann. How can I help you?"

Mom's sense of humor was always forefront. Her one-liner dad jokes and pranks were a hoot. After we both stop giggling, I told her all about Dick Clark.

"Dick Clark picked up your napkins?" she screamed. "Dick Clark?"

"Yes! Mom, think of all the musicians he's met!" I tried to remain unnoticeable to fellow employees and brought my voice down and then sulked. "Mom, I always wanted to meet Dick Clark. All the way back to Rockin' New Year's Eve 1982 with The Go-Go's."

"The Who-Who's? What?"

"Oh, never mind, Mom. I just thought I'd meet him as a singer--not like this."

"Oh, Laurie. You were destined to meet him one way or another. Wow, Dick Clark! Dick Clark! I can't wait to tell the neighbors!" She screamed his name over and over, panting heavily.

"Gotta go, Mom." I hung up and pushed my lunch away, my hunger gone. I pondered the situation. Instead of Dick Clark sitting in his American Bandstand audience, picking up my album, showing it to the camera stating, "Ladies and Gentlemen, this is Laurie Markvart," - he picked up my napkins.

So, it began--my mother's daily calls inquiring on celebrities or *The Tonight Show* guest list. She'd always shriek on cue, "Who'd you see? Wow!"

"Mom, you know you can look at TV Guide for *Tonight Show* guests. You don't have to call me every day," I said, playing with her.

"Oh honey, it's much more fun hearing it from you."

I'd indulge her. It was fun to tell her the exciting details. I knew my calls raised her mood; she was still mourning Stan. But one day she got me, "You know kiddo, watching *The Tonight Show* is like watching you. Every night I tune in, even though I know it's not live. Watching the show, knowing you're nearby when it was taped, well, I feel like I'm closer to you."

The perks of celebrity sightings and daily octane fused calls to my mom were an easy distraction from my pursuit of music, but not entirely. I did find some high-quality players through music ads. These musicians were in the same boat as me--they wanted to write, jam, play live, without the hustle of the business—but they were few and far between. Plus, my day job sometimes lasted twelve hours. Every Friday, bleary-eyed at midnight, I'd arrive home to our rented townhome in Sherman Oaks, shattered.

Neil was in a similar state. He was working long hours at his new job, too. We were both adjusting to a big city. Our town-home was on a busy street, Fulton Avenue, and our unit at the front faced the 7-Eleven across the way. We hung thick drapes in a failed attempt to soften the loud patron conversations, traffic noise and frequent sirens.

Some Saturday nights, after a long day of recuperative sleep, the most energy we'd muster was for a stroll a few blocks south to Casa Vega on Ventura Boulevard. We'd fill our bellies with hearty Mexican food and margaritas and stumble home to bed. I was learning an industry fact: in Hollywood, if you only work eight hours a day, that's considered a part-time job.

The NBC perks made up for the long hours. For a while. *The Tonight Show* would open the set and allow NBC employees to watch that night's guest band rehearse. I'd burst from my desk every day at 1:20 pm on the dot, and hustle down to the set. I'd sit with a few dozen employees in the vacant audience seats and watch the guest band rehearse, promptly at 1:30 pm. I'd giggle like a kid and tap my feet watching private concerts of Depeche Mode, Goo Goo Dolls, No Doubt and artists like Dave Navarro and Mary J. Blige.

For most bands, even though it was a one-song rehearsal, they'd still perform to us--especially Mary J. Blige. She rehearsed in a white bathrobe with her hair wrapped up in a white towel but she "performed." Moreover, she kept going into another song just for us. She got so animated, her towel fell off her head, but she kept singing. I was in awe of her enthusiasm.

Some bands requested a closed set. U2 was one of them, but I could still watch them on the video feed in the control room. U2 started a song, then stopped because their timing was off. I was tickled: even the pros screw up.

After every rehearsal, it was hard to return to my bland, tan colored cubicle. As I looked over the broadcast logs, I fantasized

I'd someday play *The Tonight Show*, too. But how? I wasn't getting there sitting in this box. I'm 33. What hope is there for me to break into the L.A. music scene now?

37

TO HONOR

Early in April 2001, Mom called and told me Aunt Nan in New York had passed. Tears welled up, and frustration loomed. I'd been out of contact with Aunt Nan over the past year. I knew she had been fighting throat cancer and had spent the last few months at an actors nursing facility in New Jersey. I wished I had called her more. Mom reassured me that she had talked to Nan often and Nan understood how busy I was.

"Oh, Laurie, she loved you and your dreamer spirit so much. In our final conversation, she asked if you would sing at her memorial," Mom said. I could barely answer, saddened by the loss and tortured by the idea of singing. I'd sung at many weddings and one funeral--but never at an event for someone with whom I was so close.

"Mom, I'm not sure I can do that."

"Honey, I'll be with you. It will be our second chance to go to New York together and a wonderful way to honor her." Easy for Mom to say. She won't have to sing.

"But, can you travel unassisted, Mom?"

She assured me that she'd use wheelchairs at the airport and she'd be fine. We'd meet at LaGuardia Airport.

Two weeks later, Mom and I joined my agent Lewis and a dozen other family members and theater industry folks at a small, modest Christian church on the Upper West Side of Manhattan for a mid-afternoon memorial. Jetlagged, nervous, mournful, and inexperienced with the song Aunt Nan had chosen, I asked Lewis if I could pass on singing.

"Kid, you *must* sing. This isn't about performing. It's about honoring." His eyes were puffy, and he radiated the aroma of liquor as he hugged me. He and many others had already united around the plastic punch bowl in a reception room that smelled of vodka, potluck casseroles, and dessert cakes.

Mom dipped into the bowl too, a modest serving, risking her semi-sobriety. She had stopped drinking after her stroke and would only indulge in a glass of champagne at a special event, like my wedding. I was nervous she was drinking, but in my grief and bewilderment, I joined her in the cozy, humid room. This was the way Aunt Nan would have preferred it: we're all a bit snockered. Half an hour later, unsteady, I sang a song in her remembrance. I swore Aunt Nan stood right next to me while I sang. Goosebumps tickled my skin. The small group applauded my effort. Some approached me afterwards, offering a hug.

Mom and I stayed a few days in New York. Our equal exhaustion from the memorial, travel and her lack of mobility kept us holed up in our Midtown hotel. I hadn't seen her since the wedding, and although she was medicating with the Vicodin and slurring her words, it was nice to hang out with her alone, catching up. But a few times, I would venture out solo and stroll the streets and wonder how different my life would have been if I had got the *RENT* audition or moved to New York City when I was seventeen like I wanted.

I was hesitant putting my drowsy, dry-mouthed mom on her flight back to Wisconsin. I knew she was abusing pain pills, as it was her way to deal with the trip anxiety. She claimed she needed them for neuropathy from the stroke, but I didn't fall for it. I just asked her to be careful and don't take so much.

"Oh, Laurie. You worry too much. I'll be fine."

We departed on separate flights out of LaGuardia. When my plane's tires left the tarmac, I knew I had left a part of my heart in New York with memories of Aunt Nan and my unfulfilled dreams.

38

PURPLE VELVET

There was nothing extraordinary about the Thursday morning in early May 2001 when I arrived at KNBC for work. Except for when I read Prince/NPG on *The Tonight Show* guest list. I set down my coffee and bolted to *The Tonight Show* loading dock. It was only 9:30 am, but maybe Prince was already on set. However, it was quiet.

I went back to my desk and couldn't finish my coffee, butterflies in my tummy. I stared at my computer screen as if I understood the broadcast schedule data, but it was garbled to my dazed eyes.

I was mesmerized by the idea of meeting Prince in person, except for the fact that I was dressed corporate and bland: black slacks, beige button-up blouse, black high-heels but nothing sassy about them. If I had known he would be a guest, I would have dressed a tad splashier and sexier. But why would Prince even notice me? Did I think that if I told him I had lived in Minneapolis and I'm a musician, maybe he'd give a shit? Wait,

I'm not really a musician anymore. Or am I? Can I give it up and take it up again?

I called Mom and announced Prince would soon be in the building. She wailed and screamed and demanded every detail once I got it.

A little before 1 pm, I went to the set early, hoping to catch Prince walking in. I hustled down to the show security guard who usually lets me pass without question. He stopped me.

"Nope, Laurie. Not today. Talent has requested a closed set. No one is going in." I stood motionless. *Dammit, I should have brought Beta tapes with me as an excuse!* Thinking of my options on how to persuade him, he shook his head like he could read my mind. I turned to walk away.

"Fine, I'll just watch on the feed," I stated.

"Hmm, nope. It's gonna be blacked out. You won't see a thing," Terry replied.

"Come on, really?" I blurted out, thinking Terry was fooling with me.

"Really." He nodded, arched his eyebrows and stuck his hands in his pockets and casually leaned against the wall. I wasn't a threat, but he wasn't going to let me go in.

I walked away, defeated. In the main hall, I paused, and leaned against a tall stack of equipment outside the big wood stage doors, plotting another way to get in. Un-expectedly, the loud clanging of drums, keyboards, and guitars, roared from inside *The Tonight Show* set. I was so taken by the sound, recognizing it was Prince, that I didn't realize until I looked down that I was leaning against his music equipment cases. Each black piece had his symbol spray painted on the exterior. Miraculously, one guitar case was open, lying flat, the guitar was gone. It had to be Prince's. If not, it's someone in NPG and close enough! I had to touch it. I felt like a kid eying up a shiny new toy.

I made sure no one was nearby. I walked up to the guitar case, and I gently ran my left-hand fingers along the inside of it, following the shape of the guitar cutout. I was tingling. The case was lined with plush purple velvet--not the fake synthetic shit, the real deal. It felt like soft butter. For a second, I was transported back to Minneapolis in 1986. I'm nineteen-years-old and holding my first acoustic guitar, the one I left in the pawnshop in Minneapolis. I remembered the smell of my guitar, its case. The clamor of Prince's most recent song played inside *The Tonight Show* set and returned me to 2001 and this NBC corridor. And the realization that this was the closest I would get to Prince and my original dream of being a rock star.

My lunch hour was over. I returned to my dreaded work cubicle, prison, on the sales floor where "civilian" people were talking about broadcast avails, rate cards, and programming.

That night, I watched Prince on *The Tonight Show* at home like ordinary people. Reminiscently, I looked at my fingers on my left hand that touched the inside of Prince's guitar case and realized then, my fingertip callouses from no guitar playing were gone.

39

PROCREATE TO VALIDATE

Into the fall of 2001, I continued plodding away at KNBC, enjoying *The Tonight Show* music guests come and go. Neil and I were adjusting to our first year of marriage and getting along well, considering we were both exhausted and only saw each other in passing.

I wasn't sure what my future held musically, but I was inspired by the Prince experience to pick up my acoustic guitar and get my callouses back. I found open mic events in Van Nuys, Hollywood, and Studio City. Usually, they were on weeknights and, if I got out of work on time I'd show up at the coffeehouse or small neighborhood bar, a bit nervous, and sign the check-in sheet and wait to perform. Some open-mics did the "first come, first to play" setup but you had to know the host to gain preference to play early. Most open-mics did the "play at random" deal which meant we put our name down on a piece of paper, and the host pulled names from a hat. It felt like a game of Bingo at a VFW hall. Open-mics were a free-for-all. One could be sandwiched between a poetry reader, a monologue actor, or a stand-up comedian. The only upside to sitting in the audience, sipping the one-drink minimum? It was an excellent way to network.

***

Neil turned the TV on in our living room at 6:45 am, in his usual fashion for background noise as we got ready for work, on Tuesday, September 11.

"Laurie, come downstairs now!" he yelled. I joined him, my groggy eyes now wide opened and fixated on the TV. We stood frozen, still in our pajamas, holding each other, and watched the South Tower fall at 9:59 am EST--6:59 am our time. We both wondered aloud if we knew anyone in or near the towers. We had multiple friends who moved from Austin to New York for TV jobs, and of course, I wondered if Lewis was okay. I got a call from my boss at KNBC. She said all employees should report to work unless they have immediate family involved on the East Coast. Within five minutes, I was out of the house with no makeup on or coffee poured and driving down eerily quiet streets to Burbank. I called Mom to make sure she was okay, knowing she'd be distraught. She answered, crying. She said she was watching TV with neighbors and she'd be okay. I was relieved she wasn't alone. Trembling, I put on NPR to get updates. I could barely drive. When I arrived at NBC, the atmosphere was dire. Employees were somber, some crying with fear-stricken faces, trying to reach NBC employees and family in New York. No one was seated at his or her desks but instead huddled around the various TV monitors. All normal programming and commercials were halted. We were on extended coverage of the *Today Show.*

For four days, NBC, as well the other TV networks remained on 24-hour news coverage. The only thing I could do for the job was adjust broadcast logs, issue credits to advertisers and make sure airline commercials that previously slated to air would not. The days of a United Airlines TV spot slogan, "Fly the Friendly Skies" were over.

That Friday after the attack, *The Tonight Show* was still off air, like other live entertainment shows. All NBC staff were asked to report to *The Tonight Show* set for an update. Production workers, administrative staff, and everyone else from housekeeping to news anchors, to *Days of Our Lives* actors filled the audience seats. Jay Leno advised the somber staff that he would go back on air on Tuesday, exactly a week after. He was soft-spoken as he announced his plan, standing in front of his stage desk, sometimes leaning on it, hands buried deep in his jean pockets. He said he didn't know how he could be funny now, but his old friend Johnny Carson had told him to "Entertain people. That is what *you* do, and that is what they need." The TV set, usually awash in loud music and a roaring audience, was motionless and mute.

The Tonight Show went back on the air one week after 9/11. We were back in full programming by mid-October and the long and intense work hours returned. I asked the temp service to find me another job, preferably not at a news station. After 9/11, I wanted to be somewhere with reasonable hours. Seeing how life can change in an instant, and the importance of family, I wanted to spend more time with my husband. In January 2002, I left KNBC.

I took temp jobs. Above all, it was nice to be home to meet Neil when he got off work. Stability in our home was welcome. Then my period didn't come.

It was a Sunday in April 2002. I bought three pregnancy tests. Well, one box with three tests included. I assumed the box was for couples like us–we weren't *really* trying but decided to let nature take its course. Both of us 34, two years into our marriage, having a baby was the obvious next step: Move forward, create life. Especially after 9/11.

I never wanted a big family. Maybe one or two kids and I thought if I can't create a remarkable music career, perhaps I could create a remarkable baby?

Neil's hands slightly shook when he took the pregnancy test box from me to inspect it.

"Why three tests?"

"Babe, I don't know. Maybe if we don't get the answer we want, I pee again? Or, you know, if one is broke, you use another one? Like, maybe they're different?" I was babbling. He raised an eyebrow.

"I'm pretty sure one is all that's needed," he said. He patted me on the shoulder like a dude pats another dude after a sporting event. He let out a deep sigh as he fumbled with the box before he passed it to my quivering hands.

"I'll let you know when I'm done." I turned to jaunt up the stairs to our bathroom.

"Okay, well, I'm gonna run over to 7-Eleven for more coffee."

"We don't need more coffee," I reassured him while I turned back and shrugged.

"I do," he said, nodding, not blinking.

It took forever for him to get his shoes on, glancing up at me every other second. I took a seat on the carpeted stairs, figuring I'd wait for him to leave. He moved like an old man, grunting when he bent over. Apparently, nervous too. He hovered at the door. I realized then; this pee stick changed his future too.

"It's all good no matter what, Neil. Okay?" He nodded, looked up at me and departed. I bounded up the stairs, touching every other step. With ferocity, I tore open the box and pulled one stick out of its plastic packaging. Placing the "everything in your world is about to change" stick gently on the counter, I yanked down my PJ bottoms and plopped down on the toilet. I put the stick below me, ready for the answers to my future. Drip. Drip? Oh, shit. I haven't drunk enough water this morning to pee. I read the box instructions again: steady stream required. *Oh, pee, Laurie. Pee.* With the might of what I would've thought a Sumo wrestler would use for a squat, I pushed out as much pee as I could from my morning coffee. I covered the stick with a trickle, not a stream, yet the pee was moving across the result window. It was enough.

Elated, I set the stick on the counter, flushed and pulled up my bottoms. The box said to wait for two minutes. I hesitated at the sink while washing my hands, looking away from the stick. As I dried my hands with a nearby towel, I counted out loud: 45, 46, 47... Leaving the bathroom, I hesitated at the door jamb and closed my eyes. ...48, 49, 50. Screw it. I hastily turned and looked at the result.

I whipped the sliding glass door open at the front of our building that faced the 7-Eleven across the street. Neil stood on the yellow curb to return, coffee in hand, waiting for traffic to pass. I leaned out onto the tiny balcony, and I screamed over a passing car, "We're pregnant!"

Neil's jaw dropped. He stood frozen, gaping at me. If I could read a million things going through his mind that didn't appear on his face, I would. I knew they were the same things running beautifully through my mind. A man who is usually reserved and quiet, smiled so huge it was like a boy who won the biggest stuffed animal as a carnival prize.

My mom once said I wasn't the domesticated type, but I fell in love with the idea of this baby. She did too. She called daily for updates, and with each report I gave her, she cried in excitement, or moaned in worry. She cried about everything. My brother had already provided her with three grandchildren, so I couldn't understand the fuss, but she'd say over and over, "Oh honey, now you'll really know what love is." I wondered who was the pregnant one.

Morning sickness--which only meant severe queasiness when spaghetti, beer, olives or mustard were near me--passed after the twelve-week mark. A diagnosis of gestational diabetes was a bummer at 27 weeks. From that point on until birth, I had to monitor my eating and couldn't indulge in pregnancy cravings of blueberry muffins and fried chicken. Insulin was not required, but I had to exercise daily to keep down my blood sugar levels. The doctor and pre-natal specialists were militant: "Your baby can't get too big or you'll have complications at birth." *What's wrong with a big baby?* I would think. I was only five pounds when I was born. My mother admitted she smoked during the pregnancy so the bigger, the better, right? What did I know?

The journey into motherhood was exciting. I was so preoccupied with baby that any thought of my music career was minimal. Although, it did cross my mind in inadvertent spurts. I felt a loss when a catchy song on the radio played, or news broke of a musician friend in Austin landing a big tour. However, I was reading *What to Expect When You Are Expecting* instead of *Rolling Stone*.

I stopped working a temporary job while Neil and I searched for a house with a yard--somewhere we could create a home without 7-Eleven as our neighbor. After intense searching in a seller's market, we found a quaint two-bedroom, one bath 1940s home in an idyllic family neighborhood in Pasadena. The house was small; the price was large. It took all of Neil's salary to afford it, but we managed.

We were spellbound moving in and creating a new life for us. For the first time in my life, with a baby inside me, I didn't feel alone. Even in my marriage, I'd had moments, if not large gaping holes, of loneliness. I knew it had been an issue with me since childhood—isolation—and Neil did work a lot, but we needed the money. He was providing. And he was doing what he loved! And previously, when I felt lonely in my marriage or life, I filled it with music. This time, it was filled with a baby. I was in the constant company of another human, a gift, a beautiful spirit growing inside me.

I was intrigued by the changes in my body, albeit some annoying like extra farts, skin tags, and swollen legs. However, I was delighted when a routine ultrasound confirmed we'd have a boy. Now I knew who was kicking my insides: a little dude. I was in love with the idea of a boy. I "got" the male human. I'd been around enough of them in bands, relationships, my husband, my brother and my ever-present strong male figure in my life, my dad.

Once settled into our home and preparing for my belly kicker, I did wonder what would happen to my music career after the baby. I loved planning for his arrival, yet the pull to play music became ever-present. I blamed it on hormones or boredom. Alternatively, maybe, my rock star lingered within. Around six months pregnant, I casually jammed with some musicians I met via online ads, and I tried to maintain the music. I enjoyed jamming my originals in a rehearsal room or playing covers for fun. Until I couldn't. At seven months, per the doctor's insistence, attaching a guitar to an ever-growing belly or standing for hours was not wise. Besides, it was harder to reach the microphone.

Since I couldn't play, I reached out to some local radio promoters I found online to share my *Intro* CD. It was still fresh, only a few years old. After a round of emails, one was very enthusiastic on the phone after listening. He thought he could get the local NPR station KCRW, a station hot on breaking new artists, to give me radio time. Then I told him I was seven months pregnant, and I couldn't do any live shows to support the songs.

"Well, no one wants to see a lady with a big belly up on stage. Call me when you're *not* pregnant," he said.

"Hell no," I replied, slamming down the phone. I shelved the new songs and prepared for becoming a mom. *Of course, I'll get back to it soon*, I thought.

In November 2002, the doctor induced me a week early. She said, "The baby has possibly gotten too big for a natural birth, but we'll try." After fourteen hours of labor, including two hours of pushing what felt like a watermelon out of a water hose, in a birthing room that resembled a pastel-painted living room more than a hospital room, the doctor insisted she'd have to do an emergency C-section.

"His head is too big and so are those shoulders. You've got him as far as he can go but he can't go further. We need to get him out."

Well, I'll be damned. I guess too big is not the best thing. The surgery room was intrusively bright to my weary eyes.

They placed me on a hard surgery bed that felt no wider than a small plank of wood. My arms were stretched out to each side of me, placed on a stretcher type apparatus and needles inserted in veins I didn't know existed. Neil sat near my head and stroked my hair. My whole body shook like I was having mild seizures. I was terrified that something might happen to the baby. The anesthesiologist reassured me that everything was normal. The medical machine beeping sounds and the voices of the doctors and nurses became louder and louder as I faded in and out of consciousness.

I overheard as the doctor gave updates to Neil. "We almost have him. We're close."

"Laurie, you're going to feel a lot of pressure from me on your abdomen. This is normal."

I thought I verbally stated, "Okay," but didn't hear myself. "Can we get some music, please?" the doctor said with urgency to her staff.

Music? Yes, music I thought. Beautiful.

The beeps and blips of surgery room equipment faded as the song *Everybody Wants to Rule the World* from Tears for Fears became louder.

When Nicholas was pulled out, his screams joined the lyrics of possibly the most excellent birth song ever. The boy was finally free! And it was one of the best moments of my life. Frustratingly though, I couldn't hold him. I was exhausted, groggy, and my arms strapped down. I knew Nicholas wasn't alone. I heard Neil with the baby, gently and lovingly telling him everything would be okay as Nicholas's cries faded just as a Beatles song came on. I couldn't make out the song, I was so drowsy, but I knew it was The Beatles and I was happy music was a part of this journey for

Nicholas. The music was interrupted by a nurse proclaiming, "Look at the dimples on this baby."

He has dimples? I faded away in joy.

I was tired but awake six hours later, lying in a bed in a small private maternity room with Neil at my side. A beaming nurse placed Nicholas in my arms. "Here's your big boy," she cooed. Instantly, I bonded. Like I never knew a human could. I felt like a silk ribbon connected us. From my head to my toes, I changed in an instant. I would never feel the same about another human. I guess this is why my mom was so devoted when she could be. And now I was devoted and mind-blown, knowing those dimples, and the cry that bellowed from his tiny, quivering mouth would be the beginning of a new life for me.

40

UNPREDICTABILITY

No sleep. No energy. No doubt I hadn't prepared mentally for how demanding and unpredictable a baby could be. I discovered being a new mom required insane amounts of endurance, quick thinking, and the ability to shift gears in any direction. Above all, it required the acceptance that anything predictable went out the front door the minute the baby arrived.

I also hadn't prepared for the deep connection I would have with Nicholas. The smell of him, even when he's covered in poop, piss and spit up, was addictive and full of splendor. But with this connection came a reawakened anxiety. I constantly worried if he was okay or if I was doing the right things. Even though Neil was a hands-on dad, involved with everything from feeding to diapering to rocking, I couldn't grasp the minimal amount of sleep that came my way. Instead, I was wide awake with worry.

Six weeks post birth, I knew something wasn't right. I recognized the depression. It came on just as it had in Austin: abrupt, like a dark Texas thunderstorm. This time it was worse.

My body ached from the surgery, my breasts were tender, and they were needed round the clock for pumping since Nicholas wouldn't take to my breast naturally for milk. My body was foreign to me. I didn't recognize the big boobs or saggy tummy. I didn't recognize Neil. My husband looked the same, but he was different with his cooing and attentiveness to the baby. We were both different. He was trying to find his way to be a new dad. We bonded over this new bold adventure with some laughs, shared concerns, and joys, so I thought we probably just needed to get to know the new person we'd both become as a parent. However, I was still bewildered with endless thoughts of my baby dying or me dying.

Through tears, at my six-week check-up, I told my doctor my issues. She diagnosed post-partum depression, and I grudgingly agreed to take the anti-depressant Zoloft, even though any drug reminded me of my Ecstasy days or my mother's illness. She also prescribed Xanax. This time, I welcomed the effect of the antianxiety into my life like a bear clutching a salmon. She also told me to get out of the house more, get a therapist, and sleep was a priority. I wanted nothing more than to be present, happy, energized. I wanted the sky to be blue again. And I knew I wanted music back in my life. But when the baby bump was gone, instead of a guitar, I threw on a Bjorn baby carrier. The guitar was unfamiliar to me, a relic from my history.

Mom visited for two weeks and helped as much as she could. Because of the stroke and her muscle weakness, she couldn't hold the baby or do housework. Her presence was loving, and it was complicated. She was confused and anxious in unfamiliar surroundings. But she gave me a reprieve and even a few laughs.

One morning over coffee, I was double breast pumping with a table-top machine that looked like a small generator. It made a loud swooshing sound with each suck. I hated pumping. Sometimes it hurt, and it was inconvenient. I wished there had been a breast pump for sleeping mothers. It pumped while you slept. *Bingo!*

I drifted off, head on hand, arm resting on the dining table until my mom reeled me back in. "Laurie, did you ever think you'd be sitting here like this getting your breasts pumped like a cow?" She giggled and softly rubbed my arm.

"Gee, thanks, Mom. No, I didn't, but I do feel like a cow. Mooooooo," I said leaning in to her. She kissed my forehead. "Moooooooooooo," she added, as we both chuckled. "Well, at least you're from Wisconsin, so this is normal," she said.

I was about to add a rejoinder when my eyes teared up. Hormones were acting up again. *Dammit!*

"Well, darling, you haven't got to the hard part yet. Wait till he's a teenager," she said with a wink. "You were a handful, kiddo."

"Really? Maybe I was reacting to you."

Where did that come from? My bluntness ended our conversation, but I didn't regret it.

She stood, touched my shoulder. "I'll be outside having a smoke."

I didn't reply. I let her go to smoke her ten-millionth cigarette that day. She'd always be nervous. She spent most of her time on our front porch smoking, in a daze, watching people pass by. *How can I love and equally loathe her?*

41

DETERMINATION

When Nicholas turned one, a joyful, energized walker and giggler, and the shock of being a mother transitioned into my reality, my longing to sing got stronger. Music was an innate part of me that being married and having a baby would not stifle. As the post-partum depression lifted, I weaned myself off the antidepressant. However, I kept the Xanax on hand, never knowing the next anxiety trigger. It was like walking through life looking for emotional landmines.

During my pregnancy in 2002, *American Idol* hit the small screen. I tuned in like millions of others. It tickled a fantasy; it might be a way I could re-enter the music world--until I learned contestants must be under 25 to audition. But I also learned of something far more pressing: my father was ill.

Just three years after Dad walked me down the aisle to get married, congestive heart failure was taking him over. Worse still was the stage-four dementia. Speaking to him on the phone, I could tell his memory was declining. I'd state the same answer to his repeated questions, and he'd become agitated. When we moved him from Texas to California so we could take care of him, his decline was apparent. His smile was diminished, and an ever-present crease loomed between his eyebrows. His once strong stride was a shuffle.

While he was at a senior-living home in Pasadena, I assisted him daily with doctor visits, grocery and pharmacy trips. He hated the restrictive accommodations and would resort to old thinking, complaining non-stop: "Only the U.S. military can tell me when to eat and shit. Who are these morons?"

His doctors forced him to give up his driver's license, and he cussed them out at the mention of it. That didn't keep Dad from trying to purchase a car. He secretly called an auto dealer, eighteen miles away, and had them pick him up. I received the call: "Ma'am, I think we have your father here? I don't think he's right. Can you get him?" I'm not sure how Dad convinced them to pick him up, but his exhaustion and dementia gave him away once he got there. When I arrived, he was slumped in the dealer chair like a teenager in the principal's office, a slight grin on his tired face. He slept in the car on the way home.

On rough days, his ability to hold back or filter his confusion could be mildly amusing. He'd stare at a stranger in the mall or a restaurant and say, "What the hell are you looking at?" Sometimes he'd stop dead in his tracks in the supermarket and fart loudly. In my embarrassment, I'd ask him to stop, but he'd say, "At my age, I deserve to fart where I want." I couldn't deny him at 82. Nor could I deny how exhausted I was.

It was on the good days, when his memory was fluid and he was pleasant that I was thankful we had time together. He'd lovingly say as he'd hold my hand, sitting on a community couch at his nursing home, "You know I'm losing my mind, right? I'm sorry, Laurie. I've kept you from your life." He repeated these comments many times.

However, one day he questioned me while confused, "Do you still make that music you do? Your music? If you don't, you should. Why don't you?" The more questions he asked, his frustration built and my lack of opportunity to respond infuriated me, but I didn't have the heart to tell him *he* was the one keeping me from it. "Dad, someday I'll sing again. Don't worry," was my routine response. It didn't seem to faze him as he'd be right back to talk about the shitty nursing home food or how bad the Cubs were playing. Somehow in his demented state, he still understood baseball and part of him knew his daughter was suffering.

Neil picked up the slack one day after my father claimed hygiene wasn't essential. Dad was no longer showering and shaving. His beard was an inch long and crusted here and there with old food crumbs. Neil tenderly placed a hot towel around my dad's face in Dad's nursing home room. "Is this okay?" he gently asked. Surprisingly, my dad nodded agreeably.

Neil took shaving cream and spread it over Dad's cheeks and chin. My dad remained relaxed while Neil applied gentle strokes with the razor. I watched this male bonding ritual with wonder, as those two had never been close. Neil continued, stopping occasionally to rinse the razor before resuming. When he finished, he again took the hot towel and wiped away what was left of the cream. My father smiled at his reflection. He touched his newly shaven face, then surreptitiously reached for Neil's hand. The whole thing was the most profoundly loving gesture I'd ever witnessed.

My brother called to check in from Wisconsin, but Dave was too far away to make a daily impact on Dad's care. My mom called often. She visited twice but appeared more interested in the bright lights of Hollywood and playing tourist. She fussed when I canceled our sightseeing trip to Malibu. I advised her the long drive would keep me away too long from a potty-training toddler and forgetful father. After her departure, I vented to my dad: "I want nothing to do with that woman ever again. She is so demanding and selfish. I want a divorce from her!"

Even in his demented state, he replied, "You can't. It will hurt her more than you know. Forgive her, Laurie. She can't be anyone else than who she is."

On the morning of March 29, 2006, Dad and I spoke softly to each other in the nursing home. It had been three years since we'd moved him from Texas. His body and heart were done. He was lucid and could talk only faintly but enough to ask me to tell his roommate to turn down the TV volume: "I don't want to die listening to fucking *Jeopardy*." I obliged.

"Dad, today the sky is so clear and blue. It's beautiful," I whispered in his ear, sitting on the side of his bed.

"Good," he replied hoarsely. He barely opened his eyes only to look at me or stare at the ceiling. His breathing was weak. His breath smelled sweet. His body was cold. I tucked the thin nursing-home blanket over his skeletal chest and arms.

"Dad, Mom is coming. She'll be here tonight."

"Good, good." He opened his eyes wide and smiled. He appeared to know something I didn't. "Now, you won't be alone." He took a profound, resolute sigh and reached for my hand.

"Oh, Dad." My tired body surrendered gently next to his body, my head cradled between his bony shoulder and head.

"Just don't fight with her," he added.

"Okay, I won't." I paused before I sat up. His face was clenched in discomfort.

"Now, go home." He weakly squeezed my hand. It was an order I intuitively understood. I put my other hand on his hardened chest and kissed his dry, bald head, knowing I would never see him alive again.

I would be strong like the soldier he taught me to be. I rose, grabbed my purse, and walked a few steps to his door. I hesitated, thinking I should remain. I slowly walked out and down the main hall to the exit, dodging eye contact with staff members. I didn't want them to see what I was feeling. The nursing home was eerily quiet, and as I approached the exit, I could hear that fucking *Jeopardy* TV show in the distance. I clutched my purse to my chest, holding back nausea. As soon I left the building I ran as fast as I could to my car. Once behind the wheel, I gripped the stirring wheel not wanting to go. I held back what felt like an avalanche of unfamiliar emotions. I wanted to cry, but he was still alive.

He died four hours later. Alone, just as he wanted. I knew he would pass. But, I had no idea his death would cause random guttural spurts of crying and explosive bouts of primal screaming, or I'd curl into a fetal position on the floor of our car, shaking, as Neil drove us to view my father's body.

Staring at his corpse in disbelief, there was nothing more I could do. I lacked the words to explain to Nicholas that his grandfather wasn't sleeping. Or that I would be immobile at my dad's bedside until Neil said, "Laurie, he's not here anymore."

With my mom in flight, I had no way to tell her until she arrived. I was scared she wouldn't be able to handle it and worried she'd be drugged up; medicated.

I sat with Neil and Nicholas in Terminal 6 at LAX. Neil kept his arm around my shoulder as I chewed my nails and fidgeted with my purse strap. Nicholas climbed up and down on my lap like I was a playground apparatus. At his tender age of three-and-a half, he didn't understand my tears that came and went.

"Momma?" he'd repeat over and over. He'd hold my face and look straight in my eyes. I was despondent but hugged him as tightly as I could.

"Hang in there, Laurie. She'll be here soon. Come on, kiddo, let's take a walk," Neil said to Nicholas. Nicholas jumped off my lap and grabbed Neil's hand. They disappeared into a massive crowd. From the other direction, I clearly heard my name through the loudness of the terminal. There she was, approaching with a steady gait of persistence, a slight shuffle on her left side. And she was sober. Mom's eyes were clear and her face welcoming and loving. She came with a look of knowing.

As she neared, I rose slowly, my body drained. "Mom," I muttered through tears.

"Oh, my love, you lost your father." She opened her arms, and I collapsed into her. My crying was harsh and uncontrollable in the middle of the arrivals section. She held me tighter than when I was a scared toddler or a heartbroken teenager. She rubbed my back and whispered in my ear, "It's okay, honey. It's okay. I'm here now." She was entirely and utterly present for me, as though the sensitive, beautiful and extraordinary woman she was had broken free from illness.

Then she added, "Well, that son-of-a-bitch couldn't wait for me, huh?" I laughed so hard, I couldn't let go of her. She laughed robustly. We became a mess of tears and laughter.

42

CIRCLE OF LIFE

We buried Dad's ashes on top of his mother's grave in Chicago a month later. At the beginning of the military ser-vice, Mom quietly wept. She sobbed louder at the gun salute. However, when they played *Taps*, she was inconsolable. My brother patted one of her hands, and I held the other. I was in tears when the sergeant presented me with the folded American flag. Neil's hands were on my shoulder, and Nicholas hugged my back. My crying softened. I wished Mom would, too.

After the memorial, we went to a Chicago pub. My father requested in his will, with some money he left, for everyone to have a beer on him. It was a small gathering of family, and we shared rousing stories as we cheered his memory. I missed him badly during the stories. Some I'd never heard before. I looked around, hoping he'd walk in the pub on this quiet late afternoon and say his death was a joke. I missed him most when Mom's emotions deteriorated during story time. He had a way of calming her. Sometimes it was a just a pat on the leg and an, "*Oh, Mary, you'll be fine.*" She never stopped needing him in that way. And neither did I. *Was it going to be fine, Dad?*

At the pub, her illness returned just as suddenly as it had left her at LAX. She withdrew from the conversations and complained of hip pain. I saw her pop some pain pills and I knew what was coming. The drugs left her a sloshy, incoherent mess. Always one to take the spotlight, my brother Dave and I tended to her. I promised Dad not to fight her, so I didn't, but I was relieved when she returned to Wisconsin; and we headed back to Los Angeles.

I went to a therapist and continued the Xanax to induce sleep and to stop the invading nightmares of searching through foggy, hazy dreams to find my dad. When awake, his death haunted me. I longed to hear him talk; his firm, resilient words of encouragement telling me everything would be okay. The man I needed to help me deal with his death was gone.

Neil was patient, if concerned, by my long crying bouts in the shower. This was the first major loss either of us experienced, grandparents aside. He took Nicholas out for extended periods of time and yet what I needed was them, to be there and to act as if nothing happened. However, who was I fooling? When they were there, I was vacant. Nicholas and my husband needed me. The stress of my father's demise had caused cracks in our marriage. I couldn't nurture my marriage or motherhood under the heavy burden of grief. I couldn't sleep in the same bed with Neil as I'd retreat to the couch, knowing I'd cry myself to sleep and keep him awake. Alternatively, long pauses emerged in our conversations in which I imagined Neil didn't know what to say and I had nothing else to offer him.

Mom was struggling, too. I dreaded speaking to her. Every time she called, she'd start the conversation asking how I was feeling and end with her weeping and eking out fond memories of her marriage with Dad. I knew she needed to do that, I listened to her, cried with her, but I couldn't handle her grief on top of mine.

In addition to therapy, I tempered the grief with music. I'd try to write songs, but they came achingly slow. Lyrics would not form easily, or almost every time I started to play guitar, sleepiness overcame me. I'd lay back on the couch, guitar on my lap and doze off.

Neil suggested I get back into the workforce. Up until now, I was a stay-at-home mom taking care of Nicholas and my dad. I agreed I needed to get out of the house. We found great daycare at Neil's work and almost simultaneously I found a temporary job as an assistant at Warner Brothers. Typical, I easily found my way back into the corporate world. Within weeks I also found myself, stunningly, pregnant.

It had only been two months since my dad passed, and I wasn't paying attention to my physical health, and I hadn't felt morning sickness. However, I did notice the absence of my period. I secretly bought the pregnancy test. I didn't want to alarm Neil. I was confused. I wasn't sure if I wanted another child right now. If I wasn't aching for my dad, I was aching for music. More than anything, I was depleted. Was I up to handling gestational diabetes again, the hormonal imbalance, and Lord knows what else comes to a woman being pregnant at 39? Reservations and all, I convinced myself if I was pregnant, it was a blessing. Indeed, the pee-stick confirmed it: ++.

My grief lifted when I told Neil the news in the privacy of our bedroom. Quietly and gently, in contrast to how I yelled across the street about my pregnancy with Nicholas, sitting on our bed holding hands, I told Neil I estimated I was three months pregnant. I was cautious in my announcement, maybe still not believing it myself. I must've got pregnant right before Dad passed.

Neil was careful in his response. His face held back a smile, "Are you okay? Are you up for this?"

"Yes, I have no choice!" I said with a nervous chuckle. "Laurie, as long as you're okay."

"Neil, for the first time in years, and after losing Dad, this is a beautiful gift. I got this."

I felt strong in my statement to him, but my gut was still nervous. *Did I have this?*

43

UNDER PRESSURE

Sitting amongst stuffed animals on his bed, Nicholas played as Neil and I told him the news. It was the beginning of my fourth month, and my joy and the size of my growing belly could no longer hide the secret.

"Hey kiddo, you're going to have a baby brother or sister," Neil told him, stroking Nicholas' smooth hair.

"How?" Nicholas said.

"The baby is in my belly," I said. "Just like you were before you came out."

"Did I come out your belly button?" The sweet, genuine expression on Nicholas' face was so precious I pulled him to me. I felt blessed by his innocence and excited that he would be a brother.

"No, sweetie, a different way," I said, giggling, kissing the top of his head. I loved the way he smelled.

"We can discuss that another time, buddy." Neil giggled too and pulled Nicholas to him for a hug. The serenity of Nicholas' subtle green painted bedroom walls and a blue *Thomas the Train* throw carpet over the hardwood floors, sunk in. Within five months, Nicholas would need to share his bedroom with a sibling. I smiled, recalling fond memories of childhood with my brother when our mom was healthy-minded. Dave and I may not have been close, but in times of need, when Mom *was* difficult, we'd sleep together at night, especially when she was at the mental hospital.

Now, when I broke the news, my mom's reaction to my pregnancy was hooting, hollering, and joyous crying.

"Oh, Laurie. Oh, Laurie. How blessed we all are! Your dad would have been so excited. This baby is a gift from God."

"Yes, I'm thankful. I'm also scared and nervous. I'm older now," I said with caution.

"Oh, honey. You'll be fine. God is looking out for you. For all of us."

Neil's parents were excited too. The news of the baby made everyone happy, and for Neil and me, any fractures in our relationship filled with hope and delight. My longing for Dad was replaced with desire and excitement for my future.

As my belly and cravings for donuts and fried chicken grew, with excitement, I impatiently waited until our next doctor visit, in a month, to find out the gender. Now at five months, I could feel slight movements of the miracle inside me.

By day, I was coasting through the temp job at Warner Bros. It brought satisfaction to be around others, and kept my mind busy, but it was just a job. When I found free time at home, I'd play guitar and write music. It came more naturally to me now that I was in a happier place. My musical ambition was far off, replaced again by motherhood, and while I hoped music would come back, my mind was entranced with excitement for the new baby and its health. But thought of my dad lingered.

One night, I had a fevered dream. I entered a darkly lit rock 'n roll bar. Faded band posters peeled off the walls of the typical floor-to-ceiling black room, its floor dirty and dusty. The dream was in black and white. No music, no tables, no sounds, no smells, no people. There was a vacant stage off to the left corner, but it was dark. I was drawn to walk through an open door to my right where a bright light was pouring out. When I entered, it was another bar, decorated just the same but brightly lit, in full color, and new. The stage off to the right was flickering with stage lights, illumining a microphone and stand, absent a performer. To my left, at the end of a black wood bar, Dad sat alone on a barstool, looking no more than 30 years of age, younger than I had ever known him, with a pilsner glass of beer in hand. He had smooth skin, rosy cheeks, and red hair. He smiled a youthful broad grin when he spotted me. He didn't speak or move, but I was drawn to him. I was excited to get to him as fast as possible, but I felt underwater.

My motions, murky and strained. I floated instead of walked. I couldn't talk. As I neared him, unknown energy moved me past him. Dad watched me move towards another open door that appeared to lead into another dark room. As I passed, his smile reduced to the glummest look of sadness. He too appeared unable to move. I was distraught, heartbroken that I couldn't stay with him.

When I awoke that next morning, I was confident the dream was a visitation from my dad. It was not the type of visitation I desired: us sitting by a clear blue stream, surrounded by flowers.

I went to work, convinced I'd shake the oppressive gloom of the dream. After lunch, my stomach was full after eating half a turkey sandwich and chicken noodle soup. I was getting to that stage in pregnancy where if I ate a little, I felt like I ate a lot. Between emails and phone calls, I suddenly had an intense urge to use the bathroom. I couldn't tell if I had to throw up or shit. I made it to the restroom, relieved to be the only one there. Nausea ceased, and nothing came out. I sat on the toilet; perspiration collected along my neck. Something was wrong. I felt pressure in my lower abdomen. Maybe I'm having Braxton Hicks, early contractions. I'd heard of this, but didn't have them with Nicholas.

I stood and stretched my elastic pregnancy pants over my swollen belly, which looked bigger than yesterday. Everything was fine, I told myself. I went back to my desk and spent the next few hours warding off vomiting and abdominal pressure. I was sweating like I just ran a 5k, and a few minutes later I was awash in chills. I called Neil.

"Food poisoning?" he said in response to my guess. "Are you sure? Is everything all right with the baby?"

"I think so. I'm not bleeding or anything, but there's a weird pressure, and it's not contractions."

"Are you sure?"

"No, I'm not sure. But it's too early for that," I said as I wound the phone cord in my fingers.

"Well, call the doctor." Neil's voice cracked.

"I will as soon as I get home. I just need to get home."

As I drove to Pasadena from Burbank, I felt an instinctual need to cover my belly with one hand. When I got home, the nausea came again, and dampness appeared in my underwear. I rushed to the toilet to find small, slimy soiling of clear fluid in my underwear. When I called the doctor, she advised me to go to the ER immediately.

I struggled through the exhaustion, cramping, sweating, and, stress and drove the four miles to Huntington Hospital. My hand again on my belly. I was trembling. *This baby will be okay. This baby will be okay. Hold your horses, Laurie. The hospital will fix this.* Once in the ER, I called Neil and asked him to come. He'd already picked up Nicholas from daycare and they were on their way. The idea of their arrival slowed my shallow breathing. I advised Neil they already moved me to the maternity ward and repeated to him what the ER staff told me, "We do not have the proper equipment in the ER for a prenatal examination, so we're moving you to maternity. It's the best place for you." I knew it was. Nicholas was born there. Everything will be fine. I had a strong desire to phone my mom, but I'd wait.

I sat on an exam table, with stirrups sticking out of the end of the table, in a small white-walled, chilly, examining room, waiting for the on-call obstetrician. I was glad I had brought a light button-up sweater, even though it was August. I fidgeted with the buttonholes, waiting. There were no magazines, no pamphlets. Not even one picture on the wall. Nothing to take my mind off the growing pressure in my abdomen. Except I could count the one by one-inch tan ceramic tiles on the floor. There were 300.

The doctor opened the door and peeked in. I sat up straight upon her arrival. She appeared the same age as me and was polite. When I spoke, she'd gently put her hand on my shoulder and never broke eye contact. She asked if she could examine me. She turned her back as I removed my pants and damp underwear and got into position on the table, inserting my feet into the stirrups, which made my abdomen cramp more.

"So, Laurie you state you're just over twenty-one weeks? Five months?" she asked when she turned around.

"Yes. My husband will be here soon with our son. Could we wait?" I said, my hands clutched together across my chest, holding back my thumping heart.

"I'm sorry, but we should get started. Okay?"

"Yes, okay. Go ahead." I swallowed loudly and wrapped my hands behind my head so that I could see her face. I wanted to see her face.

She turned on her examining headlight and delicately moved the thin hospital gown over my legs. She advised she'd be inserting the speculum and there would be pressure. I'd been down this route many times; I knew where she was going so I didn't respond. I kept a deadlock on her face.

She appeared stern while squinting through her exam glasses. She made no sound or gesture as she stared into me like a baseball pitcher staring down his catcher. She removed the speculum and inserted her fingers, like a typical gynecological exam and she felt my abdomen at the same time with her other hand. I was waiting for some comment to come from her, but she looked off into the distance as she applied pressure, moving her hands around my belly like an artist sculpting clay. A severe pain shot down my lower back into my pelvis. I gulped in discomfort and placed my hands over my warm face. A waterfall of tears built in my eyes. I knew this pain. I've had it only one other time in life. It's a pain a woman never forgets. I shouldn't have waited to call the doctor.

44

BEAT THE ODDS

The doctor removed her hand from my belly and her fingers from inside me in response to my yelp of pain.

"Laurie, I am sorry to tell you that you've dilated to two centimeters and your cervix is partially effaced. The discharge you have is the remains of the cervix mucus plug. You're in the early stages of labor."

My hands still over my warm and teary face, I was silent. *What the fuck was happening?*

I looked at her, between my legs, her hands still in blue examining gloves. Her face soft, gentle, the look of a mother telling her child their puppy had died. Her eyes were fixed on mine, not blinking.

"How? I can't be in labor, right?"

"Sometimes women go into early labor and we can stop it. I need to bring in an ultrasound. I'll be right back, and we'll investigate more, okay?" She moved away from me and removed the light blue examining gloves. The fingertips tinged with blood. My stomach sunk.

"Neil, get here immediately." I left a message on his voicemail. "Right away!" Now that I knew I was in labor I understood every damn physical symptom I had, and it made me sicker. This can't be happening. I'm not even six months pregnant! What did I do wrong? My whole-body trembled. The doctor reappeared with a nurse and an ultrasound machine.

"I need a puke thing. I'm gonna throw-up," I announced between heaves.

The nurse swiftly brought me a pink puke tray and an extra pillow and blanket.

"Here, here." She wiped my perspiring face with a paper towel as I dry heaved. Nothing came up.

"Doctor, did I get here too late? What did I do wrong?" "Laurie, that's not the issue. Your cervix is failing. You had no control over that but let me focus on the baby right now, okay?"

A knock on the door interrupted the doctor. Neil poked in his head. He was familiar enough with the Ultrasound machine that his face turned glum.

"What's happening?" he said.

"Is this the dad?" the doctor turned, greeting Neil with a handshake.

"Yes, yes," Neil replied, as he moved to my side.

"Sorry, it took me longer than I thought. I dropped Nicholas with our neighbor."

"That's fine," I said through tears. "You're here. We have trouble."

The doctor repeated the issues to Neil, who remained motionless as he listened.

"I'm doing an Ultrasound now to check the baby's health, and then I'll know what to do."

She dimmed the lights in the room and rubbed the ultrasound wand on my belly, and steadily looked at the Ultrasound screen. Neil held my hand, and I pulled the blanket closer to my face with my other hand.

"Okay, the baby looks fine. She's moving a lot. See her legs?" she said pointing to the screen.

"Her?" I cried, watching the baby kicking inside me. I *knew* she was a kicker, too.

"Yes, your baby is a girl." She smiled softly and continued the exam. Neil's face became red, and I could tell he was holding back tears.

"She is doing okay, but a portion of the bag of water has dropped through the cervix and into the birth canal. The bag has not broken, but I'm sorry, the bag cannot be exposed to bacteria. This is not looking good, but there is an option."

Now that Neil was here, my urge to vomit receded. I was ready for the game plan. Neil squeezed my hand tightly--his show of nervousness.

"We can stop the cervix from dilating, but we have to get the bag of water back into the uterus. The only way to do this without breaking the bag is to invert you. We'll lay you flat, invert the bed, head down at a 45-degree angle, and hope gravity draws the bag back in. If it does, we'll close the cervix, seal it and you're on bedrest for the remaining term of the pregnancy. This will be the best outcome."

"Are you sure it, the bag, will go back in?" Neil asked, fidgeting with his pant pocket with his free hand.

The doctor turned the lights on and paused before she spoke. "No, I'm not. I must tell you; we're looking at a ten percent chance of success. If the bag hadn't dropped, this would be a different story. I am truly, truly, sorry."

"I shouldn't have waited," I cried.

"Laurie, the bag is intact. If you waited any longer, it would have broken. You did nothing wrong."

"So, we still have a chance?"

"Yes, but I *must* be realistic with you. We only have up to twelve hours for the bag to drop back into the uterus. We must beat infection setting in."

The room was pin-drop silent.

"I'm going to step out and let you two talk, okay?" said the doctor.

"Wait, please, what if it doesn't work?" Neil said. "What happens to the baby? To Laurie?"

"Well, her body will continue the natural delivery of the baby, but we'll most likely need to induce delivery."

I assumed this doctor had dealt with this before. She walked to the side of the exam table. For the first but not the last time, she held my hand. "Laurie, if you need to deliver your baby now, at twenty-one weeks, she will not be viable, to survive. I'll bring in a pediatric specialist to discuss further, okay?" She departed the room with a softly closed door behind her.

Neil collapsed in the small chair next to the bed and buried his head in my shoulder. He didn't cry but sighed deeply over and over. My tears had dried. I was now ready for the challenge. After seeing that little girl, I must fight.

"Neil, we can do this. I can do this."

"I can't believe this, babe. What the happened?" He looked at me with wide eyes.

"My cervix is failing. I shouldn't have waited. What if I caused this, Neil?"

"No, you haven't done anything wrong. You heard her. You can't control your cervix." He grasped my hand and shook his head.

We remained silent, stroking each other's hands. He's right but I had a growing resentment for my body–a deep level of anger at my cervix. How can this same cervix hold in a big baby like Nicholas and now give up on this tiny baby? My tears formed again. My body had failed me--her, all of us. My mind swirled with anxiety and fear at what was to come to save her, or of the potential to lose her.

I had never thought much about gravity, but now it's the only thing keeping this baby inside me. Maybe I could overcome this failing cervix. Maybe I could beat the odds.

45

TRADE YOU

When the doctor returned to the exam room, I informed her I was willing to do the inversion. There was an intensity to her movements, voice and actions as she rallied the nursing staff to move me to a maternity room.

I became a witness, of sorts, to the flurry of activity around me, my body a mere vessel they needed to keep in dry dock. The staff let me stand to use the toilet and change my clothes into a pink hospital gown. Within 30 minutes after that, I was horizontal in a maternity labor room bed, with medical devices beeping, a catheter inserted before saying ouch, an IV with a cocktail of antibiotics, and medicines to prevent further cervical opening. Neil stood by and watched the commotion, not saying a lot while holding back tears.

The doctor readied me for what came next. "Laurie, we're going to invert the bed. It will be uncomfortable at first. You may feel nauseous, get a slight headache and all that is normal. The nurses are on standby for you." She handed me the nurse call button cord.

"You can have ice but nothing else, okay?" She took my hand again. She occasionally glanced at Neil on the other side of the bed.

"Here we go, Laurie." She inverted the bed. My view of the room was slanted, and I was sliding to the floor, but my pillow and the top of bed stopped me.

My mind was encased in disbelief. I was dizzy, disoriented. Tears trickled to my hairline and into my scalp. I was crying upwards. The anger brewing in my mind at the unfairness of this situation turned to invasive thoughts of rage.

They should turn me upside-down like a bat. Yup, hang me upside-down from the ceiling. That will do it! If we're going this far, let's go all the way!

I had a vision of myself hung from the ceiling with a noose around my neck. I was dead. My father's young face appeared. He smiled as if to say, "Nope, not you!"

Dad, I need you! Internally I screamed for him, and externally I fought the urge to scream. *I must calm down!* I'm supposed to be as still as possible. My body couldn't afford puking or stomach cramping or anything that resembled bearing down. It's no easy task to be still in a moment of chaos.

Neil rubbed my arm. "Laurie, you're okay. You're okay." He put a cold washcloth on my head. Its dampness provided some relief.

"Did I fall asleep?"

"A bit. You just jerked awake right now. It's only been twenty minutes since she inverted you. She said it's normal for you to be a bit out of it."

"Neil, I'm scared as hell. I'm so worried this isn't going to work."

He squeezed my hand harder, rubbing my shoulder with his other hand. The room lights were dim. I recognized the pastel room wallpaper and carpeting as the same as when Nicholas was born.

"Neil, is this the same room when we had Nicholas?"

"No. That room is a few doors down. I know, I thought the same at first."

The drapes on the window to the side of me were open, exposing the pitch black of night.

"Speaking of Nicholas, I need to get home to him." "You're leaving?" I panicked, grasping Neil's hand firmer. "I can't leave him with the neighbors all night."

"Neil, I can't be alone. I thought you'd stay the night and get your sister or someone to stay with him."

"Laurie, I have to go. *I* need to be home with him." I let go of Neil's hand, not sure of his reasoning. And yet I understood his need to get to Nicholas. This was all so messed up.

"Okay, I just, uhm, I'm scared." My shoulders shook. *Don't move, Laurie!*

"Laurie, I know. I am too. We'll get through this no matter what, okay?" He grabbed my hand and kissed my 45-degree-tilted forehead.

"When are you coming back?"

"The doctor said the pediatric specialist would be here at 10 am and they'll do another Ultrasound. I'll be here with you for that, okay?" I didn't answer as the time frame sunk in. Twelve hours of this. Twelve hours.

"Okay?" he said again, rubbing my arm. I nod.

"Neil, I need my mom. Before you go, can you call her and tell her what's happening? I'll call her back after that."

"Why do you want me to tell her?" His face resembled someone who just got scared by a ghost.

"I can't. I need her to cry for herself first. When she's calmed down, I'll call her and then she can cry for me."

Neil nodded multiple times, a knowing, as he reached for his phone and left the room, closing the door behind him. She spoke her mind, and he held things in, but they had Nicholas and me in common. They've never been entirely comfortable with each other.

Ten minutes passed, and Neil returned. His face was drawn, pale, eyes red.

"I told her you'd call her when you're ready. Are you okay?" he said as his face softened.

"For now. What about you? And how was she?"

"Well, you know, she's well, your mom." He took a deep sigh and his eyes glazed over as he stared at the floor. For a second, I was sorry for him. Guilty that I had made him call her. Sad, he was going through this, too. But I could only take so much.

300

"Thank you for calling her. I love you," I said, as I reached for his hand. He took it and shook his head and shoulders quickly in a shudder as if spiders were crawling down him. I assumed he was trying to process everything. He leaned down and hugged me again--the best he could at the odd angle.

"I love you, too. I'll see you tomorrow. Hang in there, okay?"

"Well, I'll be a pro at this by the morning." I smirked and waved him off. "Oh, Neil, wait. What are you going to tell Nicholas?"

"Just that you're going to be okay and he shouldn't worry."

"But what about the baby? He'll wonder." At the mention of this, the room felt warmer. The hall light looked brighter as it crept into my darkened room through the half-opened door. Everything was magnified. The odors of rubbing alcohol and gauze-typical hospital smell--stung my nose. Anxiety was approaching.

"Let's just wait 'till tomorrow? He doesn't need to know anything right now except that you're okay."

"You're right. Hug him as strong as ever for me."

"I will. I will."

Before Neil departed, I asked him to leave the room door fully open. He said I wouldn't get sleep if he did; the hallway was too loud. But I didn't want to be alone with the beeps and chirpings of my machines. Then a woman down the hall screamed while giving birth.

"You want it closed?" he said, nodding in the direction of the woman's sounds. He looked a mix of sad, angry, and devastated.

Tears formed, and I nodded yes. He softly closed the door behind him.

The silence was surprisingly welcome. While the room was serene, I yearned for my dad's strength too. I imagined him sitting in that baby blue hospital chair in the corner of the room: the tall one that looks like a comfy La-Z-Boy, where future dads sleep while their woman labors. I envisioned Dad telling me everything would be okay, stay strong, you can do this. The actual sound of his voice escaped me. I wish I had a voicemail from him. How could I forget how he sounded? It's only been five months since he passed. I concentrated harder to imagine his voice, in hopes it would overpower the woman's screams down the hall. My phone rang. Mom.

"Mom. Mom. Mom…" Each time I said it, it trailed off into a grumbled word, then loud tears. Tears that came from an immobile body.

"Laurie, Neil said you'd call me, but I had to call now."

"Mom, I'm not sure what I did wrong but I'm losing her."

She made an audible gulp. She coughed loudly, holding back tears.

"A girl?"

"Yes, Mom."

"Laurie, you did nothing wrong," she said with conviction, as if she was qualified to make the statement. No longer crying, she continued, "Honey, what does your intuition tell you--your mother's intuition about…her?"

A swarm of emotions swirled in my head. My body was rigid, but I had an answer.

"Mom, I feel like I'm losing her. This won't work."

I felt an urge to pee, then it went away. The catheter took care of it, but I was left with a burning sensation that dissolved. A growl in my stomach churned of hunger. Frustration at the whole fucking situation overtook me. I punched the bed as hard as I could with other hand.

"Mom, I won't accept that this is over. Fuck my intuition!"

"Oh, sweetie. I'm sorry. I understand. Calm down. Being so upset will not help."

"Mom, I'm totally fucking upset! And I'm alone in this room all night!"

I was saying things to her I couldn't say to Neil or the doctor or the nurses. Only Mom could understand. She didn't respond with the same heightened tone. Her voice was calm.

"Laurie, just hold your horses. By the grace of God, this will work. If not, you are still a mom to Nicholas, a wife, my daughter, and an artist. You have purpose."

Her crackling smoker breath hummed with rhythm through my phone. I liked it. It was 11 pm my time, 1 am her time. She must be tired.

"Mom, it's late for you. You can go to sleep. I'll call you in the morning."

"Oh, hell, no. I'm staying on this line all night. Even while *you* sleep. Laurie, if there was a way to trade spots with you, to switch, I would. I'd do anything to suffer this instead of you."

Tears slipped up my face. I fell asleep to her comforting words of *The Lord's Prayer* and her telling joyful stories of when I was young. Every couple of hours a nurse would come check on me. I'd stir and answer the nurse's questions. I'd hear my mom's breathing, still on the line.

"I love you, Mom," I'd say and fall back asleep to her similar response. Once I woke and the nurse was talking to Mom on my phone, providing updates. It had to be 4 or 5 am. I fell back asleep.

The sunlight glowed behind the heavily draped window. It woke me. It was 9 am. I was feverish. My stomach ached, and my mind filled with nerves. My phone was still cradled in my hand, near my waist. I brought it to my ear. Mom was snoring. I kept the call going even though my battery would soon die. A new nurse came in. She glanced at the beeping machines and my IV bags.

"Hi, Laurie. You have a challenging day ahead of you. I'm here for you. The doctors will arrive within the hour. Can I get you anything?"

"No, I just want the doctors to get here, that's all."

"Laurie!" Mom screamed from my phone's receiver. Startled, the nurse clasped her hands to her chest.

"Mom, hold on a second," I said, hoarse and croaky into the phone. I placed the phone against my chest.

"Has your mom been on the phone with you all night?" the nurse said, taking my other hand in hers.

"Yes, she's never hung up. I need to charge my phone. Can you help with that?"

"Absolutely. Let me know when you're ready." She paused. "You got one hell of a mom there." She smiled and left. "Mom, I need to let you go now and call Neil. The doctors will arrive soon."

"Oh, dear. Okay, okay. Just remember, I love you, kiddo. And you won't be delivering a baby today. She will be fine. You will too."

"Thanks, Mom. I really appreciate you." My words broke off into grumbled tears and I couldn't speak anymore.

46

THE BEAUTY OF A MOMENT

Neil arrived a few moments before the doctors. It was10 am on the dot. My husband was unshaven, his eyes sunken and his hand felt cold as he grasped my hot hand. I was burning up. Neil told me his family was praying and sending their best. The neighbors were praying, too. He even called his priest and asked for prayers. Surely with all those prayers, the outcome would be to our desires. I internally hummed *Jesus Loves Me*, having the memory of singing it in church when I was a child. The humming quieted my racing mind. As always, music to the rescue.

My previously quiet room was now buzzing and cramped with activity of two nurses, an obstetrician, a neonatologist and a prenatal specialist with an Ultrasound machine. Everyone was situated around my horizontal bed, like a debriefing at a conference room table, looking at the Ultrasound screen, which was just to my right, a foot away from the bed. I had a front row seat.

The prenatal specialist got to work with the scanning machine. He focused his vision, through black plastic glasses, on the screen. He remained quiet. I squinted, and there she was: wiggling around, kicking and very much alive. Neil squeezed my hand.

The doctor continued to move the wand over my belly. The more he did, his face frowned.

"Laurie, Neil, can you see your baby? She looks perfect." He smiled as he looked our way, then turned back to the screen and pointed. "But if you look here, this is your cervix, Laurie. This area here is your bag of water. It's still in the birth canal. Oh, but look at that. Your baby just stretched her arm out, and it has passed through the cervix. Wow." He appeared genuinely fascinated by her movement. I was too, but I needed more answers.

"What does this mean?"

"The bag is intact, but since it's still in the canal and not back in the uterus, I'm sorry. There is nothing more we can do." Everyone was silent.

No anger, no tears came as I watched my baby girl dance about within my belly, continuing to stretch out her arm through my cervix.

Gravity failed.

"Laurie, you'll need to deliver your baby as soon as possible. Infection is inevitable to you," the obstetrician said.

"But what about her?" I begged, pointing at the screen. Neil readjusted himself in his seat and leaned forward onto my bed.

"Laurie, she will not survive," said the neonatologist, Dr. Griffin. Standing behind the obstetrician, he appeared glum as he delivered the news. The obstetrician moved to the side, and Dr. Griffin moved closer. He leaned down to me as he softly spoke. "She is not viable at twenty-one weeks. Usually, we consider the earliest chance is twenty-four weeks. Right now, your baby cannot breathe on her own. While she looks fully developed, she is not. Parts of her central nervous system, lungs, brain, organs, and eyes are still developing." He paused and stuck his hands deep into his white doctor coat. I continued looking at her dance in my womb on the monitor. Neil's grip of my hand got tighter.

"Laurie, we cannot save your baby. We must concentrate now on saving you. I am very sorry," the obstetrician stated, this time with more fervor. I sensed an urgency in her tone.

"I'm going to remove the ultrasound now, okay?" said the specialist.

Both Neil and I nodded. I knew with the ultrasound departure I'd lose vision of her, but I'd be meeting her soon enough. Neil released my hand, and his head fell into his hands as he slumped forward in his chair. His shoulders shook. I asked if we could be alone. Everyone departed. The room was quiet except for Neil's muffled tears. He was never one to wear his emotions on his sleeve. I assumed he was holding back the real tears he wanted to shed. Neil and I did not share many words as we sat alone. We held each other's hands and stared off. I had no tears. An intense surge of fortitude came to me. I knew what I had to do. I had to deliver a baby to die.

The obstetrician came in and pragmatically announced the game plan: break the bag of water, induce labor with medication, and expect to deliver within four to eight hours. Pain meds were suggested, but an epidural was not.

I agreed. It was the most disgusting agreement to make.

"I can't believe I just agreed to end my baby's life," I blurted out. Neil squinted at me. The obstetrician grabbed my sweaty hand. "Laurie, whatever your beliefs, your baby was coming anyway. What I've witnessed in my years and how I cope with premature deliveries…" She paused as she looked at both of us. "If a baby comes early, it's nature's way of delivering a baby who was not physically ready for this life." She was convincing to my intellect, but not my heart.

She broke the water with an amniotic hook and the warmth saturated the pad under my bottom. The nurses removed it as I remained in bed. I let out a small cry of frustration and anger, but I sucked the rest of the tears back up. I convinced myself that with each action they took that I would not cry. If I did, I'd cry the whole time and it wouldn't change a damn thing. The cramping started immediately. The doctor started the IV with the medication to induce labor. The contractions came on like a punch in the back and kick to the stomach. The pain meds came next, softening the blows but not enough to extinguish the agony nor the heartache.

For four hours of imprisonment, I endured waiting for her birth. Never in my life had I felt so trapped and forced into a situation that I had no control over. I tried to think of a similar scenario, but everything I came up with had a solution, a way out. Sure, they could knock me out, I could sleep through it all, but then I wouldn't meet her. I had to meet her.

The physical birthing urge to push came, and it pissed me off. I wanted to push, to rid myself of the savage pain, but I knew I was pushing to her death. The doctor and nurses got in their formation for birth. I felt out of body. *This couldn't be happening.* Over my heavy breathing and occasional shrieks, the doctor announced that the baby had descended and they were ready.

My mind raced. Soon, we'd meet her. Compared to Nicholas's slow birth and eventual C-section, this baby's birth was abrupt, almost crude. I could feel her moving down the birth canal. Neil watched from the side. He frequently looked away, stared at the floor or closed his eyes in despair.

Here she was. With no more than a slight push, out she came into the doctor's hands.

"Here's your daughter," the doctor announced softly in the dim lit room, holding her up to us. The baby outstretched her skinny little arms like she was saying HELLO! She was squirming, her mouth gasping but her chest not moving, her eyelids fused. She was dark purple, no hair, but she was beautiful. All fingers and toes counted. It's strange how I made sure of that, even though it didn't matter. And yet it did, her hands and fingers notable and remarkable.

"Don't cut the cord yet!" I screamed. I knew the only thing keeping her alive was the umbilical cord and me. Neil jumped to his feet and reached for her. He jointly held her with the doctor's hands, tears dropping in clumps down his cheek. They handed her to me. I held her delicate, frail body, all eight inches and six ounces of her, close to my chest. They covered her with a tiny blanket, and I delicately kissed her forehead, and my tears fell onto her. We were one. In that beauty of a moment, she was alive and every part of her exquisite, sweet soul, and God were present. I felt immense gratitude and awe of her presence. She was my daughter, and I was her mother. She was still moving but barely. Even though she was connected to me, I wasn't enough.

"Laurie, you are bleeding heavily, and I need to make sure you pass the placenta," said the doctor. "I'm sorry. We must cut the cord." I gently handed the baby to Neil. His wet eyes met mine, and I knew she was his to hold now. I would never embrace her again.

The doctor cut the cord, and Neil paced the room with our baby, wrapped in a blanket, saying things to her quietly--words I couldn't catch, but whispers of encouragement and love I imagined a father would tell his daughter. I knew she was in the best hands. Oh, how I needed my father now.

My bleeding increased, and my body would not pass the placenta. The cramping intensified. I felt faint. Before I passed out, the doctor advised Neil they'd need to take me to surgery. My last look at my baby was in Neil's arms as he cried.

I woke the next morning, alone, in a typical hospital room: single bed, generic, sterile environment. The window drapes were open, exposing the overcast gloom of a hazy August morning. I felt no pain except my boobs hurt. Oh no, will milk come in? What a piece of Mother Nature bullshit if *that* happens.

My bed pad was soaked in blood. Where was everyone? Two nurses immediately came after I buzzed them.

"Your husband just called. He and your son will be here soon. You have a boy?" the nurse sweetly asked while cleaning up the mess beneath me.

"Yes, he's almost four. Nicholas." The thought of him made my heart flutter. "What about my daughter?"

"I'll have a doctor from maternity call you, okay? Just answer the phone when it rings, honey."

"Hello?" I answered the phone on half of the first ring. This obstetrician was not familiar to me, but said she'd read my chart. She was calm as she broke the news. My blood pressure had severely dropped after the birth, and they had to do a DNC before I lost more blood. I'll be okay and can go home later today. My baby--her heartbeat for four hours after they cut the umbilical cord. She *lived* four hours. Neil held her the whole time. He had to do that alone. I had no idea what he went through, but I was astounded. I wish I had been with them.

"You know, most preemies that young, don't live that long. They usually pass right away." Her voice shuddered. "She was strong."

"Thank you," I said, my voice sturdy, recognizing the baby's amazing life force.

"Before you're discharged, a maternity nurse will visit you. We have your baby's birth certificate and...her death certificate."

She took a deep inhale before continuing. "They both need to be signed." She paused, and I sighed. This must be the worst part of her job. "Oh, and we also have pictures of your baby, and foot and handprints, and her blanket, in a keepsake box. Do you want these?"

"Oh, my God, yes. Why wouldn't I?" I gripped the phone hard enough my hand shook, angered by her question.

"Oh, gosh, I'm sorry, but some people don't want the reminders."

I inhaled deeply; my anger released to appreciation.

"I want to remember," I replied, releasing my stronghold on the receiver.

The maternity nurse visited later that morning and delivered the cream-colored sturdy cardboard keepsake box, no bigger than a shoebox, decorated in delicate dried rose petals and tied with a thin silk green ribbon. I held it closely to my chest.

Once Neil arrived, I opened it. He immediately rose from his seat next to my bed and advised he didn't want to look at the contents, not now. He went to the window and stared out. He informed me Nicholas was in the courtyard with Neil's sister. We'd meet them out there when I was ready. Neil's shoulders slumped forward; his hair messy. His index finger tapped his upper lip, indicating he was deep in thought, somewhere I couldn't reach him.

After discharge, I held Nicholas closer to me than ever before. He didn't resist. Confused, he asked where the baby was. It took explaining, and eventually, he appeared to understand she went to where Grandpa went. "They are together, honey." I would tell him. I held Nicholas tightly and tried not to cry in front of him. A new level of anxiety entered me: the fear of losing *him*. I always felt pressure as a parent, but now it was outright fear. I had a painful new awareness of the precious delicacy of life. And I was pissed for him. He never got to meet his sister and lost the chance to be a brother.

Within a day after delivery, yup, my milk came in. Fuck you Mother Nature. It dried up within weeks as my body caught on there was no purpose. However, the depression didn't dry up with it. Post-partum depression hit again like a hurricane on already damaged shores. My anxiety was like walking on my own eggshells. My brain was a loaded gun and I didn't know my triggers. I refused the anti-depressants although my obstetrician reminded me, "Laurie, you have General Anxiety Disorder, also hints of PTSD. Don't take your treatment lightly." I didn't want to hear it. I was angry, pissed to be in this situation. I tried to control now what was uncontrollable before. However, I welcomed the Xanax like an old friend. I understood the blissful effects, and I wanted them. But, fuck the mind-altering anti-depressants.

47

NUMB BUT NIMBLE

To fight off the depression I took walks every day. I walked the neighborhood and hiking trails nearby like I used to around Town Lake in Austin. Xanax numbed the rest of my head, but it didn't make life better. I *must* find my purpose again, I thought. Domestic life threw me a massive turdball, and I didn't give up music for this. Sure, I had my initial reasons to drop music. My music career was waning, I was tired of the hustle. *Blah blah blah.* I thought I traded chasing a music career for a life of predictably and comfort. But that was out the window now. I loved my husband, and he'd been good to me, yet with each passing day, we dodged each other as you would a stranger in a grocery store aisle—your head down looking at a shopping list for things you're not sure you need or where to find them. We had been to hell and I wasn't sure we had got back.

Mom called daily and checked in. Our conversations were brief. She knew I was aching, and my loss was something she couldn't fix. Her voice was welcoming until she turned to tears which was pretty much every call. She lost a grandchild, too, I would remind myself.

I sank into my head during my long walks. Winter leaves crackled under my feet as I forced each foot ahead. I was lonely, as usual, and not sure who I was. I wasn't a singer anymore. I was still a mom, though contorted with grief, and Nicholas was my shining light. His energy, enthusiasm, and curiosity for life were beautiful and breathtaking. But I couldn't bank everything on him, like my mom did to me. I knew there was only one thing I could do. Music. I must do music again. Somewhere in the music, I'd find me.

Months after the loss, the local Pasadena community college held auditions for their opera program: a six-week course for approximately twenty opera singers, cumulating in a weekend of four shows. In memory of my dad's love of opera, I auditioned half thinking they'd laugh me away, a 40-year-old, with my rendition of *Les Misérables*, *I Dreamed a Dream*. Contrarily, the director welcomed me in as a mezzo-soprano to sing four-part harmony ensemble roles in Mozart's *Marriage of Figaro*, Donizetti's *L'elsir d'amore* and Leonard Bernstein's, *Candide*. I was shocked. I heard opera but I had no experience singing it!

When rehearsals started, I realized this was a once-in-a-lifetime opportunity--and a great distraction to my grief. I was even more thankful that my early piano lessons provided me the ability to read music. However, it was daunting to memorize Mozart, no less, and extend my voice to a dynamic new level.

There were times at rehearsal when my insecurities mounted, and my anxiety swarmed my mind like a disturbed beehive.

My yellow highlighter dried up from noting my parts and integral sections in the music. I took notes on the sheet music in a frenzy to keep up. The twenty-somethings with operatically strong voices, appeared in their element, never breaking a sweat, while I looked for the exit sign. However, I stayed, stubborn to figure out my vocal part, just like when I was a young girl sitting under Beethoven's bust, practicing piano in Wisconsin. I was determined to master my parts.

One night, early in rehearsals, the piano accompanist pulled me aside during a break, asking me to come to her piano which sat off to the side in the rehearsal room. She was a bit frumpy with overflowing scarfs and layered clothing. Her greying dark brown hair pulled into a loose bun gave away her mid-60s age. She had always been pleasant, and I admired her quiet confidence. Due to her doctorate in musical arts, she was referred to as "doctor" by the program director. I was intrigued that she desired to talk to me.

"Laurie, why are you doing this program? You're not registered for a music degree at this school, and your voice is more suited for musical theater." I stood with a blank stare not sure of the purpose of our discussion.

"Laurie, this program will get harder as we go. I'm a woman of decency, and in respect of the music we are recreating, I need to know what your intention is?"

I was flabbergasted. Was I that bad? Or was she just too serious? Then again, this was opera. She had asked with a genuine tone, and I assumed *her* intention was not harmful. I informed her of my desire to honor my father and to challenge myself musically and I needed something, *anything* to remind me that I can sing. My personal desires appeared to resonate with her when she smiled and nodded.

"Well, you can read music, and you can sing. I'll help you as I can," she said, sipping a warm beverage in one hand and opening the music to *Marriage of Figaro* with the other.

She placed her travel mug decorated with musical notes on the piano bench. "Okay, let's start with opening your mouth wider. As so." She opened her mouth like cat yawning, and I giggled at her example. Yes, there is still a silly, teenager at heart within me! There I am! She placed her hand on my mine which sat on top of her black upright piano. She became serious. I liked the feeling of her hand on mine. It was maternal, and I felt supported, accepted.

"Laurie, you need to give more. I understand why you are here, but I need to hear it. Now, sing." Straight away, she played my vocal part in the *Marriage of Figaro*. On cue, I sang.

She found my voice.

Mom flew in from Wisconsin to see the performances and share in the dedication to Dad. The production included four shows over one weekend--one on Friday evening, two on Saturday and a final matinee on Sunday. After the last show, as I wiped away my bright red lipstick, removed my formal purple gown, and let down my poufy operatic hair, I was satisfied with the conclusion. It was by far, one of the most profound musical experiences I'd had. I learned about expanding my voice in technique, breathing, and dynamics, but in the end, I told myself to stick with rock 'n roll. I would never have a big enough sound for Opera, and that was fine with me.

As my singing legs gained strength and confidence, I found the occasional open mic or sang at a local variety show. I met a talented, easy-going guitarist who had a small digital recording studio in Redondo Beach. We recorded three of my songs there. It was incredibly satisfying to record; however, it wasn't enough to feel like a working musician again or how it felt to be in a band. I wanted to be in a group again, but that idea seemed the dream of a teenager.

Along with music, I accepted a permanent administrative position back at Warner Brothers. It made sense to bring in money, and Nicholas was now in school so I didn't need to be home. Also, it was good to be around people, making friends. However, after all these years, music still drove my desires and purpose. I was older, but I had to put myself out there. Quarterly, I still received a royalty check from my CD *Intro*. It was for when a department store played one of my songs as background music. I was still legit, in a Macy's kind of way. However, I needed more, to fill the lingering gaps in domestic frustration. Neil asked often if I wanted to try for another baby. I couldn't do it. I wouldn't bear the loss again. He didn't push. There was a knowing.

One night I was watching TV with Nicholas, and I saw another reality TV singing show, *America's Got Talent*. It had been six years since it first hit the airwaves in 2006. I was inspired at the time, but I couldn't do anything with my father being ill and then the loss of the baby. However, now? Maybe I should audition for one of these reality shows.

Although it went against my music principals, I was intrigued by these shows even as I knew they were crafted soap operas. There was always a dramatic story behind each singer--a tale that often trumped their talent. Except for the stellar one-of-a-kind singers whom I thought would've still made it somehow: Kelly Clarkson, Jennifer Hudson, Carrie Underwood, Adam Lambert. But they were all in their twenties when they broke in. Then came Susan Boyle in 2009. If she could make it at 48, with her unexpected appearance and operatic voice, maybe I had a chance too. At this point, what did I have to lose? For years I'd been watching and waiting.

I called my old songwriting partner and guitarist Aaron in Austin for his input. He agreed the shows lacked sincerity and that the process might be intense for me considering all that's happened, but added, "Hey, look, if I were in L.A., I'd probably do it. Why not, right? Just don't take it to heart, you know?" I brushed off his take it to heart comment.

I read online about an upcoming open audition in Los Angeles for the first-season reality show *X-Factor*. This show might be the key, the access I need to take my music career to the next level. These reality shows were like hitting the warp drive button on a music career. The exposure, the potential record contract, all coming at the winner within months of auditioning for the show. At 43, with no better music options, I needed it. And so did my aching heart.

ACT THREE

THIS LIFE
PRESENT DAY

2011

48

HERE WE GO

I met Stephanie through my Warner Brothers job. Her cynical humor and candid honesty drew me to her. She said the things I wished I could and told exciting tales of her personal and creative adventures. We fell into instant rapport. She was the sister I never had.

The *X-Factor* audition was approaching. It was easy to ask Stephanie if she could attend and provide emotional support. I also suspected she'd love the chance to observe the eclectic array of thousands of aspiring music stars auditioning.

However, in the days before, she was concerned about the auditions.

"Laurie, have you heard what they're saying on the news? There might be over ten thousand people going, and it's a two-day process. The first day, Saturday, is for registration. Sunday is when you sing. Are you up for this?"

"You know, Steph, I appreciate you're willing to go with me, but if you can't do it, I'm completely okay with that."

"Well, I'm thinking of you too. Like, will *you* be okay? Mentally?" Steph knew I suffered with anxiety.

"Yes, right now I'm fully ready to rock 'n roll."

"Okay. But my Friday night plan may still be with me Saturday morning. So, I'll let you know."

Now on the morning of registration day, I hesitate before sending her the text, knowing there's a chance she won't reply.

I'm now up and will be leaving in the next 30. You still in?

The irony, of course, is an audition is a sole experience. You can't bring a spouse, mother, agent or friend and let them hold your hand while you sing. You are as alone as you will ever be. Yet having her with me for the expected wait time would be an incredible comfort.

I stop nervously tapping my phone on the nightstand as I stand up to stretch. The cold floor radiates up my legs, reminding me of the time I stood on the ice and sang the national anthem before a professional hockey game in Austin. The memory is a beautiful reminder that I can handle this audition, even if I'm on my own. I'm up for the challenge; it's just more fun when your friend is along.

I'm surprised when I get an immediate reply from Stephanie: *All good. In.*

I'm relieved she's already up and ready to go; though I will soon find out she had hardly been to bed at all.

I pull myself together, thanks to planned details for the makeup I'll wear, carefully chosen clothes, and the touchup to my hair I styled last night. At times, I get a bit sensitive over my age as a performer; but right now, I'm resilient.

As I get closer to leaving, I make a final adjustment to the bag I've packed for the day. It resembles supplies for a day of hiking, more than for registering for an audition: a change of clothes, extra shoes, steel water bottle, snacks, sheet music, and extra makeup. Everything is in this bag but my heart. That I'm wearing on my sleeve.

The drive from Pasadena to West Hollywood to pick up Stephanie is not long by L.A. standards, and on a good traffic day, it should only take twenty-five minutes. Of course, all travel in L.A. is about how long, rather than how far. The sixteen-miles could take twenty-five minutes one day, or an hour on another day. The only thing one can predict in L.A. is there will be some form of traffic. Simple as that. The one thing I could never have predicted is living in L.A. at all. I'd always imagined I'd live in New York City. This makes me think of my husband's comment before I left this morning. That he was proud of me and to "break a leg." I reminded myself, again, I'm someone who is getting the chance to audition for a TV show. A show with potential fame I hope will be enough to fix things. To fix me.

As I make the bend on the 210 freeway west through the sweeping mountains out of Pasadena, on the way to get Stephanie, the valley below is a grand, pretty sight. At eight in the morning, the downtown L.A. skyline appears peaceful and still. The rising sun sets a soft glow on the east side of the buildings. The City of Angels has not quite woken up yet, and the serenity I'm observing is misleading. Somewhere close to downtown, masses of people are lining up with the same goal as mine.

I am not too fond of rushing to a destination, but this morning, I press the gas pedal harder and turn on classical music to ease my anxiety.

Stephanie informed me via text she'd only slept an hour. And I thought, *shit*, that is not sleep--that's a nap! She's an enigma: a creature of great stamina to even be conscious, let alone willing to do something solely for my benefit. I'm surprised I see her already walking to the Hollywood Coffee Bean when I arrive at her street. She spots me, fumbling to open my car door. Without a pause, she starts to ramble. "My phone is gonna die. I didn't charge it last night, I hope you have a charger 'cause I'll freak if I don't stay connected."

"Wow, you look great for only a catnap," I say. "But, no I don't have a charger. And I'm not sure there will be anywhere to plug in today. But we can go back to your place and get yours?"

"Oh, hell. Nah, I'll make it, I just need coffee," she admits, waving her hand to shake off my suggestion.

I study Steph's appearance. Considering her lack of sleep, she looks remarkably kept, except for her long wavy hair slightly tousled. By L.A. standards, and the same age as me, Steph is natural: nothing on her is fake, plumped, or stretched. She's feminine but not prissy. She loves fashion, but she's not a slave to it. She'd rather design her jewelry or handbag than empty her bank account for *Louis Vuitton*.

Steph's usually rockin' some fashion-forward outfits and today is no different. She wears a flattering pencil skirt with a boxy top, and some wacky, colorful tights. Instead of her regular pumps, she's shod in chic, low-heeled boots. A smart choice.

"Did you bring the camp chair or folding chair or soccer chair field thing, or what is it?" With a snarled lip, Steph looks visibly confused at her own words.

"Yes. I'm a mom. Always prepared. I also have a blanket in the car if we need it. Shit, I also brought along a bag of snacks."

"Whatever's. I just want the chair. My back goes out quick. Especially after last night," she winks.

She settles into the car seat, holding her phone close to her chest, and guides me to the Hollywood Coffee Bean's parking lot. Steph dashes to grab her coffee, turning back to shout, "Do you want anything?"

"No, I'm good."

I already had coffee, and don't want to add to my anxiety and nervous stomach with more caffeine. The nervous audition tummy leads to nervous bowels, a performance dilemma.

As I wait for Steph, I'm left to obsess about the days ahead. I had prepared for the audition by reading the show's online blog. They emphasized the importance of song choice since participants will have mere seconds to impress. Seconds.

Each *a cappella* song I have portrays a slightly different style of my voice, but I can't decide if it's best to showcase my bluesy-rocker sound, my Broadway-style or my singer-songwriter voice. It might've been a mistake to read their blog because ever since

I've worried continually about both my song choice and my outfit of army-camo-styled Calvin Klein cropped pants, black wedge high-heeled boots, and black short sleeve deep V-neck embroidered blouse.

"Sorry it took so long. Those Coffee Bean people piss me off. The Bean is just slow. But at least this Hollywood one is entertaining while you wait. There is always someone strange in there. Or at least a celebrity, which is sorta the same," rasps Steph as she pops back into the car.

She always makes me laugh. And I need a good laugh right about now because I'm way too serious about the day ahead.

Exiting the parking lot, we fly fast to the freeway. This drive would typically be treacherous, but since it's so damn early on a Saturday morning, we confront little traffic.

We make small talk for the remainder of the ride downtown. My nervous chatter bounces off Steph's recap of the previous night. It's airy and humorous and lessens my anxiety.

When we exit the freeway just south of downtown, ahead of us traffic is backed up at a standstill. Event parking lots on all sides display large signs advertising prime parking for $10 or $20. After a few blocks, we see a large mass of people gathered in the parking lot outside the Los Angeles Memorial Sports Arena. We're at the right place.

"Oh, my God, Stephanie, this looks crazy. Like all the people who should be inside the arena are in the parking lot! What is going on?"

"Whoa," moaned Steph as she gazed out the window.

"I need to find a parking spot STAT. We need to get in there," I say. I simultaneously scan parking lots for the perfect spot, navigating traffic, cops, and J-walkers.

I spot a parking lot. It's not too far from the arena, and since it's $10, a good deal at this point, I make a quick entrance. Some attendant guides us into our spot, and we start unloading the car in a rushed frenzy.

49

IN THE DRIVER'S SEAT

"Sweet Lordy! Thank God, it's here!" Steph chirps, as she grabs the folding chair. She gives it a brief hug, then places it gently on the ground. I roll my eyes in acknowledgment of her declaration and slightly shake my head with a short laugh.

Looking at the distance we need to walk, I suddenly grasp the challenge of wearing heels while carrying a lot of crap. It's a good thing that by my age I have mastered the high-heel walk.

"Well, at least you have flat boots on," I say. "I wore fucking heels! I may need the chair before you do."

"Nope, I called it, and you brought it for me," announces Steph. "This chair is mine. Besides, I don't have one of these things. I'm not the soccer mom. I'll also need a nap."

"Well, I'm a proud soccer mom, but for today, I'm a rock star." I grinned.

"That's a slight overstatement," she says doubtfully, playfully nudging my arm.

"Yeah, probably."

To our left, two college-aged looking guys urgently pop out of their car. Instead of gathering loads of bags or furniture, as we have, they position their simple backpacks in place, and are ready to go.

"Why can't women be that simple?" I ask.

"Cause you love hooker shoes and I have a bad back, that's why," replies Steph.

To my surprise, we still make our way out of the parking lot with the same timing as they do. Instead of walking to a corner with a stoplight and crosswalk, Stephanie and I J-walk like many of the others, bursting across the street.

We walk at a slower, even pace as we file behind others near the arena parking lot where I get a closer look through a tall iron fence. I'm surprised everything is so quiet. There's energy surrounding us, but no loud sounds--not the clamor I'd expect from a crowd I presume already numbers well into the thousands.

Footsteps shuffle behind us. The two college boys have kept pace on the narrow sidewalk. They most likely need to pass us. I turn to them, "Hey guys, go ahead and pass, we're going kinda slow here."

"No worries, we'll all get there," one acknowledges. They maintain their stride behind us. These two kids shock me; I wouldn't expect them at an audition. They look collegiate, even sporty, straight off-campus, or a university football game. They're strutting college hoodies, Nike high-tops, baggy jeans; one is wearing a TX Longhorn baseball cap. They're not dressed hip or stylish, and yet they're not nerdy looking either.

Am I too old to get their look? They seem like good, decent, college kids. I wonder what type of music they perform. It makes me laugh at myself and all the effort I've put into planning what I'm wearing today and tomorrow.

We approach the entrance to a paved parking lot, holding a sea of people, thousands, all facing straight towards the arena. It strikes me as eerie, like a massive group of zombies with their backs to us.

A highflying banner flaps back and forth in the wind over the entrance. It gallantly displays *X-Factor* front and center with a smaller WELCOME below. My mind spins, anxiety sparking by the sheer number of people standing on the other side of the banner.

We pause, trying to get our bearings. There are three groups within the parking lot, kept apart by wood street barricades. Before we can decide, we're ushered by security to the group straight ahead.

Of the three groups, each is about 75 feet deep and 40 feet wide. There are no lines within each group; rather people are just standing where they can find room. It doesn't matter where one stands; the goal is to move forward and get behind the nearest person *or zombie* ahead of you.

Steph and I proceed to the end of the crowd and stand. Side by side. I have never felt so odd merely standing. When I've stood in any line before--at the grocery store, the bank--there's a purpose, a destination I can see. This line is not a line at all, but a massive clump of people. I have no idea why we're all just standing here.

The college boys have arrived at the same area; they remain directly behind us. They're courteous, and I can tell they're checking out the situation, too. I look around, many people are trying to get oriented. Stragglers are reaching out to others, asking questions. No matter what, at this point, all of us are at the mercy of the crowd's flow.

At the end of the group, we have a decent amount of standing room. People are within arm's reach. I wonder when we may eventually become too close to each other. I dread the personal space invasion–when you're so close to others, packed subway tight, you can't sneeze, cough, burp, fart or barely breathe.

Standing on top of each other at a concert is a different thing, altogether. Like at the Rush concert when I was a teen. Beer spilled, hands in the air, toes stepped on, elbows ram into backs or bellies. It's rarely an issue, as it's all in the name of rockin' out--an expected part of the experience. But being too close to strangers when you have no idea how long you'll be there, and you are in actual competition with most of them–this is daunting. More people arrive, filling in the space behind us, but we remain at a standstill. Twenty-five minutes go by and we haven't moved.

I stand on my tiptoes and try to look over the crowd. Another section to our right, about the same amount of people, seem more compact, like they've been here longer. Their section is closed by a barricade, whereas our group is still open and accepting people.

We settle into our respective stance and personal space. Now, it's cloudy 70 degrees. The college guys are still behind us. One has a look of concern on his face that mimics ours. His furrowed brow toughens as he slowly shakes his head.

"Dude, this is nuts. How long we gonna be here?" fretted the one in the red hoodie.

"Man, I don't know, but I'm not liking it," answers the guy in the Longhorn baseball cap.

Without hesitation or pause, our conversations join.

"Look, there are a decent number of people coming in behind us. I guess we're not the last ones to get here," I say to Steph and in the general direction of the guys.

"Yeah, I guess not," red hoodie guy replies, while his friend nods.

"I still think we're kinda far back from what's going on up there though," Longhorn cap says, "I'm hoping we're not too late. We drove way too far for this."

"Where did you guys come from?" inquires Steph.

"Well, I drove in from Arizona yesterday and met my friend Jacob in San Diego last night." Jacob in the red hoodie gives us a smile and wave.

"And we made the drive up here to L.A. this morning," Longhorn cap finishes.

"Wow, that is a hell of a drive," I jump in. "I feel bad fussing about our drive this morning."

"Where did you come from?" probes Jacob. Both Steph and I giggle.

"Hollywood. I'm Stephanie," she reveals. "I'm Trey," Longhorn cap replies.

Trey looks more intense than Jacob. His hands are forced deep into his pant pockets, making his body appear rigid and uptight.

"Well, I'm Jacob," Red hoodie chimes in. He's a good-looking guy, nice hair, hazel eyes, with a laid-back demeanor. His arms are softly folded in front, as he gently rocks back and forth on the sides of his feet.

"I'm Laurie," I say, with my hand out. I notice a nice-looking tall guy standing right behind Steph. He's fashionably put together in black jeans and a purple V-neck sweater. He looks around thirty-five, and I can tell he's seasoned by how he carries himself: shoulders back, head held high. He's occasionally listening into our conversations but doesn't comment, but I include him as well.

"Hello, and who are you?"

"I'm Jackson," he beams, waving to the group and acknowledging everyone.

"Where did you come in from?" inquires Trey.

"Vegas," Jackson says. "I flew in yesterday and leave tomorrow night."

"Cool. What do you do in Vegas? Any big shows you've been on or auditions?" Trey replies.

"Honey, let's just say my audition résumé is longer than my performance résumé." He says as he flicks his raised hand like he's waving off a notion. He continues, "I sing and wait tables. It's a typical pairing. So, who all is auditioning here tomorrow?"

"He's singing," Jacob confirms, pointing to Trey. "I'm just along for the ride." He smiles, giving Trey a nudge.

"I'm along for the ride, too," says Steph.

As the reality of their drive and overnight travel sinks in, I'm impressed at the effort these guys made to get here for this audition. Their determination is noteworthy. They remind me of that grit I once had, at seventeen, to be in a band, to take on the world. I break out the lawn chair for Stephanie. She hasn't complained yet, but I need to unload it from my shoulder.

Shaking his head, "You guys brought a lawn chair? Seriously? Can you do that?" Jacob says.

"Who's going to step into this sea of people and tell us we can't have the chair?" I remark.

After I set up the chair, it becomes centerpiece to our group, as we all stand around it facing each other. Steph doesn't miss a beat to sit, and I'm now quite glad I've brought it; not only for her comfort but some sense of an island in this vast sea of people. At least an hour has passed, and we have yet to move forward.

The crowd behind us has grown to twenty-plus deep, with at least 50 people across. It's become cramped. People are closer to each other, almost touching distance. Happily, no one is pushing their way in front of anyone. We're like a school of fish, ending up at the same location no matter how we go about it. We are a group of strange, curious folks; lambs hoping to not end up at the slaughterhouse. Almost on cue, a roar of cheers erupts from the front of our group. Something is happening.

We quickly grab the chair, our bags, and move forward in pace with those next to us. We share smiles and thumbs up and high five slaps until we stop after very little progress.

"Seriously, did we just move like twenty feet?" grunts Trey. "Yeah, I think so." Steph surveys the crowd.

It's not a lot of progress but it's movement in the right direction is all I can think.

The warmth of the sun turns hotter as the day progresses. I crave a cool breeze. Space. Everyone is checking their phones, and I check mine for the time. I text Neil an update, filling him in with all the details. My cell is like a lifeline to the real world. The world I put on hold, thinking this world may be better.

50

ROADKILL

"I'm getting restless in here. I'm gonna walk out of the crowd and check things out. I'll be back," Stephanie says.

"We'll be here, obviously," snorts Jacob.

Stephanie waves and moves through the crowd. Within seconds, she's out of sight. I wonder if she'll find food on her adventure. I dig into my bag to look for my orange.

I sit down for the first time on the parking lot to give my feet a rest. Our pile of bags occupies our chair. Trey plops down next to me. He acts bored, twisting his shoelace around his finger, and probably frustrated with the situation.

"So, you sing, too, huh?" he quizzes. "What kind of stuff?" "I mostly do rock, pop, original stuff. I'm a songwriter. I

mean, I've done everything. Weddings, funerals, even a metal band. But now I do singer-songwriter stuff."

"Me, too. Well, except for the metal stuff or weddings. Or funerals," he replies. His shoulders dance up and down as he laughs.

"So, what's your style?" I say.

Trey sits up from his laid-back position and awkwardly folds his arms across his chest.

"I'm a songwriter. Play guitar, sing. Yeah, my dad has a studio, so I do a lot of studio work." He pauses and looks down at his shoes. "My dad actually called me last night, telling me how much he loves me and how I deserve this because I'm such a good musician." He half smiles. "He'd been drinking, of course, but whatever."

Trey's left leg starts to pulse and his foot taps to a mystery beat. I decide not to bring attention to the drinking comment, nor my familiar issue with my mother. "So, your dad has a studio; is he a musician too?"

"Yeah, he's a producer. He does a lot of recordings for other people, companies, and artists. He's so cool about my music, and since I work in his studio, he said I don't have to go to college. I should concentrate on music."

"Wow, my parents weren't like that. You're lucky." "Yeah, I guess so. I never really thought about it."

Trey reshuffles his legs and looks away again. My claustrophobia kicks in, as I look at all the other people standing above us. I squirm to get up, hoping Trey won't find me rude.

I hadn't noticed Stephanie return, but she is busy explaining our day jobs to the rest of our group; what the company is like and how we met. Before we know it, the crowd makes a hard shift to move forward. We jump again to grab our gear.

"Here we go," Jackson yells.

We progress rapidly from baby steps to full-on walking. The crowd eases into the motion without pushing but maintains a brisk control over the direction. I sense people are more protective of their place in this crowd, after having stood here for close to three hours. I feel the same way.

We continue to walk forward another twenty-five feet before we come to a dead halt. A variety of sighs, boos, and even some applause comes from the crowd. The frustrated have become impatient, and the optimistic recognize this is our furthest movement yet.

The front of the line is only ten feet away; we have moved a lot and are now shoulder to shoulder. With a loud, booming voice on a bullhorn, a security guard in front of our group announces welcoming words at this point: "Everyone, you are now moving onto the next group to enter the building. Please do not push, and please respect those around you."

As he opens the barrier, the crowd doesn't push; although some advance forward beyond their usual placement and fill in the sides.

Within our small group, we're separating.

"Let's stay together," I shriek. "We've come this far."

"Grab the back of my backpack," Jacob orders Steph, as he falls in behind Jackson and Trey. Stephanie pulls me to her. I stay behind her, and all of us stand behind each other like train cars.

"Yeah, stay with us girls," Jackson yells, leading the pack.

The others around us are excited. Conversations have amped up. The crowd makes another surge forward, clapping erupts, and we are just fifteen feet from the arena. Suddenly, our cheers muted by the frantic yells of a woman outside of the mass. "Jessica! Jessica!" she screams. She's there with four young children under age ten, and they also yell out Jessica's name.

"Help me! I can't find my twelve-year-old daughter. She is missing," the woman yells. Her face is red, and her eyes are tearing. The crowd yells out Jessica's name, and people start to circulate news within their groups about the lost child.

"Oh, my God, I saw that whole family earlier today when I walked in," Jackson rants. "I laughed at the time because she was pissed at one of the kids for getting crazy. She told him she would 'choke him out' if he kept acting up. Now she's lost one."

My stomach does a somersault and my head becomes heavy, and I'm faint. I grab Stephanie's arm.

"I don't feel so good. I need to get out of here." "Oh, shit. Are you having a panic attack?"

"I don't know. I don't know. She needs to find her kid. She needs to find her baby." Beads of sweat gush from my hairline.

Steph holds me tightly to her in a hug, whispering in my ear. "You're okay. You're okay. You need to stay here. We're too close. Just ignore her. Here, drink water." She passes me her water bottle, and I sip what I can to hold down my stomach.

"You, okay?" Jackson yells over his shoulder.

"She'll be okay. It's just that the crowd is getting to her." Jackson doesn't appear to buy her reply. His eyebrows narrow.

"Hang in there, girl," he says to me.

"Do you have Xanax with you?" Steph asks.

"Yes, but I can't take it now. Not now. I can't be groggy. She just needs to find her baby."

My head is spinning, and my thoughts are jumbled, and I can't tell if staying in Stephanie's embrace is helping or if I'd rather run. Run as fast as I can from this crowd, away from my memories, and this woman who is so fucking stupid to bring her children here.

The crowd is still yelling Jessica's name, here and there, but is quickly interrupted by the mother yelling out the child had been found.

"Thank you, everyone, thank you. We have Jessica."

The crowd of hundreds erupts in a roar of applause and now triumphantly chants "Jess-i-ca." The mom is walking away with five kids in tow.

Stephanie is still holding me in a hug. My heart-beats slow, knowing the mom found her child. My sweat slows down, and my dry mouth moistens.

Steph releases me and dabs my face with her scarf. "You better?"

"Yes, I'm better. Thanks," I mumble.

The college boys hadn't noticed my episode, and I'm happy about that for my sake. The incident is over within minutes, although I have mounting anger within me. Nothing in this world is worth losing your child.

51

WRISTBAND

We move towards the doors, and the vast horde narrows into four separate lines. Our group gathers to walk through together.

"Move as far to the right as possible. Keep moving, keep moving," shouts an event organizer. Just inside the door, he continues with hand gestures and directions, advising us to move to the back of short lines leading to registration tables. The lobby has been turned in to a makeshift enlisting area and smells like a locker room. There are only eight tables. They hold a dozen or more staff members to accept the registration papers from the dazed audition hopefuls.

"Fill into the right, keep it moving, keep it moving," the guy states firmly, with tedious redundancy.

I'm surprised at the limited number of staff on hand to register people. Clearly, this has caused today's long wait.

At this point, our group separates into the shortest lines we can, yet we try to stay close together. I'm pleased I've made these acquaintances today and how we've shared these hours, but I don't lose sight of why I'm here.

Within minutes, we are at the registration table.

"Hi, how are you?" the administrator politely inquires. He appears friendly as he reaches across the heavy-duty plastic folding table for my paperwork and ID.

"I'm fine," I reply, happy for the warmth he exudes. "Are you a singer or guest?"

"The singer," I reply.

He reaches for my right wrist and attaches a purple paper wristband with the show logo on it. "You'll wear this wristband, which denotes you as auditioning. Do not remove it," he admonishes. "It's the only thing that gains you access to the arena floor to sing tomorrow."

I look back at Stephanie and smile. A ping of excitement soars when he mentions the actual audition.

"Now, this is your seat ticket showing where you sit in the arena while you wait to audition. These tickets have been issued in order of attendance today." What he hands me resembles a concert ticket, with a specific row and seat number. Another piece of paper has audition details.

"That's it. Good luck," he finishes with a smile. His eyes quickly move from me, and he leans his head to the left to get a look at the person behind.

As I step aside, he engages Stephanie in the same dialogue. "I'm a friend. Oh, I mean guest. I'm not singing," she advises as she taps her long blue painted nails on the plastic table.

He reaches for her right wrist to attach an orange wristband. "Wait, what's this for? I'm not singing. And it's orange. Like, neon orange." She darts a look at me and mouths silently, *sorry*. I wrinkle my nose back at her.

"Everyone must wear a wristband. It's how we identify those who are singing and those who are guests. And don't remove it or you can't get back in tomorrow," he clarifies, no longer smiling.

"But I'm not auditioning. Oh, hell. Okay. Put it on. I'd rather have the purple though. I'm going out tonight and this will clash with what I'm wearing."

He stares at her and doesn't blink. "It's regulation. Purple is for singers, orange for guests."

"Okay, got it." Steph reshuffles her stance and thrusts her wrist at him. He wraps the wristband firmly around it.

"Next." He looks around to the person behind her.

As we walk away from the table, she tries to move the band around her wrist, but it's so tight she can't. She lets out a grunt. "What a dick. Could he put it any fucking tighter? Sorry, Laurie. I'm kind of bitchy. Long day."

"Hey, you're holding up way better than I would in your condition. Bitch all you want. You know, it looks like a wristband you'd get at a club, so it's not too weird." I'm not sure I can reassure her.

The guys appear at the doors to leave at the same time we do. We compare tickets. We're all seated next to each other: same row, seats in numeric order. Either the tickets were distributed in the exact order as our arrival or fate is keeping us together.

"Wow, this is crazy," I say. "We're all sitting together."

"Totally," agrees Trey, examining his ticket.

"Bizarre, but cool," beams Jackson.

As we exit the building, we exhale. The previously dense crowd behind us has dwindled to a few hundred. We get our bearings, reorganize our bags, and Trey talks first.

"Well, I guess we'll see you guys tomorrow. We're gonna go eat and hit the hotel." He reaches out to give hugs.

"Food, yes; that sounds good," Steph says with a smile.

Trey and Jacob smile and throw a hand up for a final wave.

Their hurried departure is no surprise.

Jackson heads in the same direction as Stephanie and me. Walking towards our cars, we pass through the parking lot, which has become a desolate trash zone, like after a huge tailgating party-covered in bottles, food, candy wrappers, cans, and cups. For the seagulls, it's a Vegas-style buffet. The crowd's energy is gone, but there is still electricity in the air for tomorrow's audition.

We exchange earnest hugs with Jackson and agree to meet in the morning at 8 am, the time suggested in the instruction paper. Stephanie and I continue silently towards the car.

"Hey, you don't have to come tomorrow if you don't want.

You hung this entire day, and I appreciate it."

"Oh, hell no," Steph swiftly replies. "I still want to come back. I mean, I don't know about eight o'clock, but I want to

see how this all turns out."

"Ha, okay. Cool," I say, happy *and* relieved.

52

WHY ISN'T THIS LIFE ENOUGH?

When I finally reach home, my mind has gone wild worrying about the next day. Combined with my angst and exhaustion, I can hardly speak to my husband as I enter our kitchen. What's left of the day's sun trickles through the curtains of the two small windows over the sink. He looks up from preparing our dinner and raises an inquisitive eyebrow.

"One day down, one more to go," I offer. "How'd it go?" asks Neil.

"I don't know. It was a long day of waiting just to receive a wristband, a ticket, and a piece of paper."

"Yea? How many people were there?"

"Thousands--so I have no idea how long tomorrow could take. I honestly have no clue how they can possibly audition so many people."

Our kitchen is small, maybe seven-feet by ten-feet but it's enough for me to begin pacing. I'm starting to comprehend how dreadful tomorrow might be. I carry on as my husband listens, continuing our dinner preparation.

"I really need to be ready for this, and I feel *off*. I just don't know if the songs I've prepared are right, and I'm starting to question everything."

Neil stops stirring the pasta on the stove. He runs his hands through his thick hair, a typical gesture when curious. "Well, you still going to do it?"

I stop my pacing. "Yes! I still want to audition." I resume pacing, even faster. "Besides, I don't want today's process to be for nothing. But I'm messed up now about which song to sing."

My husband looks at me and smiles sheepishly, returns to his stirring, after checking his wristwatch. I'm sure he thinks I'm being overly dramatic.

"I need to spend tonight concentrating on the songs, practice them more and narrow down what I'm going to wear," I say, turning to leave the kitchen.

"Wait," he interrupts with a gentle tone. I stop and turn to him, my hand wrapped around the door frame from the kitchen into the dining room.

"Laurie, you've been planning this audition for weeks, rehearsing over and over, and you're still going to rehearse more tonight? Don't you think it's a bit overkill? Why don't you relax, and let tomorrow be what it will be? You know, go easy on yourself."

I stare at the hardwood kitchen floor. I nod in acceptance but not in total agreement.

"Where's Nicholas?" I ask.

"He's in the backyard with his friends. He's fine. Just relax, okay?"

I wish I could. I dart out of the room to the bedroom to change clothes.

"Hey, Laurie, dinner is almost ready so don't go too far," Neil yells. I imagine him shaking his head.

The smell of roast chicken wafting into the bedroom and the sound of dinner plates clanking on the glass dinner table rouse me to return to the dining room.

"Mom!" Nicholas yells as he leaps out of his chair to hug me. "Ah, kiddo." I bury my nose in his dark brown hair. He smells of outdoors: grass, dirt, sweat. The aroma of him, a healthy, energized eight-year-old, makes my anxiety disappear. This life with them, why isn't it enough? Is a TV show really the answer? I still lust for the performance high and the attention, but at what cost? If I get on this show, I know it will be all-encompassing. Can I handle it? Can my marriage handle it? But something in my gut aches, telling me I must try. Maybe it's a foolish wish, but maybe this show can fill the holes in my heart.

53

BUDDHA IN A SHOE

At 6:00 am sharp, Ennio Morricone's *Love Theme* is growing louder and louder. I love waking up to this song. It brings such serenity. But today I'm ready to scream, *Shut up!* I fumble for my phone on my nightstand to silence the alarm; my purple wristband looks like a bruise on my arm. I have an hour to get my game face on and get on the road.

On the dining room table, I again pack my bag of performance essentials--extra makeup, change of shoes, clothes, curling iron, snacks, and water. I plot my drive to the arena in my head. Stephanie is going to arrive on her own time.

My husband appears and gives me a sleepy but reassuring hug before going to the kitchen to run the coffee grinder. The crunching noise startles me. My adrenaline is already pumping, probably much too soon. I reach for my bottle of Xanax in my purse. I don't want to lean on the med today to get me through the stressful parts, but I'm tempted to take one, to take the edge off. No, I can't be groggy. I must do this clean. But, I decide to bring the bottle with me.

"Say goodbye to Nicholas," I say to Neil, hustling to the car. "Will do. Break a leg," he answers, as he leans out the door. His tousled hair, wrinkled t-shirt, and sweatpants remind me it's Sunday; usually reserved for a relaxed routine of coffee, newspaper reading, and idle chatter. I wave goodbye.

Arriving near the arena, it is absolute mayhem: heavy traffic, large groups of people walking, traffic cops, street barriers, helicopters, friends and handwritten family support signs hung off cars and poles.

I'm not sure where to park, but I'm willing to pay the hefty price to leave the car as close to the arena as possible. I scan the nearby parking lots and screech into one with a quick hit of the breaks. "How much?" I ask the attendant.

"Thirty dollars and you're my last car. Pull straight ahead," he says, collecting my money.

I couldn't get any luckier. Being older and having money is working to my advantage. If I were my nineteen-year-old self in Minneapolis, I'd be taking a city bus here.

Gathering up my bags, I take a deep breath before opening the car door. The momentary silence is peaceful, soon be lost to a thousand voices across the street.

There is energy in the air, even from here, and my heart flutters with nervousness. I take another deep breath, close my eyes, and blow out through my nose. *Hold your horses, Laurie.*

There's my mom's voice creeping into my head. I had told her on previous days about the audition, but I kept her at arm's length in the details.

I walk directly into the sea of people making their way towards the arena. There is the copycat Michael Jacksons, flamboyant Lady Gagas, the country star cowboy hats, the long-haired metal heads, the drag queens and the Mohawk punks. I'm a conservative dresser in comparison: part rock 'n roll with skinny black jeans and lots of jewelry, and part singer-songwriter with a floral patterned long-sleeve blouse that's fitted at the waist.

We slowly shuffle into yesterday's parking lot, now transformed into small group areas sectioned off with yellow caution tape. Each area displays flying *X-Factor* flags and banners.

Trendy pop music, blaring out of strategically placed speakers, ensures no one can escape the music or occasional announcement. As we walk in together, we are told to move to the closest group on the left, and we follow instructions. We obediently stand in place waiting for more directions. When we're quarantined by tape to close off our section, it becomes clear they are herding us like cattle. Again, it's oddly reminiscent to the day before, except now I stand between Freddie Mercury and Madonna lookalikes.

Why would the show want us to stand outside again? I have a pinch to ask questions and push to the front, but I'm also patient- to see how this rolls out. Looking around, the same bewilderment is on most of the faces.

Stephanie calls, a sense of relief overcomes me, seeing her name on my phone. "Hey, how you doing?"

"Oh, I'm fine. It's early to wake up, but I'm managing. I don't think I'll be there any time soon, though. Maybe in an hour or so." Her voice is slow and grainy, sounding tired yet alert.

"Well, from what I can tell there is no rush for you to get here. I'm standing in the damn parking lot again. There are thousands of us, and no one knows what is going on. Occasionally they announce things will get started soon. Who knows what that means? Oh, and unless you like LMFAO pounding in your ears, you can probably take your time."

"Oh jeez, nice. Okay, I'll get coffee and start on my way at some point."

"Okay, cool. See you in a bit."

An announcement over the loudspeakers interrupts the end of our call.

"Welcome to audition day," proclaims a lively voice. When I catch a glimpse of the guy on a stage, sixty feet or so away, it's a young, blonde, Ryan Seacrest-looking guy. The crowd goes wild with applause and cheers. I applaud, too, this is finally starting!

"We're going to start letting everyone into the arena soon, so you can have your audition to be the next huge singing star..." The crowd again erupts, and he continues after a calculated pause. "But, first, we ask for your cooperation in helping us get some camera shots for the show to prove Los Angeles has the best singers in the world!"

Now the crowd really hoots, and I'm cheering with them. If this is what we must do to get in the arena, I'm game. Pop music still blasts over the speakers, and enthusiastic blonde-guy is screaming on top of the music: "Show the cameras how good you can dance! Show us your moves!"

A boom camera is grazing the top of the crowd near the stage. People's arms are raised high, indeed showing their moves.

Blonde guy's voice keeps overriding the music with a repeated, "Show us your best!" It's hard to resist when the music is loud, and excitement is in the air; so, I'm grooving, but I came here to sing. Others appear to have the same attitude. We're not making it on camera, so why expend any energy on lackluster dancing? Although, multiple Michael Jacksons in my area dance their hearts out. I wonder if they sing as good as they move.

The commands continue—dance! scream! clap and jump! - as cameras roll for crowd shots I assume to use in the show's opening sequence. *This* is why they got us here so early? To ask everyone to do the same thing over and over? And to scream? Really? Haven't they got the damn shot already? I'm done with feigning dance movements and I'm not going to scream along to any song. I need to preserve my voice.

In my area, dancing has stopped. Instead, those waiting to audition are talking to their supporters-or listening to their phones-or doing nervous sways back and forth with steely concentration on their faces.

It occurs to me, at this point, I need to preserve my feet, as well as my voice. I've been wearing 4-inch pumps, thinking I should be in full-audition mode, but we've been standing here close to an hour now. I pull them off and put on flats from my bag. As I place the black MRKT wedge pumps in my bag, I notice an inscription on the insole.

> \mär-ket\ - (noun) Date: 12th C. 1 (1): An open place where wo/men convene to believe in what's possible. (2): In the MARKET: potential to be seen. Act of discovery. I m a g i n e.

Holy shit, it's like Buddha in a shoe! It's serendipitous and so relevant. I want to show my shoe to the people around me, but Freddie Mercury and Madonna have moved away. Now, I wish Steph were here. She'd like this: my shoes are a public service announcement.

Without the nerve to show off my insole to strangers, I place them in my bag. I'm frustrated and uncomfortable standing so long. I cover my ears to muffle the same annoying voice pouring from the loudspeakers. Tick-fucking-tock: time is moving at a standstill.

Steph calls, spurring me to a happier place.

"Hey, I parked, and I'm walking in. People are still in the parking lot?"

"Yup, we're still here. It's been a dance-along for the cameras. Come on in," I say sarcastically.

"Are you kidding? They haven't opened the doors?" "Nope. This is fucked up," I reply with contempt. "Where are you exactly?"

I guide her on the phone until we finally meet up. She's distracted by all the colorful costumes and the crowd. The intense sound of a helicopter nearby makes it impossible to hear anything. "They're doing a flyover of the crowd. Those assholes. They want us to act like idiots," I shout.

By the fourth flyover, the crowd has lost all interest. A lot of impatient scowls everywhere I look. Some now protest by flipping off the helicopter as it flies over. I'm laughing and sighing at the same time.

We've been standing outside for close to two hours with no progress moving inside. Restless and annoyed, I have no problem raising my middle finger in the air at the next flyover.

54

A GOLDEN TICKET

After waiting three hours in the parking lot, Steph and I finally set our feet inside the arena. An intense smell of hot dogs and popcorn permeates the welcome air-conditioning. For a while in that parking lot, I felt like one of the forgotten thousands, the wannabees. Is there *really* anything special about my singing? About any of us? However, at long last, my impatience and doubt morph into importance and purpose. I have something to prove. The energy in the lobby is like right before a rock concert.

People dart in and out of the crowd, racing to their seats. They scamper everywhere, shouting instructions and directions to friends. Some are already in tears, probably due to stress.

Steph and I stop and take a breath, as more people swarm past us into the arena. I grab Steph's arm to guide her in the direction I think we should go, but realize we need to walk halfway around the arena to find our seats.

"I wonder if the guys got in?" questions Steph. "I'm sure they're somewhere."

Walking to find our seats, people are in nooks and corners rehearsing and preparing. Some have brought folding mirrors to practice in front of or put on makeup. Others are deep in absorption, looking at sheet music or listening to their phones. A hipster teenager listens to a cassette Walkman. *Wow*. I can't help but ponder how each person, like me, has a wish and expectation for this day, and most will never even make the show. It's daunting to look too long at any of them, I feel their heightened awareness of what is about to happen.

When we reach our section and enter with a view of the full arena, I'm taken aback by the number of people in seats and the deafening noise level. The house lights are glaring, making it feel like a sporting event. Steph distracts me.

"Hey, look. I see the guys. There's our section right above us."

Sure enough, there sits Jackson, Jacob, and Trey. They look like lifeboats in a sea of craziness. They stand and wave us over.

"Ladies! Welcome," Jackson beams, extending a friendly hand.

"Wow, so these are our seats? We sure *are* all together! How long have you guys been here?" marvels Steph.

"Not long, maybe twenty minutes or so. How are you feeling, Laurie?" Jackson asks.

"Fine. Tired, but fine," I answer. "The whole wait outside was ridiculous, but at least we're in. How are you Jackson, Trey? You ready?"

"I'm ready to sing, girl! But whew, what a wait," Jackson proclaims as he fans his face with his hand.

"Yeah, I don't think I could have stomached another obnoxious pop song, but I'm ready to roll," Trey chats, giving a thumb up.

I take my seat furthest in from the aisle. Stephanie follows, one position closer to the guys. Jackson sits next to her, then Trey and Jacob by the aisle.

As I slip back into my high heels, I realize I've never been in here before. I understood it opened in the late 1950s and the city is considering tearing it down to make way for a new one. There must have been glorious past concerts and sporting events here. This place is legendary, but for now, the seats are tiny, hard, with cracked, blue vinyl cushions that lost their padding long ago. The armrests are fatigued wood, profoundly marked with dents and stains. My knees touch the seat in front of me, and I'm not that tall at 5'6". Jackson is over six feet, two-hundred pounds and some change and stuffed uncomfortably like a grown man in a highchair.

People file into seats next to us, above us, below us. The frenzy picks up even more, as I realize the auditions will start.

We are on the second level up from the floor, the loge level. Looking down, I can see every section below us is full, encompassing the whole circumference of the arena.

"Guys look at the booths on the arena floor. I guess that's where we'll audition?" I say, pointing.

"Ya, I just counted and there are twenty-four booths," said Jackson. "That's not enough to get all these people through in a couple hours. We're here for a long-haul, people," he proclaims.

"Well, at least the temperature in here is good," I say. "It's comfortable. Better than outside."

We all sit still, awestruck. Event workers mill around the arena floor. They wear protocol black t-shirts, black pants. Then producers of the show appear and start entering the booths, two at a time. They are dressed professionally: some men are in collared shirts or suit jackets over white t-shirts, women in dresses or trendy clothes. How can there be so many producers? I wonder about their qualifications and what instructions they have received from the top brass. Have they been advised only to consider singers with big voices? Alternatively, just younger singers who they think will have the stamina for a career?

"They asked us to prepare three songs, but I don't know how anyone would get through one. There are just too many people," Trey says, perhaps sensing what we're all processing.

"Yeah, I don't know either, but don't you think one song is all they need to tell if you can sing or not?" speculates Jackson.

"I guess that's why it's so important to choose the right song," I reply. The statement pushes a gulp to my belly. "Meanwhile, I'm heading back out to the ladies' room. There was a long line when we came in. Of course, I'm sure you guys noticed the men's room had no line."

"Hey, actually I heard they're going to open up some of the men's rooms for the women or just make them unisex. As they should be anyway," Jackson advises.

"Agree, Steph, you need to go?" Steph waves me off, opting to stay behind.

I make my way back to the corridor, still bustling with activity as more people arrive. Thankfully, there is no line when I arrive at the ladies' room. I'm unsurprised to find a bevy of women clamored up to the mirrors. They reapply makeup and take their first of many repeat glances. Thank God, there is a full-length mirror. I inch in and grab a glance at the woman reflecting. Am I a super star singer? Am I the "one?" Flipped blonde hair from another woman flings into my face, testing my nerves. She doesn't apologize, and I use it as a cue to leave and to stop taking this audition or myself too seriously. Yet, the excitement in the air is like standing in line before a roller-coaster ride.

I duck and dodge to the sink. There are teenagers all the way up to a 70-year-old looking woman, all trying to put on their best faces. The aromas of perfume and makeup powder remind me of musical theater and curtain calls. I talk myself out of the urge to apply more makeup, not wanting to cake up my face so early in the day.

I arrive back to our seats just in time to observe the crowd settling down. The organizers have taken the floor and are asking for everyone's attention.

"I think this thing is going to start," Trey exults, clapping. We all stand.

"We'll see," Jacob whispers.

"Welcome everyone! Welcome! We have finally reached the audition stage," resounds a man with a microphone standing on the arena floor near section one. His hip business suit and resilient, deep radio voice indicate he's *the* official event producer. When the applause of the excited crowd quiets, he continues.

"We hope all of you know how important this day is. This is the day you will be discovered. The day we will help new singers, new talent, and the next entertainment icon fulfill their destiny. This audition is very important to our show, to the entertainment industry and, most importantly, to you, the gifted talent who have come before us!"

I laugh out loud at the talent comment. "Talent? Really? If I recall correctly, on their website, it referred to us as contestants." Trey and Jackson both nod but continue gawking at the announcer. He continues with propaganda talk, then finally gets to the much-needed specifics. "We will audition by sections, starting with the section directly in front of me, section one." The people in that section give a unified loud roar.

"We will go row by row, within each section, and move on to the next section in numerical order. When we finish this first level of the arena, we will move on to the second level."

We share desperate looks, and I start doing the math. There are at least eighteen sections on the first level. We are in the ninth section on the second level. Twenty-six sections will audition before we have our chance. There are twelve seats per row and at least twenty-two rows to each section. With approximately 264 people per section and twenty-six sections, that is almost 7,000 people. Considering half of those people are guests and family, that leaves nearly 3,000 people ahead of us to audition. This is nuts.

"I do want to remind people to please remain patient. We will eventually get to your section. You are all important to us. Please keep in mind, in fairness, your seat and section are based on your arrival time yesterday," he goes on, the hoopla sounds patronizing.

He continues to explain that only the person auditioning will have access to the floor where the booths are. Their companions must remain in their seats. Further, you must show your purple wristband to security, to prove you're the one auditioning, along with a seat ticket, to prove you're in the appropriate designated section to audition.

The audience has remained calm, focused on these instructions until this point. "After your audition, two things could happen. One, you may be given a gold ticket and asked to continue to the next level," he reveals. Cheers and applause erupt around the arena. He holds his hand up to calm the crowd and continues. "If this is the case, you will be guided to another area in the arena to continue. If the unfortunate happens, and you are not asked to continue, you will need to leave the arena immediately," he says with calculated gloom. Boos echo around the arena. "If this happens, you cannot return to your seat, so please bring your personal belongings with you to the audition floor or leave them with your guests. They will need to meet you outside. Once again, if you are *not* asked to continue in the competition, you will leave the arena immediately and cannot return to your seat."

"That's cold." Jackson cringes.

"Thank you for coming, everyone, and let's get this audition started," he says, handing off the microphone to a production staffer. The producer raises his hands high above his head and claps strong and consistent like a cheerleader until Top-40 recorded pop music erupts from the sound system. Thunderous applause from the arena crowd takes over. Some people are hugging and some high-fiving.

"Well, here we go everyone, here we go," Jackson yells over the applause and music.

I nod and rock my body side to side, just as anxious as the next person. We all eye the floor to watch the remaining producers enter the booths. Security personnel begin to line up auditionees from the first section into lines in front of the twenty-four booths. Within twenty minutes, they start sending contestants into the booths, followed by instant applause from the crowd.

Moments later, one of the first to audition comes out of his booth with an enormous smile. He thrust the first gold ticket high up in the air. The arena explodes in even more thunderous applause. The ticket indeed is gold and shiny and large enough to remind me of *Willy Wonka and the Chocolate Factory*. The song *I've Got a Golden Ticket* dances into my mind. It's a sweet song, reminds me of childhood. With each couple of minutes, more and more auditionees come out of other booths and put their hands high in the air, showing off their gold tickets.

When leaving the booth, some scream in excitement or perhaps shock as they exit; others do their version of a happy dance. A good many look up at the sky, pointing to their idea of God above. The arena applause continues to support those on the floor, but each round gets less and less clapping from us high up in the arena.

"So, is everyone getting a gold ticket?" I remark. "It almost looks that way," Steph replies.

"Maybe everyone in section one *is* that fantastic?" Trey joins in with a bit of sarcasm. "Seriously you guys, not one person has walked the other direction. I find it strange that all of them sing that good."

The crowd flares up, again, into a massive roar, and we all take notice of commotion on the floor. A tiny and frail old woman, bending over her walker, has just come out of one of the audition booths. Her one hand balances and holds her walker, as her other hand shoves her gold ticket as high up in the air as her frail arm can push. I applaud to support her sheer effort and ability, not for singing, but for merely standing. Did she wait through this whole audition process, standing in the parking lot yesterday?

"Okay, what is going on here?" blurts Trey. "That's great for the old lady, but can Grandma sing *that* well? It's a mercy pass putting her through. Um, and a little late in life to chase your dreams?"

I stare at Trey, flabbergasted by his ignorant comment. "Hey, everybody has dreams, Trey. Can't take that away no matter the age," I chime in.

Trey looks at me, then at his feet. I hope he's embarrassed. The crowd's cheers and support die down a bit after grandma.

As people continue to stream out of booths, holding up their gold tickets, the crowd now responds with minimal applause. Most people have taken their seats.

"Oh, oh wait," Stephanie yells out frantically. She points towards the arena floor, her finger moving up and down. "That woman down there we've seen around the last couple days. She's about to go into a booth. Laurie, remember her? The trashy, drugged-up-stripper-looking lady who was wobbling all over the place yesterday, and we saw her again this morning!"

I scan the floor in the direction of Stephanie's finger. "Oh, hell yes, I remember! She was a mess, right? Actually, how is it she is in the first section?" I ask shaking my head.

"Who knows, but there is no way in hell she'll get through. She is not here to sing. The way she walked around socializing. I think she's here just to say she was here."

All our eyes are fixated on this woman as she enters her booth. As if her audition will be deciding the legitimacy of the entire competition. In less than a minute, trashy lady comes out of her booth. She pauses and looks around, as if not knowing where to go. She is led by security in the other direction, the *No* direction, the walk to leave the building.

She walks in a fast pace in her spiked heels with a flutter in her step; appearing slightly embarrassed, shrugging, though not terribly tainted by rejection. She acts as if she has somewhere else to go; her hands boldly waving to the crowd sitting above the exit corridor. Even waving off some of those giving a supportive clap in her direction. For a fleeting moment, my heart sinks for her.

55

REPRESENTATION

"Oh, I know those guys!" Jackson blurts out, interrupting the silence and boredom. He points to the third section making their way to the floor. "Where?" I ask.

"Look, those two guys, both wearing black in the back of the line for booth two?"

"Ah yeah, yup, see 'em. Who are they?"

"Actually, they're two fantastic singers who are singing as a duo. I know them from one of the shows I did here in L.A. a few years back. They have representation, so that's how they got in that third section. They didn't have to sit through yesterday," Jackson finishes.

As I sit stunned by Jackson's comment, I realize I was a fool to think we were all here as part of an open audition. I take my eyes off the guys on the floor and jerk my head towards Jackson.

"So, you mean they're planted? Their reps got them the audition, so they just walked in today to an assigned seat?" I cross my arms and wait for his response.

Jackson is feverishly texting as he continues to look up from his phone and back down to the floor. He pauses before he answers. He finishes the text without looking at me, his eyes on the floor. "Yup, they're a walk in, and they're good, too. I'm sure they'll get through. I'm texting one of the guys now."

He jumps up and raises his hands high above his head, as he tries to get their attention. One of them looks up at our section taking a moment to find Jackson. He throws his hands up and waves.

"So, aren't you at all bothered they just walk in, and we had to sit through yesterday and today?"

Jackson looks resolved as he shrugs and sits back down. "No, I'm not bothered. They're good, and they have a rep. They deserve to be there. If I had the right rep, I would have done the same thing. I'm sure there are tons of people who have reps and skipped the initial process. That's part of the game. Laurie, all the shows do it! This show isn't different," confesses Jackson. He gives me a sweet wink. "Come on, Laurie. You know the deal, you've had representation. You'd do it too if you could. Unless you find sitting here more enjoyable?"

Trey and Jacob listen intently, while Jackson continues reluctantly. "Look, Laurie, just because my friends are in that section doesn't guarantee they'll move on or make it on the show. It just gets them into the process faster."

By the time he is done talking, the duo has walked into the audition booth. With less than a minute passing, they come back out holding up their gold tickets. Jackson leaps out of his seat and applauds loudly. He gives a fist pump in the air and finishes with a wave. They wave back and beam with smiles so large, their teeth gleam. "Yes!" Jackson screams loudly. I never rise from my seat. I remain with my legs and arms crossed.

As he sits back down, he continues. "See, I don't like sitting up here either, but seeing that they are going through gives me hope. Now I know the producers recognize genuine talent. If they recognize those guys, they'll recognize me. I don't care how people get in the door. It's what they do once they're inside."

I'm not at all okay with this setup, but Jackson has a point. There was a time I had a talent agent in San Antonio, Austin, *and* New York.

56

TOO OLD FOR THIS SHIT

Trey rapidly rises from his seat. "I need some air," he interrupts. "This whole audition process is bizarre and listening to you two talk about representation. Fuck this. I'm going for a walk." He departs down the stairs without waiting for a response from anyone.

"I'll come too." Jacob runs to catch up with Trey. It must be hard for them to learn this audition might not be as open as they thought.

Jackson watches the boys depart down the stairs. He doesn't appear concerned with Trey's comment, and his demeanor is calm. However, I'm still frustrated. He looks at me and continues speaking. "Don't worry, sweetie; we'll move on, too. This is no different from any other audition except you and I are up here. The door wasn't already open for us to breeze in and display our talent. But, we will, we will."

Damn, he is convincing. But the longer I sit, the less convinced I am that I'll be able to display my talent.

I pause to center my thoughts. Jackson smiles warmly, and I'm encouraged to go on. "Jackson, maybe I'm getting too old for this shit, and I just don't have the patience anymore."

He reaches over and gently pats my leg. "Sweetheart, we all are, but I'm not dead yet, so I'm still gonna try."

What is getting to me now is the time I could be focusing on my music: writing and playing guitar at home. Instead, I'm sitting for hours, waiting to sing a few words to convince someone my wait was worth it to them. Alternatively, to convince myself the wait was worth it for me.

"Steph, do you want to take a walk?" I ask, thinking of food and singing.

Steph moves out of her seat and stretches. She's been quiet through the whole Jackson exchange, though she looked up on and off between texting.

"Jackson, you want to come too?" Steph asks.

"I'll stay and watch our stuff. I might even take a cat nap," he says with another smile. His calmness and stamina are attractive, and I hope, contagious.

After buying nachos for Steph, we find a semi-quiet place to sit on the corridor floor. Various small groups have clustered together to eat, chat or rehearse. Some are asleep. There is even a couple making out.

We sit in silence as we eat and watch the comings and goings around us.

"Hey, I'm going to run a couple of these songs by you. I'll sing right out here. Everyone else is." I take a few steps back from where Steph is sitting, and I start to sing the first song.

Stephanie is a captive audience or pretends so, as she listens to my *a cappella* version of *Make You Feel My Love* by Bob Dylan, while continuing to enjoy her nachos. One nacho at a time, she keenly watches and intently listens. She never breaks my gaze, reaching for each nacho, quietly munching.

After I've finished a few bars, Stephanie sets down the nacho remains. "So, is that the song you'll audition with?"

"Well, it's one of three. It's the one I like a lot, but I don't know if it's the best for me."

"Well, you have such a strong voice, Laurie. Like when you sing Janis Joplin songs and the hard rock stuff is amazing. Not many people can sing that strong. You sing this song nice, but I don't know why you're not doing something more rock. Just saying." She turns back to her nachos. Her interest seems genuine, but so does her hunger. Also, she's right. I sang strong as hell in the metal band. Damn, where is my mojo?

Steph put the empty nacho container to her side. "So, what else do you have?"

"Okay, check this out. This is an old bluesy rock song I used to audition for *RENT*. It got me call-backs, so I must be doing something right with it." I start *Guilty*.

It is so strange to sing directly to one person, almost too intimate. It's easier to sing to a thousand than to one. You don't know if you should look straight into someone's eyes. Should you keep your eyes closed the whole time? It's always been a weird predicament at any audition or intimate performance. Standing here in the middle of a crowded corridor with people passing to our left and right, and various sounds coming from all directions, singing straight to Steph is like trying to serenade someone on a corner in Times Square.

"Well, I like that one better," beams Steph and applauds. "But, it's still not like rock or strong as I'd expect from you."

I drop my shoulders in frustration.

"Oh, I'm sorry, Laurie. I don't want to confuse you anymore. I really shouldn't comment. I'm not a musician. I don't know what I'm talking about."

"Steph, no, you're right, and you don't need to be a musician to know when something sounds right or not. I'm just not prepared for this. I should be walking in here all balls-to-the-wall with attitude, knowing exactly what I'm doing. Like Jackson. I thought I was ready for this!" I plop back down to the floor, defeated.

"Laurie, I didn't say it was bad. I just said it's not what I was expecting. Please, don't assume that Jackson is all that confident. He's nervous, too. He keeps wiping his hands on his pants like his palms are wet. Oh, let's not even get started on Trey. He's so young--this is probably one of his first auditions ever. Just relax. You'll be fine, no matter what." She smiles and gently rubs my arm before getting up to toss out the empty container.

She's right, and yet so wrong. She's right that the other guys probably have a decent amount of nerves about all of this, and maybe they're not as prepared as I think they are. However, she's wrong that *I'll be fine no matter what.* I'm worried. This is my last chance at music success. My Hail Mary.

"I'm going to the bathroom. You need to go too?" Steph asks.
"No, I'm gonna call my mom. My head is swimming. I'll see you back at the seats."

"Okie-dokie." Steph departs, I dial my mom and walk to the glass doors looking out to the parking lot. The sunlight is uplifting.

"Oh, Laurie. Hello! Your number came up. That is so neat."
"Yup, caller ID is kinda cool, Mom, isn't it?" I say. Now in her seventies, I marvel at her awkward adjustment to technology.
"Yes, but I haven't figured out everyone's number yet, but I

got your number," she jokes. "You get it, Laurie? I got your number?"

"Oh, my God, Mom, yes. I get it."

After I share my current feelings of audition dread and insecurity, she offers her support as best she can.

"Why, you're so good, honey. You shouldn't worry! You'll be on the show, and I can't wait to see you on TV!

While she may think, her words are uplifting, I take as added pressure to make her happy.

"I'm getting too old, Mom. Like this isn't my thing anymore. I'm out of sync. I don't know who I am!"

"Well, honey, you have to make choices. Maybe it is time to hang the whole thing up."

"Wait, all of it? The music?"

"No, not music, but pursing some big dream. Maybe you should be at home focusing on your marriage and be with Nicholas. You're the one who chose that path." *She* is saying this?

"But why can't I have both?" I whine.

Now I'm filling with frustration. I called her for support and am getting conflict. This reminds me of the grind of the business: the choices to stay in or not, the lovers to keep or leave. Most of all, the need for acceptance.

57

TICKET EXCHANGE

Sitting back in the arena, Jackson and Steph have lost themselves in cellphone video games. We're now at four hours. I've been trying to settle in at my seat, coping with stress and boredom. I hear guitar playing in the distance and the aroma of weed tickles my nose.

Jacob and Trey spring up the stairs and swiftly make an announcement. They've found a flaw in the system that will possibly enable us to audition within the next thirty minutes to an hour.

As the three of us sit with our mouths gaping, Trey packs up his backpack like a teenager on last day of high school. Jacob takes a deep breath before continuing to explain.

"Check this out..." He lowers his voice when he notices people behind us listening in. "You know how we all have a wristband and a ticket? Well, the three of you singing *need* that purple wrist-band to get on the floor, but you also need a ticket, too, to prove you're in the section that is currently auditioning.

That is the key to audition sooner: the ticket. All you need is *a* ticket *from* that section that is auditioning in the next half hour or so."

"Huh?" puzzled Stephanie, leaning in more closely.

"Well, we know that everyone here has a ticket to a section-auditionees and supporters," Jacob goes on. "Auditionees need to show their purple wristband *and* their ticket that shows their section to access the floor. The auditionees represent only half of any section's tickets. The rest are supporters. The supporters don't *need* their tickets now that they are in their seats. The event people don't know which section people belong to until it's time to go to the floor. So, when the time comes to go to the floor, if you have that purple wristband *and* that section's ticket, that's all the event people look at: the wristband and the ticket."

We sit still, quietly listening. I'm not sure what to make of the situation. Jacob tilts his head to the side.

"So basically..." he pauses to find the correct words. "We made a deal with some people we met down below. Their section is about to audition in the next fifteen minutes. One of the supporters of one of the auditionees has given Trey their ticket to *their* section, so when that section is called, Trey will jump in with them and walk down to the floor. He already has the purple wristband. All he needs is that section's ticket," Jacob pauses, smiles. "Now he has it."

With that delivery, Trey looks at all of us and in a matter-of-fact tone says. "I'm going now, guys. I can't wait anymore. I found a faster way in and I'm taking it."

Jackson, Steph and I trade surprised glances.

"Well, hell yes!" Jackson announces suddenly. "Good for you, Trey! I'm gonna go find a friend and get a ticket, too." He pauses for a beat and adds in Trey's direction, "Well, after you *actually* get past security." He finishes with a laugh. Trey doesn't look at Jackson. He's ready to roll.

Trey hugs Jacob and gives him a fist pump. "Thanks for sticking with me, man." He nods at the rest of us. Throwing his bag over his shoulder, he darts down the stairs.

Jacob stays back and nervously places his hands on the top of his head before he plops down in his seat. "I hope this works for him, since he's rushing it and all."

The rest of us are stunned. We sit in silence. I'm nervous for him to pass security, but I'm also concerned about his audition. I hope the kid is ready. I don't think he took any time to warm-up and prepare.

As we wait and converse, Jackson notices Trey near the arena floor. It's only been about twenty minutes since he left.

"Look down there! He is walking in with that group. Oh, my God, he did get past security," Jackson exclaims, rising to his feet. "Whoa! Look at him! He's there!" Stephanie joins in and stands up.

"Holy shit--he made it," I say, stunned. I slowly rise out of my seat watching him on the arena floor.

Trey proceeds to one of the groups waiting in front of the many audition booths.

Trey ends up being the tenth person in line behind one of the booths closest to our side of the arena. He looks up in our direction to find us. Jackson starts dramatically waving his arms down towards Trey, and the rest of us join in.

"I just got a text from Trey. *Hold up*. He says he sees us, but he doesn't want to draw attention to himself by waving," Jacob reports. "Oh, he also says someone in a booth one over is doing the same audition song *he* is. He's nervous now. No more texts."

We take our seats. Time is passing in slow motion as Trey makes his way, one step at a time, to the actual audition booth.

When Trey finally enters the booth, I hold my breath. Other booths are still releasing contestants with gold tickets, but more and more are being released in the other direction, not advancing. If Trey makes it through this first stage, it not only means he's good enough to get to the next level, but his plan opens the opportunity for all of us to audition sooner.

The people behind us stir, and talk softly, assumingly about us. They've become more aware that this kid, who was just sitting with us, is now auditioning. Their curiosity makes me uneasy. I'm afraid they'll figure it out and tell security. Before I can become too interested in their conversation, Trey comes out the other side of the booth.

He pauses for a brief second, looking down at the floor. Next, he holds the gold ticket high in the air with his left hand. He makes a fist with the other hand and pumps it in the air.

We erupt in screams and clapping. Trey gives a big wave up towards us with a big, beaming smile. He starts to jump up and down, his fist held high, swinging the gold ticket like a victory flag.

Jacob's eyes follow Trey as he walks in the direction the gold ticket holders are ushered. "I just got another text, guys. I should meet him down below quick before he moves to a different part of the arena for the next audition."

Jacob takes off down the stairs to meet Trey, and we plop back in our seats. We high-five each other joyously.

"Whew, that was crazy!" gasps Stephanie.

Jackson doesn't get too comfortable before he blurts out, "Ladies, I'm going in, too. I'm going to the bathroom to spritz my voice, mist this handsome face, and find a ticket friend."

"So, you're going to go *smitz*?" I ask with a laugh.

"Ha! Yes, darling, *smitz*," he replies with his hearty laugh. "I like that one. Did you just make it up? Because I'm gonna steal it."

"Yup, it's all yours, my friend."

Jackson stands. "Well, my time sitting in this smaller-than-small with small sauce seat has ended. My ass is moving on to bigger things." He looks in my direction. "Either I see you at the next level, Laurie, or I'm out the door walking the exit of shame." I smile back at Jackson, but my heart sinks. I have no doubt *he'll* be going on to the next level. I'm just not 100 percent convinced that I will.

"Are you going to try too, Laurie?" Jackson says. "I don't know. We'll see."

Jackson's bags are in his hand. He gives us both a hug. "Okay girls. I'll post updates on Facebook."

"Go get 'em, Tiger!" Stephanie says.

Without a look back, Jackson bounds down the stairs with the strength of a linebacker and the grace of Gene Kelly.

Steph and I sit in silence, eyes glazing over. I'm trying to digest it all and feel lost without Trey and Jackson. I thought we would all be auditioning at the same time, all on the floor together. Anything that resembles community, a band, brings me comfort.

Jacob returns and joins us. "So, I saw Trey, and he is on his way to the next round. Looks like I gotta stay up here until the main arena auditions finish. Then I can join him."

"How long before he auditions again?" I ask.

"I'm not sure. They told him it could be hours before Round Two and to prepare for an all-night process."

"All-night process?" I squeal. "So even if I jump ahead as he did, I'm still looking at an all-nighter if I make it past this round?" Jacob nods reluctantly. "Trey will be texting me through the whole process. Yeah, believe me, I gotta wait here all night, too.

There is nothing I can do, he's my ride."

"There is no way I can pull an all-nighter here with you, Laurie," Steph inserts as she gently places her hand on my arm.

"Steph, you can leave any time you want. I would never expect you to sit here all night."

"Well, I've stayed this long, I'd like to watch you get through the First Round. But if you wait for your normal time slot, I don't know if I can wait that long."

"I know." I have no other words to offer. I'm too nervous. This is happening too fast.

"Do you want me to go find you a friend in one of those sections below, so you can do this now?"

I shrug, still nothing to say.

At least twenty minutes have gone by when Stephanie announces a Jackson sighting. "Look way over on the other side of the arena. You can see him, in his green sweater, standing in the second line."

Jacob and I stand, surveying the other side of the arena. "I see him!" I say. I'm so happy he made it to the floor, and I'm not surprised he made a friend and was able to get a ticket.

"I'm looking at his Facebook post. He's ready to sing his ass off," Steph says.

Jackson moves through the line faster than Trey. *Maybe the auditions are running faster now?* I can imagine producers in those booths are getting tired, too.

When he's at the booth entrance, we lose sight of him, though he must have entered. But, we can see the exit side of his booth and the wait for him to exit, pure torture. At least four minutes have passed, and Jackson is still in there.

"I wonder what's taking so long," says Jacob.

"Who knows? Maybe he has more to sing," I add, with no idea what is taking him longer.

With a sudden burst, Jackson struts out of the booth, regal and glorious like a lion. He's holding a gold ticket in the air with pride, smiling from ear to ear.

"Yes!" I yell. I'm so proud of him. Stephanie and Jacob give shouts and clap along.

"Well, you're next, Laurie. You wanna try this?" Stephanie raises the question again. My mouth goes dry and my chest tightens.

"I don't know, Steph. I'm not one to go up and ask someone for their ticket."

Stephanie replies with a huff. "Well, I am. I don't give a fuck so it's easy for me!"

"Okay, okay," I finally concede waving her off. That seems to ease her tension and she gives a thumb's up. Jacob, too, lets out a sigh of relief.

58

NOW OR NEVER

While Stephanie searches for a ticket friend, Jacob has been telling me about his relationship with his brother. I have a genuine interest in what he's saying but my attention goes in and out. I dart my eyes between his face and the staircase leading up to us. I've become nervous as all hell.

I need to prepare: to warm up and get focused. If I'm going to do this, I might as well be tip-top. Before I can get in that head space, I need to know if Steph was successful.

"Laurie! I got the ticket!" Steph blurts out, running up the stairs. "I made a trade, but you must go now." She doesn't give a shit who can hear her around us.

Jacob and I shoot each other a quick glance, then look down at the ticket. He smiles in reassurance. I return the smile.

I jump to my feet. "Where?" I ask, grabbing my stuff.

"That section down there." Steph points to a section below us, close to the center of the arena. "They're the next section going so we have to hurry and get down there."

Without delay, I grab my bag and purse and ask, "How did you do it? How did you get the ticket?"

Steph replies with more ease, now that she's taken a breath and calmed down. "I just started chatting with this lady and her family, but it doesn't matter, let's go!"

"Okay!" I exit the row, stop dead in my tracks and turn to Steph and Jacob, "Guys, guys, I haven't even warmed up. Shit, I haven't even looked in the mirror for hours. I'm not ready at all!" The people in the row behind us again take notice of our commotion. They are now intently watching us, but this time I don't give a shit. I'm more concerned with my own predicament.

"I don't know what to tell you, Laurie. I mean, I don't know what it takes for you to get ready, but if you want to jump ahead in this process, you need to do this now. This is it," barks Steph.

"Go for it," adds Jacob. He shrugs and grins.

I look at both with surprised confusion. I'm getting advice from the two people in the group who are *not* singers. I need a sane artist's mind right now because I think mine is about to make a wrong decision. Then again, when is an artist's mind ever sane?

"Steph, let's do this."

We hustle down the steps in a hurried mess, jumping over camps of people who have moved from their seats and taken over landings and hallways. As time progressed, fire codes and security efforts have lost out to mass numbers of tired auditionees taking over the arena. Maybe this is an excellent time to jump a line. Why wait? Waiting fucks things up anyway; this I've learned.

59

GAME ON

Steph and I enter the next level down in the arena and make our way to an opening above the last row of seats going down to the floor. Steph points to the section I need to go.

"You need to get closer to that group as they're now starting to get up from their seats. They'll soon be walking this way. Just get in line when they pass. I swear, no one will notice. I've been watching this process for a while," she says softly, covering her mouth.

A staff worker strides towards us with auditionees following. He's leading that section to move to the floor. He's looking down, his hand up to his ear holding a walkie-talkie. He doesn't notice us standing to the side.

He passes, and a group of auditionees trail behind him in a loosely formed but straight line. Their nervous, anxious faces suggest the anticipated audition is nearly upon them. They wear the same-colored wristband as me.

"This is your group," mutters Steph.

I look for an opening. If I jump in front of anyone in the line, it will be strange and noticeable. Yet everyone has their heads down, as if sulking, moving along, led blindly.

The end of the line appears--my chance to jump in. Except another staff member brings up the end of the line. There is no way I can cut in front of him unless I lie that I was in the bathroom and I'm jumping back in my group.

Suddenly, the line stops hard. Thirty or more people ahead pause, and the effect trickles back to us like dominos and the staffer at the end moves to the front to assist. The congestion is from the contestants stopping to show their ticket to a security guard; he grants access down an additional flight of stairs to the arena floor. We're stuck, and this couldn't have worked out any better.

I pass Steph a look and give her a nod. I assume she knows what I'm thinking: I'm joining the line right here. She backs away to stand up against the wall, and I examine the people in line behind me. They haven't noticed my position. Most have earbuds in, heads down, singing to themselves.

The line moves again and, without hesitation, as if on cue, I become part of it. I don't gaze back to see where Steph is. I don't look any other direction but straight ahead, where an imposing security guard in black jeans and t-shirt awaits, looking at tickets and wristbands. Game on.

60

STAND ON THE X

Eyeing the staffer at the head of our group on the arena floor; she doesn't appear ready for us yet; she's still gathering people to her. I up the volume of the music on my iPhone and wait. Two full days of laborious waiting have led me to this moment. Finally, now at 5pm, I'm here.

Before I realize it, her lips are moving. I yank out my buds. "So, you can pick any booth you want. Just let us know as you reach the front of the line." She pauses for a moment and looks over the jittery group like a schoolteacher. "Once in your audition booth, only speak and sing when directed, okay? At the end of your audition, you will either be provided a gold ticket to continue to the next round, or you will be told to leave the building, and your journey is over. Most importantly, please do not question the producers, staff members or security for answers beyond this. A security member will guide you where to go after your audition." With a tinge of annoyance in her voice and a look of disgust like she just smelled a bad fart, she delivers her final command. "And please, do not touch the producers." She nods our direction to make sure we've all understood her comments. I look around to nodding heads, amused. I'm here to sing, not touch anyone.

I take a couple of heavy breaths. The acoustics from this concrete floor must be horrible when you're in the booth. The ability to hear yourself limited. Looking at the twenty-four systematically placed private booths at this closer range, staged side-by-side, twelve on each side of the arena, enclosed by black drapes that appear thick and heavy, I can see this setup is hardly ideal for singing. The entrances to the booths are on our side, the exit on the other, like a carnival funhouse. And with my cold and unsteady voice = lousy combo.

I look to the front of the line where people are choosing their booth. I'm about twentieth, and they are moving people quickly, progressing much faster than I would have thought. I have no time to fix my makeup or hair.

I'm next in line to choose my audition booth. It's like the lottery or, worse yet, Russian Roulette. The producer in one booth may totally hate me, he's had enough rocker, bluesy-type singers today, but the producer in the next booth over may love me because she hasn't seen enough. This is crazy! My stomach aches: pains of stress poke my insides like a knife. I'm my own worst enemy. I always have been.

"Do you have a booth choice?" A voice breaks through my thoughts. Asking is a tall, bearded and pleasant twenty-something production guy, in the same black clothes attire as the security guard and the rest of the show staff. Before he has the chance to ask again I blurt out, "Booth seventeen or eighteen, right there." I point and smile.

"Alright," he smiles. I move around him and walk ten feet to take my place in the next line. A new mix of people are in line with me, and the frantic looks on their faces just about matches how I feel inside: excited, nervous, energized, riding the audition high and freaked the hell out. Is this really what I want? To be on this show?

My legs tremble again, like a soft earthquake, my mouth goes dry, and my palms gain all the moisture that left. To slake the continuing dryness in my mouth, I reach into my bag for my steel water bottle; it's empty. *Shit.* Maybe I look as nervous as Venice Guy told me I did when I first got on the arena floor.

As I wait, the sounds distract me. More clapping and cheering from the crowd above and Walkie-talkies buzzing on event worker's belts.

A male contestant, a few booths away is singing the Journey song, *Don't Stop Believing.* He sounds just like Steve Perry. I'm encouraged, hearing the lyrics. Moreover, soothed by the familiarly in his voice, reminding me of my teen years and that first rock concert, Rush, that changed my life. Now I feel this moment is another life changer.

The closest audition staffer on the arena floor wearily looks in my direction, "You're next in the audition booth. Wait for me to tell you to go."

Next? On cue, my legs tremble. Again. I've only been on the arena floor thirty minutes. I firmly place my hands on the top of my thighs, hoping the pressure will stop the shaking.

The singers occupying the booths in front of me sound drastically different. The singer in booth 18 is good. She has a big voice. She's doing a Whitney Houston song, and even though she's not as spectacular, she's just as loud. I'd prefer not to follow her. I can barely make out what the one in 17 is singing--her voice is faint--I need her to finish so I can get in there so my damn legs will stop shaking and I can do what I came to do. Sing! My voice may be cold, but I'm ready to roll.

When the contestant in eighteen finishes, they gasp in excitement and then there is a lull from inside the booth. A conversation between the producers and the singer: soft talking, whispers. It's hard to tell what is going on. However, the energy is high. I sense they're wrapping things up, but booth seventeen is quiet. I crack my knuckles and stretch my neck back and forth. Dammit, I wish I had some water to soothe my dry throat.

I can't see the entrance to either booth. Since I'm standing between them, I'm not sure what to expect. I let out another deep sigh to regain my composure. I hear Mom say: *Now, hold your horses, Laurie. Hold your horses.*

"Okay, go ahead." The staffer waves me to the opening of booth 18. I stay put. *Booth 18? I want booth 17!* I don't want to follow Whitney Houston voice! Possibly I misunderstood in all the chaos.

"What booth?" I yell over the arena loudness.

"Eighteen!" He yells with his hands held up to his face like a bullhorn.

Oh, shit. Well, I guess 18 holds my future. I shake my head to clear my thoughts and use the forearm of my blouse sleeve to blot my oily forehead. I walk into the booth with gentle, steady progression. I'm hesitant yet controlled and displaying confidence.

I get one stride in and abruptly stop at the opening. I'm incapable of taking another step. My breathing halted. The obtrusive arena sounds grow silent while I stare. First, there is just one producer, and I assumed there would be two. Second, he is strikingly handsome—handsome like a Ralph Lauren model. *What the hell? Who's he? Why doesn't he look ordinary like most producers?*

Now I'm not *just* a singer about to audition, or a woman trying to find her greater purpose in life. Instead, I'm befuddled in front of a hot guy. I may feel secure about my looks, but that doesn't make me immune to a teenage response. He appears in his late thirties. Silver temples dash his dark brown wavy slicked back hair. Some strands fall to his chiseled chin.

While sitting on a wood bar stool, he appears tall and does not rise as I enter. There is no table in front of him. He holds a clipboard as he balances one foot on the stool, the other anchored to the floor in his well-traveled Western boot.

With the most welcoming and soothing Australian accent, he asks, "Hello love, what brings you here today?"

What brings me here? Did he just ask that? He awkwardly read- just his footing on the stool. The look on my face must have encouraged him to rethink his approach.

"Hello, how are you?" he mutters. His question is asked so sweetly, I can't help but think he's sincere, which is unusual.

Before my mind can go off any further, my audition robot takes over, and I give a straightforward and polite, "I'm fine, thank you. How about you?"

He smiles. "Good, good, thanks."

The arena sounds emerge again as if someone opened the door to a concert hall. With a free hand, I cover my ear to extinguish it. I remain near the booth entrance and grip my purse close to my chest with my other hand. My black and gold checkered blouse clings to my sweaty back, and my bag of performance essentials hang off my shoulder, an additional weight on my burdened body.

He points to a black folding chair in the corner, aware of my encumbrance. While containing my nerves, I softly place everything on the flimsy folding chair.

I turn to him. With a giant thud, all my belongings sink into the folded crease of the chair and simultaneously collapse the whole shebang to the floor. I wince at the sound, but don't look back at the flopped heap or try to correct it. All I can muster is a shrug. He narrowly smiles.

"Please stand on the X," he instructs.

I move to the duct-taped X, a familiar and welcome audition symbol. I let my arms fall to my side, even though I'd rather use them to cross my chest to form a barrier between us. We are a mere seven feet apart. I'm close enough to get a slight whiff of his cologne, and yet too close to sing to him.

"So, what do you think you have to offer that we haven't seen?" There is kindness in his tone. He looks down at his clipboard but stops when I speak.

"I think I bring a lot of raw emotion and energy to my singing and songwriting that people can relate to."

Before he replies, he squints his hazel eyes at me. Then with a blank stare he asks, "Do you think *you* have what it takes to be the next big singing sensation?" His delivery is artificial. He appears too comfortable and unmoved, swirling his pen between his fingers, asking such a question. My hands, held low, now clasp in the front of me.

I look down and close my eyes. I feel bewildered, frustrated and with a touch of anger brewing in me. I have lost so much and faced such uncertainty in my personal and music life that his question feels whimsical. *Really? Do I have what it takes?* I can tell him I have what it takes for *my* music. I have what it takes to survive the deepest sorrow and to dream the biggest dreams. But, I'm not going to tell him my personal story, so he can make it *their* story. I came here to sing.

I stare straight into the handsome Aussie man's eyes and release my hands into soft fists. With a playful and proud smile, I repeat the question: *"Do I have what it takes to be the next big singing sensation?* Well, how about I just sing?"

He smiles back coyly. "Then have at it."

61

CONCRETE AND SOLITUDE

I shake out my shoulders, which is like moving boulders and relax my hands at my sides. I close my eyes, make sure my knees are slightly bent--certainly not locked--and readjust my throbbing high-heeled feet to hip wide. I remember in the metal band in Austin, the DJ handing me the microphone at Liberty Lunch, which means, I'm *on*. I look up at Aussie man, and without thought, out comes the Randy Newman bluesy-rock song, *Guilty*.

With decent strength, energy, and what feels like the right key, I sing.

As I plow through the lyrics, I sing directly to him. My arms are animated, and I'm emotionally involved in the song. I love this song. It got me Broadway auditions and made it on my album *Selfish*. He doesn't know this, but I relish the thought. He looks down to write on his clipboard, piquing my curiosity. He closes his eyes and leans back his head. I can't tell if he's enjoying the song or stretching.

I start the second verse, but I sense a pull in his energy, like he's no longer listening. On a hunch, I stop.

He starts to talk, then pauses, gazing at me with soft eyes. He drops his head to his left like he's going to ask a question. His thin lips pursed. He looks off in the distance past me, as he lets the clipboard fall to his thigh. It's scribbles and doodles on the white paper. *What the hell?* He looks at me again. With no expression, he blurts out, "I'm sorry love, not today. I don't think today is your day."

Knocked against the head with rejection, everything comes at once: deafening silence, my legs lock, I can't blink. Vulnerability overwhelms me. I continue to stare at him until I catch my breath and the obnoxiously loud sounds of the arena march back into my ears. His flat expression doesn't change. He doesn't move but continues to look directly at me with his poker face. He waits for my next move, like pulling my feet out of wet concrete. Oddly, I am relieved. Pissed, but relieved. Fuck them. I don't have all night.

I offer a fake smile and a nod. "Okay, thank you," I mumble, retrieving my bags off the floor. I don't reset the collapsed folding chair.

I abruptly walk out the booth door, where a security guard awaits. He guides me-a hand placed gently on my damp lower back--toward the underground walkway leading outside. It's a funeral pace. Many remaining contestants wait above in the arena. They look down at me with sullen glances. I'm the poster child they'd like to avoid.

I want to scream at them: *I'm actually a good singer. Don't think I suck because I didn't get a fucking golden ticket!* I catch one last look of desperation on a teenage girl's face. I smile at her and wink with the gentleness of a mom and the experience of a professional: *You'll be okay, kid. Don't let them define you! Sing for you!* As soon as I get out of her vision, my smile retreats. I'm still shocked. The freshness of the letdown kicks into gear. A familiar inquisition after an audition. *What went wrong with my singing? Did that dude even know what he was doing? What the hell just happened?*

The security guard's job done, he returns to the arena as I stare down the damp and empty tunnel. It's dimly lit and dismal. There is no question which direction to proceed. I am forced to walk forward alone to what feels like a musician's graveyard.

The passageway is barely wide enough for a car to drive through. The noises of the arena fade behind me as I drag my feet into the deafening silence. I share the space with concrete and solitude.

Ten feet in, I pause and squat down, my back against the wall. Bending over, I can't tell if I'm ready to cry, vomit or scream. I don't want anyone to see me weak, so overcome with emotion, and certainly not for this damn show.

I straighten up and wipe my eyes, deciding no tears. I knew this could happen. I don't want this one audition to eclipse my years of experience or my memories of playing live. Or how great writing a song feels, even a song no one will ever hear. Or how incredible it is to be in a band with your best friends, to record your songs in a studio or to sing at a wedding. Or even, a memorial. Yet, it's hard to hold back the rawness of this letdown. To hold back being human.

I sink to sit crisscross on the concrete, and cry--not loud, bellowing cries, but humble, knowing sobs. Sobs that one only does alone. The ones that make your shoulders shake and your stomach hurt. I don't cry for the loss of this show. I cry for the loss of my dad, the baby, and the parts of me that disintegrated after they passed.

I lean my head back against the wall, drop my bag to my side, and let out a hefty moan that echoes loudly. I came here to resurrect a music career and myself. I thought this show would fix my pain, loneliness, and anxiety. I assumed my music resurrection would equal my overall redemption, and provide acceptance, perhaps the approval I've longed for since I was a child. Flashes of my face at different ages--invariably wearing a hungry expression pass through my mind. But now, being rejected by a stranger, I'm faced to realize, no one can accept and approve of me genuinely, but me.

In this unusual moment, I realize my personal pain or faltered music career is not a problem to be solved by being on a TV show or achieving fame or gaining everyone else's approval. It's *my* approval on my terms that will bring me back to…me.

Looking inward, accepting myself, I'm overcome with a wave of peace, gratitude, and recognition. I breathe it in slowly, deeply. I am the only one who knows the outcome. I'm sure Stephanie and Jacob didn't see me leave. Sitting in this damp, cavernous tunnel, I don't owe anyone an explanation. Not my mom, Neil, this show, anyone. I feel like how I felt when I first started music. I may have started to appease my mom, but once music got a hold of me, it was for me. I just didn't know it then. All the solitary practice in my youth, the rehearsals, and that performance high was all mine. And *this* moment is all mine.

It's not without irony my blissful "alone" moment is interrupted. "You need to clear this area," a security guard announces, approaching from the arena. He's waving his finger at me like a pissed high school teacher. "You can't stay here," he continues, intruding on my calm space. I slowly get up, wishing I could linger in this tunnel of cool, damp awareness. "Please, lady. You need to leave." I put my hands up in recognition of his words and nod.

I stagger along to an opening that reveals a loading dock to the outside. There's a barricade at the end with another security guard. This one silently ignores me as I head towards the sunlight that's pushing its way into this arena darkness.

There are no cheering crowds, no excited family members, no waiting friends here. Instead, two policemen lounge against their cars.

I emerge into the sunlit parking lot where we stood for hours and hours. Now empty, it's silent and layered again with pieces of trash. And Seagulls.

The sunset paints the sky with pinks and reds, stirring up tender feelings of acceptance and excited feelings of anticipation of what I still can do with my music, with me. I smile.

62

BREATHE

My phone vibrates. I've missed seven calls from my mother, two from Neil, and three texts from Stephanie. I text Steph, reporting my whereabouts.

I call and break the news to Neil. "Are you kidding me?" he erupts.

"Look, I'm okay. I really am. I'm actually better for this."

"You are?" he says curiously.

"Yup, I'll tell you more later. I need to call Mom."

"Yeah, she's called here, too. Well, hang in there. We'll see you soon."

His words are welcoming, and I'm ready to go home. Even though home is unsettled, it's still where I'd rather be right now with my family, my guitar, my songs.

I ring my mom. Even though I'm at peace, I worry the disappointment could devastate her.

"My God, Laurie. What is happening? I've been so worried!" she begs, a crack in her voice. She takes a deep puff off her cigarette and releases it, and it helps me release my breath since I'm not sure how to break it to her.

"Laurie, are you okay?"

"Oh, Mom." I pace small steps.

"Well, tell me! I'm on pins and needles. The neighbors have stopped by to ask, and I told them not to worry--you'd be amazing and be on TV soon!"

"What? Mom, why would you say *that*?"

"Well, because you are amazing. You're my daughter!"

"No, that I'd be on TV. There was no guarantee." The phone line grows quiet. "Mom, I didn't move on."

She releases smoke from her mouth, like the sound of a soft fan. I hear her set her ceramic coffee mug down with a thud on the wood dining room table.

"You didn't move on? You?" "Mom, I um..."

"No, Laurie. You're a fantastic singer! Who the hell do they think they are? Turning you away? Well, well, fuck them. You'll sing somewhere else."

My stomach tumbles, and I sit down on the curb. Her hysterics always make me uncomfortable.

"Mom, I completely agree with you. I'll sing somewhere else. But, earlier today, you said I should go home and concentrate on my marriage and not pursue some big dream. I thought--" I hesitate and can't complete my sentence.

"You thought what, honey?" Her voice drops many decibels lower. It's calmer.

"I thought, I know all my auditions have meant a lot to you. And this show meant a lot. You hoped it would bring you something too. Come on, Mom, you have a shrine of my headshots and show performances on your living room wall!"

The line is silent, except for her breathing. Calm, paced, without smoke crackle. I love to hear her breathe. When I was a child, I'd sometimes sit next to her bed when she was depressed. I'd listen to her breathing and wait. If she was breathing, I knew she was okay and then I'd be okay.

"Laurie, no matter what you do, I'm proud of you. You've had such heartbreak and you keep going. I never had the balls to do what you do." There is a pause in her voice. "I may have put a lot of pressure on you to do things for me, and I'm sorry. But you are the best of me. You are special."

"Mom, I'm not that special." Her words trigger tears, but I don't give in. I've come too far.

"Nonsense, you're special to me! And you have something I never had: a voice — a choice. Not just to sing, but to be…you. You do things I can't even imagine. No matter what you achieve, it's more than I can dream." She sniffs back tears. Tears I sense she sheds for herself. For the first time, I understand her, and I accept her for all the moving parts of the extraordinary woman she is, including her mental health.

"I love you, Mom." I stand up. My feet ache but not my heart. "Well, Laurie, I love you too. Now, I need to get off the phone. I need to tell the neighbors that my daughter just auditioned for a

TV show in front of thousands of people, more people than live in Waterloo."

"Mom, that's not exactly how it went down." I smile imagining the quirky smile on her face.

"I don't care, that's how I see it. Kiddo, you keep dreaming, and I'll keep believing."

After the call, with composure I remove my shoes. I pleasantly moan in relief. My bare feet, red and swollen, have completely rebelled against my high-heeled MRKT wedge pumps, but my spirit hasn't. The inscription on the insole is correct: this was an act of discovery. But a TV show didn't discover me, I discovered myself.

I sit back down on the curb and close my eyes. I raise my knees close to my chest. A subtle, warm breeze moves around me. I hug myself and I feel my inner strength. My stomach tightens with adrenaline the good kind like when you're blowing out birthday candles or kissed for the first time. I hear my breath. It's strong, steady, comforting. I hear my voice say, "You'll be okay."

This is my journey, my music, and my dream. I have never felt more like an artist than in this moment. I open my eyes and face the distant sun and welcome the warmth on my skin. It reminds me of stage lights and a newfound passion for what's to come.

AUTHOR'S NOTE

I started writing this book in 2011 but paused in 2014 when my mother became ill with COPD. Although she always asked me for book updates, I wasn't sure I would return to the book. My focus was on her. I'd tell her, "You know, I'll get back to it, Mom. Don't worry." But I knew she was worried. She knew the book meant a lot to me, but I also learned how much it meant to her.

In June 2016, on her deathbed, she said to me sternly, "Laurie, finish that damn book." She was never one to mince words, and I never wanted to disappoint her. So, I promised her I would. It was one of the last things I said to her. In the years to follow, I started writing again.

Mom's death had an impact on how I wrote her. Through mourning, her memories became more precise and poignant, but it didn't change that the book ended in 2011 or that she'd never be able to read it. But if I could tell her something now, it would be, "Mom, I finished the damn book."

ACKNOWLEDGEMENTS

To the exceptional editors who guided and molded my words AND me as a first-time author: Shelly Cofield, Robbie Tucker, and Dana Issacson. Thank you for magically whipping me into shape.

And to those who supported, listened, encouraged, inspired, read the book, re-read the dang book, talked it out, and sometimes cried with me – THANK YOU! In no specific order: Amy Sharp, Sara Stiffler, Paul Linke, Jessica Colp, Shawn Lucas, Charles Salzberg, Vinita Khilnani, John Bryan, Francine Aron, Joe Wilson, Hank Phillippe Ryan, Paula Munier, Aaron Barrera, Kimberley McCaskey, Jay Thompson, Chris Erskine, Mike Carlin, Jenna Seid, Sara Haskell, Charity McGhee, Edgar Recinos, Craig Dillon, David Markvart, Jennifer Valdiviez, Sharon Fanto, Bruce Newlin, Jude Chacon, Andrea Evans, Robert Parker, Jesslyn Bundy, Ellen Considine, Alex Swart, Lisa Wilson, Debbie Sagar Lopez, Matt Lopez, Liz Militello, Kathryn Russ, Joseph Silva

And thank you to the countless wine bars and coffee shops from Boston to New York City to Los Angeles for letting me stay long after my glass or cup was empty. Because of your generosity, I was able to bury my head in my laptop, fingers tapping away, disappearing into my words, and finish this damn book.

ABOUT THE AUTHOR

LAURIE MARKVART is a professional singer, musician, published author, songwriter, blogger, and poet. She thrives through life with GAD (general anxiety disorder) and is a social media advocate for positive mental health awareness. She is also a recent breast cancer survivor and talks about it openly. Laurie is Midwest-born but now lives in Los Angeles with her son and two cats, Sir Freddie Mercury and Lady Annie Lennox.

The audiobook of *Somewhere in the Music, I'll Find Me: A Memoir* is available on Amazon.

For more information on Laurie's future books and publications:

Social: @lauriemarkvart
www.lauriemarkvartdiary.com

RESOURCES

National Suicide Prevention Lifeline
Call, text, or chat: 988 - 24/7

NAMI (National Alliance on Mental Illness)

24/7, confidential, free crisis counseling
Crisis Text Line: text **HOME** or **NAMI** to **741741**

SIMS Foundation
Emotional wellness and support for the music community in Austin,
Texas.
www.simsfoundation.org

Made in the USA
Las Vegas, NV
08 February 2024

85420559R00246